& Review

Corvallis Gazette-Times

the Journal Times

T4-ADE-418

television 3

THE BISMARCK TRIBUNE

ityJournal

The Montana Standard

ona Daily News

NSIN STATE JOURNAL

9 KGMB

The Ottumwa Courier

rnal

atine, Iowa

KM3TV OMAHA

STAR

Southern Illinoisan

Lee's Legacy of Leadership

THE HISTORY OF LEE ENTERPRISES, INCORPORATED

by Wilbur Cross

edited by Ceila Dame Robbins

GREENWICH
PUBLISHING GROUP, INC.

©1990 by Greenwich Publishing Group, Inc.

All rights reserved.

Printed and bound in the United States of America.
No part of this publication may be reproduced or transmitted in any form or by any means, electronic or mechanical, including photocopying, recording, or any information storage and retrieval system now known or to be invented, without permission in writing from Lee Enterprises, Incorporated, 130 East Second Street, Davenport, Iowa 52801, except by a reviewer who wishes to quote brief passages in connection with a review written for inclusion in a magazine, newspaper or broadcast.

Credit is gratefully given for use of the following photographs:

Chapter 1	p. 8	The Bettmann Archive
	p. 11	The Bettmann Archive
	p. 13	Musser Public Library, Muscatine, Iowa
	p. 14	The Bettmann Archive
	p. 15	The Bettmann Archive
Chapter 2	p. 24	Bachrach
	p. 30	The Bettmann Archive
	p. 33	(left) The Bettmann Archive
	p. 34	The Bettmann Archive
	p. 37	Mrs. Karl Strohhehn
Chapter 3	p. 44	Fabian Bachrach
	p. 46	Art Fischbeck
	p. 51	F. W. Guerin
Chapter 4	p. 62	Fabian Bachrach
	p. 71	Bachrach
	p. 74	The Bettmann Archive
	p. 75	Jeff Cook, Quad-City Times
	p. 77	Bradford Bachrach
	p. 78	De Longe
Chapter 5	p. 83	(bottom) Phil Hutchison
	p. 98	Joe Boll
	p. 102	Phil Hutchison
	p. 105	Jim Koenigsaecker, Quad-City Times
Chapter 6	p. 110	Bachrach
	p. 115	Fabian Bachrach
	p. 118	The Bettmann Archive
	p. 121	Bill Mitchell
Chapter 7	p. 161	Larry Mayer

Design by Thomas C. Brecklin
Typography by Silver Eagle Graphics Inc., Butler, Wisconsin

Library of Congress Catalog Card Number: 90-82816
ISBN: 0-944641-00-8

Published and produced by Greenwich Publishing Group, Inc.
                           Post Office Box 9
                           Essex, CT 06426

First printing: August 1990

Foreword

The story of Lee Enterprises is meant to tell the history and legacy of the company so that all of us in 1990 can better understand its background and foundation.

Since I've spent all of my life in association with Lee and have known all of the principal players with the exception of A. W. Lee, I'd like to point out a common theme I find running through the story.

All these men have shared a fine and strong Midwestern value system based on caring, kindness, integrity, truth and toughness. They have also encouraged a strong feeling of family awareness, and instilled and followed traditions that are valid today — and yet those traditions have not been stagnating. None was avaricious for either their bank accounts or egos. This may be outmoded behavior by today's standards, yet it is still true in Lee.

The strong feeling of family among employees is unique. Newcomers to the company readily accept Lee's values, traditions and family feelings; they even welcome it, for Lee is a great place to work. One person is always ready to help another in times of change, transition or crisis.

Lee people have always had fun together, forming lifelong friendships and not just business relationships. There is a camaraderie and continued communication among retirees.

Today Lee has 4,800 employees, who take pride in their accomplishments and face the future with confidence. They are maintaining historic values while living in a less-than-perfect world. These people and all who went before them have made the company great.

What would my grandfather, father and Laura Lee think today? They would be pleased and proud that Lee eagerly marches ahead into the next 100 years.

Thank you to all the people interviewed for this book. There was no orchestrated pattern of interviews and no one was intentionally omitted.

Betty Adler Schermer

Contents

7   *Chapter One*
The Tradition Begins
Alfred Wilson Lee — 1890-1907

25   *Chapter Two*
An Instinct To Build
Emanuel Philip Adler — 1907-1949

45   *Chapter Three*
A Believer in Broadcasting
Lee P. Loomis — 1949-1960

63   *Chapter Four*
The Compassionate Consolidator
Philip D. Adler — 1960-1970

91   *Chapter Five*
Seeing Beyond The Horizon
David K. Gottlieb — 1970-1973

111   *Chapter Six*
A Winner Who Doesn't Know There Is A Second Place
Lloyd G. Schermer — 1973 -

160   *Chapter Seven*
Growing The Leaders Of The Future

173   Index

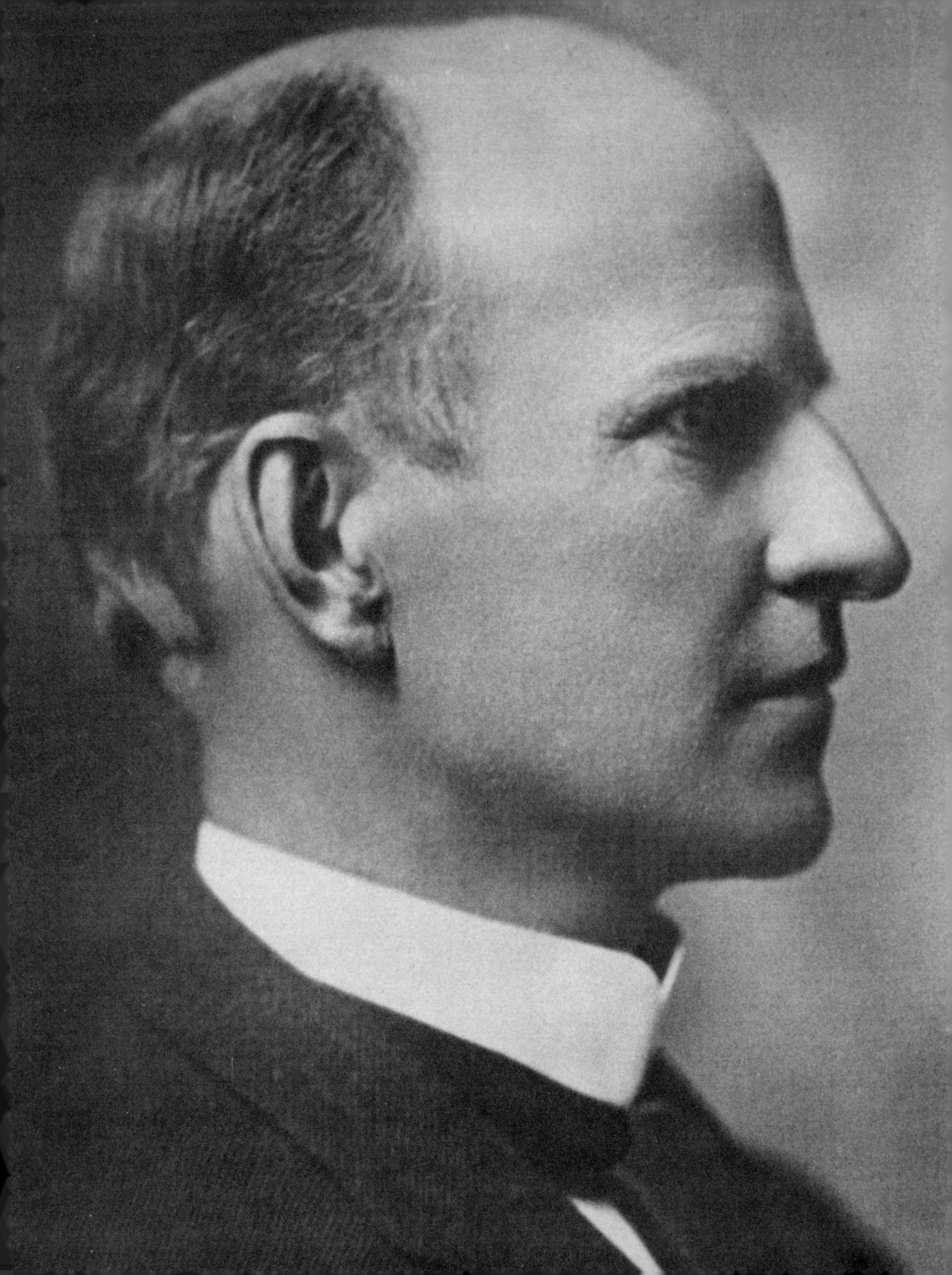

Chapter One
the Tradition Begins

1890-1907 *Alfred Wilson Lee*

Born July 8, 1858, on a farm in Johnson County, Iowa. Son of John B. Lee and Elvira Branson Lee, formerly of Philadelphia, who moved to Iowa in 1853.

Brother of Anna Lee (born 1845), who married John Mahin, later editor and part owner of the *Muscatine* (Iowa) *Journal*.

Graduated from Muscatine, Iowa, public schools and entered the University of Iowa at age 13, where he completed his freshman and sophomore years.

Moved to Chicago to work on the *Chicago Times* in 1880.

Worked in the post office in Muscatine, during early 1880's, under his brother-in-law, John Mahin. Later, worked part-time at the *Muscatine Journal*.

Married Mary Ingalls Walker, known as Minnie, daughter of W. W. Walker of Cedar Rapids, Iowa, June 4, 1885.

Father of two sons and one daughter: William Walker Lee, who died at age two, Alfred William Lee, who died at age nine, and Laura Anna Lee, who survived him.

Held positions as stockholder and officer of the Journal Printing Company, publisher of the *Muscatine Journal*, 1885-88.

Purchased *Ottumwa* (Iowa) *Daily Courier*, April 1890.

Acquired the *Davenport* (Iowa) *Times*, July 1, 1899.

Acquired *Muscatine Journal*, January 1, 1903.

Acquired Hannibal (Missouri) *Courier-Post* and *La Crosse* (Wisconsin) *Tribune*, February, 1907.

Died of heart failure July 15, 1907, in Nottingham, England.

"You can have the freedom to publish accounts of almost anything under the sun," A. W. Lee was wont to remind his editors and reporters, "as long as it is news, is reported fairly and objectively, and can be fully supported by facts that you have compiled before you even set pen to paper."

Lee's statement reveals the personal integrity that became one of his distinguishing characteristics. He was, first and foremost, a newsman, and one who expected of himself and inspired from others the highest journalistic standards. His career — and the story of the Lee Company — began at a time of growth and turmoil in American journalism.

The environment of A. W. Lee was far removed from the world of today — culturally, intellectually, and morally, as well as chronologically. Yet there were factors that invite comparison. On the domestic front, industries and new technologies that would affect newspaper publishing were beginning to flourish across America. Internationally, news reporting was becoming broader, as Western ideologies were being challenged by the philosophies of the East, brought more forcefully to public attention because of strong currents of Asian commerce, notably from Japan, China, and India.

The last decade of the nineteenth century saw the beginnings of a demand for constant, continuing, and effective communication. Too often, newspapers resorted to sensationalism and embellishing fact with statements and stories that were open to question — later referred to as "yellow journalism." Yet it was a time when the American newspaper flourished and when competent editors and reporters were achieving measures of greatness. While some publishers like William Randolph Hearst were finding they could sell papers by resorting to the sensational,

Using yellow paper and outrageous cartoons was the ploy used by some American newspapers in the 1890's to attract readers. A. W. Lee denounced this blatant "yellow journalism" when he established that Lee papers would publish straightforward news and avoid the sensational.

This undated cartoon, titled, "The Newspaper Padded Room: What an innocent man may be brought to by the sensational press," echoed Lee's feelings.

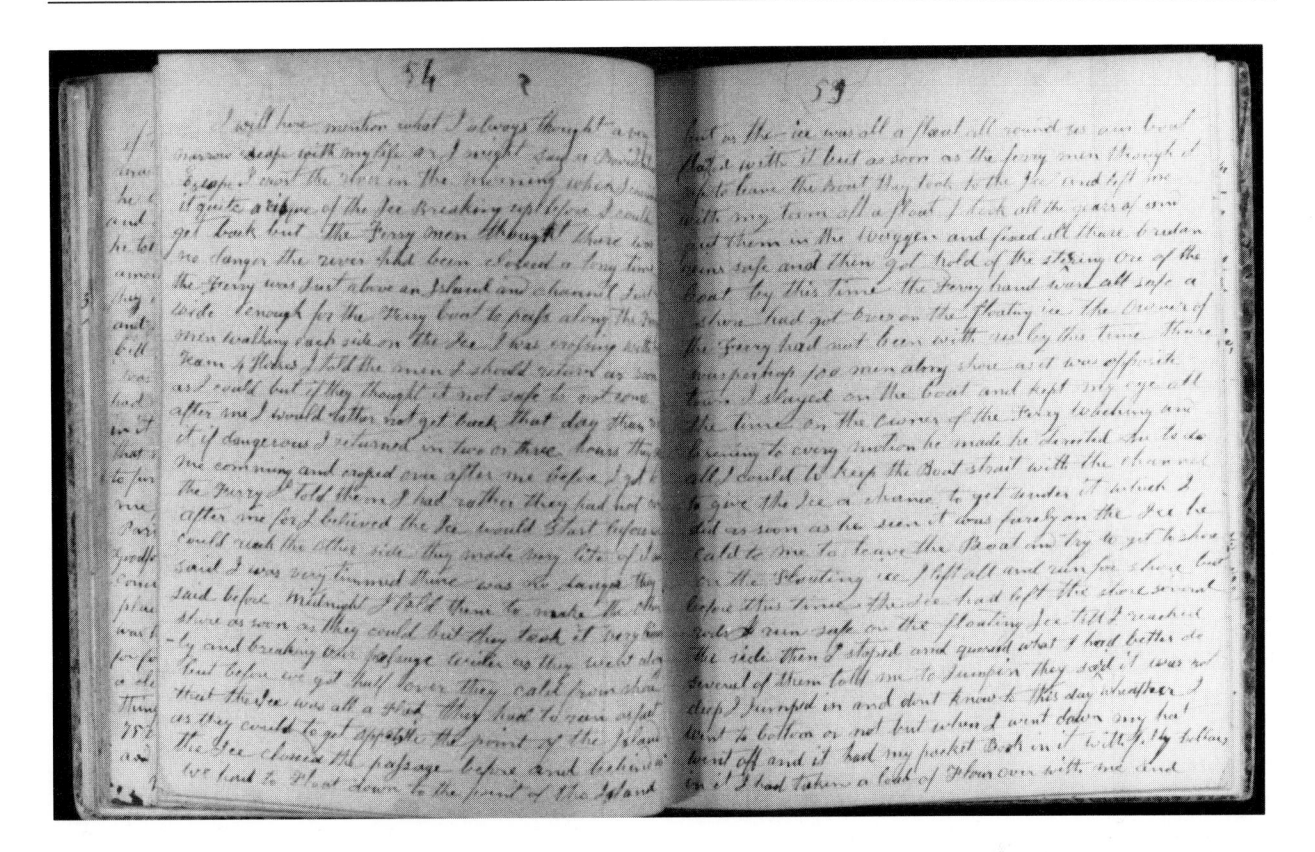

John B. and Elvira Branson Lee moved West in 1853 to start a life for themselves. The move came about because when Elvira agreed to marry John in their hometown of Philadelphia, she decided to leave her parent's Quaker church. Their displeasure at the union made living nearby uncomfortable, as did the disapproval of John's aristocratic parents, who were upset that the young couple had eloped.

They settled on a small homestead near Iowa City and became pioneer farmers. It was here, on a prairie farm, that A. W. Lee was born in 1858.

This photograph shows the diary John B. Lee kept throughout his adult years. It is a chronicle of his life and the lives of his family and relatives. His meticulous attention to detail was passed along to his son, who applied it first to bookkeeping, then to publishing.

Although there is no record of diaries kept by A. W. Lee, he did have a reputation as a prolific writer of notes. "He seldom advised, corrected, or applauded his associates by word of mouth," notes The Lee Papers. "Almost always it was through the medium of written notes." One of his most notable communications was the commendation he wrote to E. P. Adler, as follows:

"Mr. Adler—I am much pleased with your work and feel that you deserve congratulation and commendation. Your pay will be $12.00 per week beginning Monday. If you keep up your present effort and spare no opportunity to acquire information (by that I mean the information that comes from study and reading), you certainly have a future in newspaper work.
            Sincerely yours, A. W. Lee"

E. P. Adler eventually succeeded Lee as head of the newspaper company.

other publishers such as William Allen White were writing columns and editorials that reflected a growing pride in community and public service.

It was in this historical context that A. W. Lee bought his first newspaper and began to form journalistic policies and procedures that would take root and grow throughout the company he was developing in Iowa and later in other parts of the Midwest.

When a company can thrive in the late 20th century by taking sustenance from traditions going as far back as an entire century, there is good reason to explore the roots and study the heritage that has made this kind of robust longevity possible. It has long been acknowledged that Lee's corporate legacy owes much of its derivation to the founder of the company, A. W. Lee. Strong and enduring patterns took shape under his hands and became a lasting inheritance passed on, strengthened, and adapted by subsequent generations of leaders.

Lee, born July 8, 1858, on a farm in Johnson City, Iowa, was precocious as a child, a quality that was strengthened and enhanced by his strict upbringing under his father, John B. Lee, bookkeeper for the *Muscatine Journal*. He distinguished himself early in life when, at the age of 13, he entered the State University of Iowa, the youngest student who had ever been admitted. His newspaper career began at this time, first when he held part-time jobs at the Muscatine paper and later when he graduated and joined the staff as an assistant bookkeeper under the stern tutelage of his father. He learned his art well and later, when his father retired, succeeded him as head bookkeeper.

Ralph Waldo Emerson (1803-1882)

Ralph Waldo Emerson was an American poet, essayist and philosopher. Educated as a minister, he later resigned his pastorship in order to develop his philosophies about life and religion. He became known for his challenges to traditional thought in his essays and lectures. He summarized many of these ideas in his first book, *Nature*.

As the "Sage of Concord" (Mass.), he became chief spokesman for Transcendentalism, the belief that everything in man's world is a microcosm of the universe, that man could see the world itself in something as minute as "a drop of dew." Emerson adopted "Trust Thyself" as his guiding motto. His philosophy was characterized by its reliance on intuition as the only way to comprehend reality. Among his chief works were *Essays* (First and Second Series), *Poems, Representative Men, English Traits,* and *The Conduct of Life*.

A. W. Lee's nephew, Harold J. Mahin, remembered that Lee, "was a great devotee of Emerson and had a full set of his essays printed in small pocket books and almost always carried one of these with him wherever he went." Lee used to mark passages that were most meaningful so he could refer to them quickly.

William Allen White (1868-1944)

William Allen White emerged at the end of the 19th century as one of the brightest journalists of his day. His writings influenced A. W. Lee's decision to become a newspaper publisher.

White was a liberal Republican who spent most of his life in Emporia, Kansas. He first won national attention with an editorial, "What's the matter with Kansas?" which helped McKinley to win the presidency. His poignant editorial tribute to his teen-aged daughter, who died as the result of a riding accident, received enormous acclaim. He was also known for his editorials underlining community growth and service, as well as his sharp profiles of people.

Despite a natural bent for mathematics, Lee visualized himself as a writer and editor. One of the most significant influences in his early life was Ralph Waldo Emerson. Emerson's belief in the "divine sufficiency of the individual" formed an open attitude toward life that today exerts itself in the philosophy of what we know as "the power of positive thinking." Lee's acceptance of Emerson's motto, "Trust Thyself," echoed his belief that individuals could improve their lives if they believed strongly in what they were doing and what they hoped to achieve.

Lee was similarly impressed and influenced by the journalistic accomplishments of William Allen White, who was close to his own age and living proof that a man did not have to experience years of toil and turmoil before he could become a respected and successful publisher. Inspired by White, Lee envisioned a newspaper network of independent, small-town dailies that would be published by enterprising journalists with dedication and mission in mind.

He saw such newspapers as perhaps the most effective instrument in the nation for furthering the development and growth of the Midwest where he lived. Lee's interpretation of journalism as a means for enhancing the lives of people would, in effect, lay the groundwork for the current Lee Enterprises philosophy that community service and involvement are prime responsibilities of newspapers and broadcasting stations.

Lee's first job as a journalist was at the *Chicago Times*, where he gained experience as a reporter and later as a staff writer and part-time editor. He had several opportunities to advance in the business office because of his bookkeeping skills, but preferred the excitement and stimulation of working more closely with the public and interviewing those who were making news.

This rare view of Chicago's State Street, from an old Stereoscope viewing card, shows how the city looked just prior to Lee's arrival in 1880.

At that time, Chicago attracted many aspiring young journalists to its "big city" papers. Although A. W. Lee was one of these, it took him only two years to decide that rural and small-town America was where he wanted to live and pursue his calling.

Ottumwa Daily Courier.

TWELVE PAGES.

WEEKLY 43D YEAR — OTTUMWA, IOWA, TUESDAY EVENING, APRIL 14, 1891. — VOL. 27, NO. 7.

LAID TO REST.

The Remains of Colonel P. G. Ballingall Interred Today,

THE SORROW MANIFESTED.

The Tribute of Respect Paid the Late Coal Palace President by His Fellow Citizens—The Funeral Sermon and Eulogy—Other Incidents.

All that is earthly of the late Col. P. G. Ballingall was consigned to the tomb today. The sorrow was universal in the city and even nature seemed sad, enveloping the city in a pall of fog and mist. All night there were bursts of rain and the morning was damp and cloud laden. It was evident that inclement nature with its forbidding aspect would deter many strangers from visiting the city to pay their last respects to the departed philanthropist and public spirited citizen. Yet the vast concourse

HON. P. G. BALLINGALL.

of people which crowded the coal palace and stood with bared heads in solemn stillness as the remains passed by in palace or on public street, attested the fact that of the certain hold the deceased had upon the hearts of the people among whom he had moved for so many years.

Biographical.

The history of Col. Ballingall's life is so fraught with experience to comfort and inspire the boys who are struggling for competency and position in the world that a sketch of his career will bear repetition.

Col. Ballingall was born in Glasgow, Scotland March 3d, [illegible]. At the age of seven years in company with his mother and stepfather, he came to America, landing in Quebec. From Quebec the family went to Montreal, thence to Port Hope, on the bank of Lake Ontario. After a short sojourn there his mother, brother and himself walked fourteen miles to Brighton and from there proceeded to Helderman Four Corners, where the colonel earned his first money selling matches.

Walked to Chicago.

Before he was eleven years old he walked from Coburg, seventy-three miles below Toronto, to Chicago by a roundabout way, which involved a distance of seven or eight hundred miles. After arriving there he was employed in various capacities in different hotels and proved himself peculiarly adapted to this calling. He advanced from one position to another and in the course of time was appointed receiver of the Lake House, which position he filled acceptably until 1835. Upon leaving he was presented with a fine gold watch, the letter accompanying it being signed by some of the most prominent men in the city. After leaving the Lake House

GOV. HORACE BOIES.

Mr. Ballingall spent three months traveling, going through most of the southern states, and while off the coast of Cape Hatteras was driven by a storm to Bermuda. After visiting the with his hotel operations he had at one time seventeen government licenses for separate and distinct branches of business which he made successful. For nine years he was proprietor of the stage line from Ottumwa to Bloomfield, and during that long period through sunshine and storm never missed a trip. In 1870 the railroad crowded this stage line off the track and he withdrew his stock. He ran a line to Sigourney, a distance of twenty-two miles, until the completion of the Chicago, Milwaukee & St. Paul railroad, when that, too, was withdrawn. In 1864 Mr. Ballingall erected the Ballingall House on the corner of Main and Green streets, which he operated for ten years. He then leased it, but retained the management of the Depot hotel.

His Political Career.

While never an aspirant for official position the deceased was frequently honored by his party and fellow citizens with local office. For many years he was a member of the state democratic central committee, and contributed liberally of his time and money to advance the interests of his party. He was a member of the general assembly in 1883. Previous to this, however, he was elected alderman of Ottumwa and re-elected several terms. He originated many of the impruvements of the city and urged them with a zeal that insured success. In the spring of 1873 he was nominated for mayor, but was obliged to decline the honor on account of pressing private business. He had also been nominated for senator on the democratic ticket and ran over one hundred votes ahead of his ticket against a party majority of over 200. On the 18th of March, 1873, he was presented with another fine gold watch and chain of superb workmanship, elegantly engraved with the inscription: Hon. P. Ballingall by his guests at the soldier's reunion at Des Moines in 1880 and others in Iowa as a token of esteem." Prior to this a chain manufactured to order in New York was presented him by the citizens of Ottumwa. Later Mr. Ballingall visited the west for rest and recreation, spending about six weeks on the Pacific coast. Upon his return he interested himself organizing the militia of Iowa. In this, as in the greater part of his undertakings, he distinguished himself and was appointed major of the Fifth regiment in 1876, being promoted two years later a colonel. He was soon afterward presented with a gold mounted sword by the Sheridan Guards. The following year he was elected major general, but the governor assuming supervisory power to revise the returns placed his competitor in the place to which Colonel Ballingall was legally elected by the organized citizen soldiery. The officers and soldiers of the different brigades testified in many ways their belief in his just claim by banquets in his honor and notably in one case by a presentation of a magnificent badge set with precious stones.

Sucessful as a Boniface.

As a hotel man Mr. Ballingall took an interest in everything pertaining to the business and was principally instrumental in securing the present law for the protection of landlords. He was elected first president of the Hotel Keepers' Association in 1878 and was annually reelected for a series of years. In 1881 he was presented with another gold chain, consisting of forty-six flat links, on either side of which is the name of a hotel and its landlord. This costly gift was presented by the association. In the last three national democratic conventions Col. Ballingall had charge of the Iowa delegation and in appreciation of his services the delegates at Chicago presented him with a cross and star set with diamonds, engraved with the coat of arms of the state of Iowa. The Wapello County Agricultural Society selected Colonel Ballingall for its first president, and he devoted much time and means for its advancement. Indeed, there are few public enterprises in which he was not actively interested and contributed generously his time and means. He was naturally industrious and was an incessant worker, frequently devoting from fifteen to nineteen hours a day to his business affairs and public enterprises. In the spring of 1886 he made a trip to Europe, and in 1887 he made a trip around the world. Mr. Ballingall also visited other places of interest abroad, taking subsequently a journey through Old Mexico and through various republics of South America. Had he lived he would have completed his third trip to Australia and the Orient. Mr. Ballingall's honors did not cease, for the more he grew in years the more indefatigable were his labors. He became a candidate for senatorial honors on the Democratic ticket and was elected to the Twenty-third General Assembly. His worth as an alert, wide awake, aggressive and exhaustive worker and organizer was so marked that when in the last legislature the senate wished to name a man for the Iowa commissionership of the world's fair he was the unanimous choice of that body irrespective of party. This honor he had to forego because as a senator he could not accept an office created by the legislature of which body he was a member

ing classes, as a prominent figure among the hotel associations of the United States, as president of the Coal Palace, as the foremost citizen in this city, he is deeply mourned. But aside from this he had taken a deeper hold upon the masses as a philanthropist of the genuine stamp.

The Colonel's Death.

As has been related in THE COURIER Col. P. G. Ballingall died at sea off Hong Kong on March 7th. The circumstances are now well known to his own citizens but that the many visitors in the city may known more of the details we append the official log of the steamer Kong Benj on which he died, and also Consul Simon's letter stating the manner in which the body was received, interred, exhumed, embalmed and sent to America.

The Official Log.

COPY OF OFFICIAL LOG, STEAMER KONG BENJ., SATURDAY, MARCH 7, 1891, 12:45 P. M.—Latitude 17 degrees, 7 min. north, Long. 110–56 east.—The Hon. P. G. Ballingoll, native of Glasgow, Scotland, citizen of Iowa (Ottumwa) U. S. A.,

He came on board at Bangkok, on Saturday 28th Feburary, 1891. Complained of being very tired aud fatigued with being about very much in the sun in Bangkok; and grainally grew more weak and languid. Was treating himself with some patent medicines he brought on board with him. On Tuesday, March 3rd, 1891, being the anniversary of his 61st birthday, he drank some port wine, and on Wednesday evening, the 4th of March, it was his wish that Mr. Dean, chief officer, and Mr. Ingles, chief engineer, should come aft to the indoor and drink some champagne in commemoration of his birthday and some state event of great interest to himself. It occurred on or about the same date. He seemed to be all right. Had a fair dinner and was dressed and wore his decorations, and was in very good spirits throughout the evening. On Thursday morning, the fifth of March, he complained to me of weakness, and said that he thought he had a touch of the sun. I treated him by giving him a good dose of castor oil and giving him ice to suck and kept bathing his head, neck, face and hands in ice water. And afterward kept some ice in cloths on his head.

At noon he felt quite well and during the day he supped about one and one-half pints of chicken broth; also two soup plates of sago and milk besides. In the evening before going to

bed, I gave him one mild purging pill. He went to bed at about 9:30 p. m., and rested very well throughout the night. The next morning, Friday, 6th I gave him a black draught, and after this medicine operated he seemed to get stronger. Through the day he supped his chicken broth twice, and sago and milk twice through the day. From the first he began to complain of thirst and had meal water, made for him to drink. In the evening, I asked him if he would take another pill. He said "No. I guess I will do now till I get to Hong Kong." After asking me "when I thought I would be in Hong Kong?" I told him 'on Monday at noon."

On Saturday morning, 7th of March at 7 a. m. he came out of his room and sat talking about the different places he was going to visit, and at 7:30 he supped a plate of sage and milk. At about 9 a. m. he drank a hot whisky punch, and ate two small biscuits. We sat talking a little while, and I thought he was rambling in his talk. I sent for Mr. Ingles, chief engineer, as I thought he was looking worse and had fever. I tried the thermometer and found his temperature at 102. I at once mixed the fever mixture No. 2 Medical Guide, Nitrate of Potash 1½ drams, Swett Spirit of Nitre 3 drams, water 6 oz. and gave him one

lain quiet and began to sweat he never spoke one word or expressed a wish till the time of his death.

[Signed] J. B. JACKSON, Master.
H. DEAN, First Mate.
G. T. ENGLES, chief engineer.

Washed, dressed and coffined the remainsand all was finished by 4 p. m.
[Signed same as above].

Consul Simons Letter.

Consul Simons has written a detailed account of the disposition of Col. Ballingall's remains after they arrived at Hong Kong. His letter shows him to be a large-hearted and thoughtful gentleman who reflects credit on the great country which he represents. The letter is as follows:

CONSULATE OF THE UNITED STATES,
Hong Kong, March 13, 1891.

Mrs. M. J. Phillips, Ottumwa, Iowa.

DEAR MADAM: It has become my painful duty to give you such details concerning the death of the Hon. Peter G. Ballingall as have been furnished me by the officers of the ship, "The Kong Benj," of the Scottish Oceanic S. S. Co., which you will find enclosed herewith, having been compiled from the official log. The cause of death is supposed to have been sun-stroke. This may have been the immediate, but enough causes were found upon examination to be connected with the condition of the heart and arteries. On Monday, 9th inst., I received notice from the Master, Jackson, of the settlement, upon which or as soon thereafter as possible, I took possession of the remains, together with personal effects and telegraphed you. The remains were placed in the hands of an undertaker who prepared them for burial in the Protestant cemetery, in which they were interred on Tuesday. 10th of March at 4 p. m. The Rev. Benefield reading the usual service. There being present besides others a representative of the United States consulate. Should it appear to you that the burial was proceeded with with undue haste, I have only to say in explanation that it was done in compliance with the local ordinances, which require interment when possible, within forty-eight hours. On the following day instructions came from the Hon. Wm. F. Wharton, assistant secretary of state, Washington, directing me to exhume, embalm and send the body to Ottumwa, Iowa, with which I proceeded to comply and all will be ready for the S. S. Rio Janeiro, which sails for San Francisco, Sunday, 15th inst. at daylight.

Notwithstanding the body had been buried in a casket lined with lead, decomposition had so far advanced that neither the undertaker nor any other person engaged in the business of em-

L S Hanchet, Waverly.
J B Harsh, Creston.
A G Kegler, Bellevue.
M J Keley, Williamsburg.
Wm G Kent, Ft Madison.
J S Lawrence, Sioux City.
Edgar E Mack, Storm Lake.
L B Mattoon, Elgin.
Ben McCoy, Oskaloosa.
J D McVey, Lake City.
A F Meservey, Cherokee.
Wm D Mills, Marshalltown.
J J Mosnatt, Belle Plaine.
Matt Parrott, Waterloo.
G W Perkins, Farragut.
Richard Price, Winterset.
Rob't G Reiniger, Charles City.
James A Shields, Dubuque.
Wm O Schmit, Davenport.
J H Smith, Cedar Rapids.
Wm C Smith, Eagle Grove.
Joel Stewart, Grinnell.
Wm H Taylor, Bloomfield.
B R Vale, Bonaparte.
Thos Weidman, Red Oak.
P B Wolfe, De Witt.
John S Woolson, Mt Pleasant.
D W Jones, Manchester.

Those who were not able to be present sent their regrets, and Senator Dodge, who had the matter in charge of inviting them to be present, received but few regrets.

Manifestation of Sorrow.

The manifestations of sorrow were conspicuous about the city. There was a lavish display of the emblematic hues of mourning, the business blocks and some private residences being decorated in heavy festoons of sombre black, or relieved with bands and ropes of white. The threatening rain of the morning held off until noon and then the murky sky grew brighter although still lowering. Street Commissioner Padden had a force of men at work early, preparing the streets for the funeral pageant and the line of march from the Coal Palace to Court, thence north on Court to the end of the paved district was placed in the best condition possible. Although the street committee of the city council had taken every precaution to fill in all the bad places on Court street with cinders to make it passable for the funeral procession, it was decided to abandon the idea early in the day. The committee on arrangements, consisting of S. A. Flagler, Calvin Manning, W. T. Fenton, Capt. S. B. Fvans, J. C. Manchester and Hon. J. J. Smith held a meeting at the Coal Palace early in the day and it was decided not to attempt to drive out to the cemetery. Superintendent Daum of the electric street railway was in council with them and it was soon agreed that the best plan would be for the procession of carriages to halt at the junction of North and East Court where there would be four cars awaiting them. The remains and pall bearers would occupy the first car, the relatives the second and the governor and staff, the senate, and the Iowa State Agricultural Board the remaining cars. The militia band and the rest of the funeral cortege, were to take the side walk and proceed to the cemetery in advance. At the cemetry the hearse and carriages were to be in waiting and thence the pageant would proceed to the grave where the body was to be consigned to its last resting place. This order of program was carried out.

Viewing the Casket.

At ten o'clock the doors of the Coal Palace were thrown open for the public to view the casket. Superintendent George Withall had everything in order by that hour and his genius of arrangement was again manifest. The stage had been extended as on president's day and chairs had been arranged for the governor and staff and the senate, members of the Iowa Hotel Keepers Association, Coal Palace directors, the Iowa State Agricultural Association, the Wapello County Agricultural Board, and others. The Palace, too, bore visible signs of sorrow. Great festoons of white and black hung mournfully down from balcony and pillar as if indica-

o'clock beginning with those that arrived in the early morning brought in great crowds of people from the surrounding cities. Although the Rock Island ran a special train to acommodate the people from the west, the regular train too was heavily loaded. On the special that came from the west at noon were one hundred people from Oskaloosa alone. Train No. 3 on the Q. carried three extra coaches and the whole train was crowded. No. 10 from the west, had several extra coaches all of which were filled with people from different points along the Q. The Milwaukee, Central and Wabash all brought strangers in on each train till by noon there was a vast assemblage of people, reaching in the thousands, from the surrounding towns, Numbers 3 and 10 brought in the most people on the Q., the Rock Island special and the regular freight from the east on the Rock Island, while on the other roads the crowd was about equally divided among the regular [illegible]. The Pella band, the representation of the Iowa Agricultural Association, the governor and staff, and a large number of the senators were aboard the Des Moines special which arrived at noon. At that hour all the banks and business houses of the city closed, business was suspended till five o'clock.

HON. J. J. SMITH.

Flags on the various buildings of the city were suspended at half mast and those on the Ballingall were covered with crape.

[Continued on second page.]

The spring opening at the Manhattan Shoe House has drawn great crowds of people for the past three days. One to look in the show windows couldn't help but enter the store where the displays of fine shoes were much prettier than those in the windows. They carry an immense stock of all grades of goods, and can please every one. You can't find any cheap truck in this house like advertised by other shoe dealers, but you can find a stylish and good wearing shoe for just a trifle more than what you [illegible] cheap truck in other stores. [illegible] a decided specialty of the work[illegible] ed J. & T. Cousins' shoes [illegible] misses and children. In gen[illegible]'s foot wear of the finer grades they carry large stocks from the factories of such well-known firms as Strong & Carroll, Johnston & Murphy, Hathaway, Soule & Harrington, and many others. Their sales of fine footwear will foot up more than the sales of all other stores combined giving evidence of the fact that for the best, most stylish and serviceable footwear they must patronize the Manhattan Shoe Store. With their spring opening they presented three remarkable values, such as 475 pairs ladies fine Tarris kid hand turned button operas and New York toe, price $2,50, worth $3.50; 367 pairs ladies Tarris kid button, price $2.00, worth $3.00; 295 pairs of misses fine Tarris kid pat. tips, spring heel button, price $1.50, worth $2.00. Those wanting stylish and good wearing shoes at low prices should always patronize the Manhattan.

Diarrhœa, Dysentery, Cholera, Flux.

Maguire's Bene Plant for over 50 years the

The price tag for the first Lee acquisition was $16,000 when the Ottumwa Daily Courier *was purchased in 1890. The paper kept this name until the 1970's, when it was changed to the present, the* Ottumwa Courier. *Seen here is the front page of the paper as it looked on April 14, 1891.*

After two years of working for the *Chicago Times*, and now in his mid-twenties, Lee decided he would like to become a publisher on his own. He returned to his hometown, Muscatine, Iowa, and used this location as a base for researching potential newspaper markets. Characteristically, he evaluated many towns in the three states that he knew best and narrowed his choices to the newspapers in Hutchinson, Kansas, and Ottumwa, Iowa.

When he purchased the *Ottumwa Daily Courier* in 1890, he did so in part with his own savings and in part with money invested by several prominent residents of the town who believed in his journalistic ability and shared his communal objectives. As its publisher, he sought suggestions and critiques from those who worked for him, along with any criticisms or personal complaints they might have. As for the citizens of Ottumwa and surrounding areas reached by the daily, he made it known that the *Courier* was *their* newspaper and he believed it had not only a right but a duty to provide the most reliable and most provocative source of news possible.

In a letter stating his personal policies, he emphasized that a newspaper publisher and editor must pursue "a hearty, honest, and kindly cooperation with unflagging zeal and a wise appreciation for the rights and interests of all."

This came as a surprise to many citizens who, whenever they bothered to read a newspaper at all, were accustomed to being deluged with misinformation, ranging from biased "news" to editorial bombast and personal vendettas. Lee brought them a new level of journalism, characterized by innovation, integrity, and professionalism.

Above all, Lee's business was news. Although he was himself modest and conservative by nature, he did not hesitate to present the news as graphically and objectively as possible, even when he was covering unpopular causes. One story illustrates his early success with investigative reporting. It occurred soon after he purchased the *Muscatine Journal* in 1903.

Muscatine, Iowa, as it looked in 1901, just prior to A. W. Lee's purchase of the town's Journal *in 1903. The paper dates back to 1840, when Muscatine was an important riverboat town. In the paper's early days, the publisher was John Mahin, Lee's brother-in-law. Samuel L. Clemens (1835-1910), who wrote under the name, Mark Twain, spent several years working at the* Journal.

Bootlegging was an explosive issue in Iowa in those days because of official corruption and various miscarriages of justice. Lee's *Muscatine Journal* began to accumulate evidence that certain federal agents, attorneys, and judges were hiring "professional witnesses" in order to secure indictments and levy heavy fines against purported bootleggers. When A. W. Lee received numerous letters from readers claiming that they had been arrested without cause or wrongfully convicted, he decided there must be good reason for their complaints and the paper should investigate.

One of the steps taken was to assign a reporter, Charles Dale, to participate in a raid on the home of a suspected bootlegger. His objective was to ascertain whether the raid was set up in such a way that paid witnesses would be involved who would later testify illegally against the defendant. When the story broke and confirmed the practice, the government officials involved were livid.

Bootlegging was a constant source for news in Iowa at the turn of the century because of the state's strict prohibition laws. The term arose from the practice of stuffing a flask in one's boot.

The Women's Christian Temperance Union, founded in 1874, was an important force in the prohibition movement. They started the Anti-Saloon League in 1893 and were finally successful in encouraging lawmakers to pass the 18th Amendment in 1917, which became effective in January of 1920.

Lashing back — and at the same time demonstrating how corrupt the system really was — they saw to it that Dale was arrested for impersonating a federal officer. He was sentenced to 15 months hard labor and fined $800 in court costs. However, they agreed to suspend the sentence if Dale agreed to leave Iowa, which he did after A. W. Lee personally paid the $800.

Characteristically, A. W. Lee retained a meticulous file of all the proceedings relating to this incident, just in case the paper was ever sued for misrepresentation of fact. But it wasn't, although Lee was subjected to some nasty correspondence from people opposed to investigative journalism. Lee was satisfied with the outcome and was gratified to learn that his reporter, Charles Dale, got a job with the *Chicago Tribune* largely as a result of his role in the incident. The Lee reputation for going after the news was becoming entrenched.

Lee, once described as "an angular sort of fellow who would have made a fine evangelist," had an open and kindly nature guided by an intense and fervent interest in helping people — especially young men who were starting their careers — to utilize their education and their personal potential to achieve success.

A characteristic example is that of John Huston, who was employed by Lee in the *Ottumwa Daily Courier* office doing odd jobs. Although he had visions of becoming a reporter, he was tempted to leave the newspaper and take a job as a letter carrier, which paid good wages and was well protected under federal regulations and policies. He mentioned his intentions to Lee, expecting no more than a cursory "good luck."

To his astonishment, Lee not only protested but gave ample evidence that he was fully aware of his young employee's record on the job and his potential as a journalist.

Despite crowded conditions, clutter, and poor lighting, newspaper offices attracted many young people who aspired to be reporters and help make the news.

Because there were no competing media and because reliable statistics and data were hard to come by or nonexistent in many cases, reporters often used their own imaginations to color their stories. In an age when "yellow journalism" flourished and it was more important to titillate readers than to provide accurate facts, editors rarely required that reporters document the copy they handed in.

"John," he commented, "it's true that you can earn more money as a postal carrier than you now make here. However, I want you to know that you will make a good newspaperman one of these days and that you will make more money with the *Courier* than you will ever make under Civil Service."

"I accepted his advice," recalled Huston, "and learned before too long that Mr. Lee's judgment in this matter, as usual, was very good." Huston later became publisher of the *Courier* and had a lifetime career with Lee.

The nature and quality of the inspiration Lee imparted can be seen in the recollections of the man who was destined to be his successor, E. P. Adler. Adler went to work for the *Ottumwa Daily Courier* as a printer two years after the paper came into Lee's hands, having had some press room experience in Denver until a depression idled some of that city's plants. "Late in the fall of 1893," he recalled, "I learned that the *Courier* needed a reporter. So I went to Jim Powell, my foreman, and asked if I might talk to Mr. Lee and have a chance at the job.

"Mr. Lee had a college education and did not believe that anyone like me who did not have either high school or college training could ever write or become a reporter. But the man who had been engaged for the job failed to appear and in desperation Mr. Lee decided to give me a trial.

"Then there came another problem. I was getting $12 a week as a printer and Mr. Lee said he could not pay me more than $9 as a reporter because I had no experience. I went home with this news, and my father was indignant to think that I could not earn as much money as a reporter where I had to wear clean shirts two or three times a week when, as a printer upstairs, I earned more money and did not have to wear good clothes or to change shirts more than once a week. But my mother, whose word was always law at home, decided I should have this opportunity that I had been seeking."

The Mahin family

John Mahin was born at Noblesville, Indiana, December 8, 1833, the son of Jacob Mahin, who moved his family west when John was only four. Young John apprenticed in 1847, at the age of 13, as a printer at the Bloomington (Iowa) *Herald*, thus starting a long career in newspapers. He was publisher of the *Muscatine Journal* for 50 years and was an important figure in journalism until retiring in 1900.

He was the son-in-law of John B. Lee, A. W. Lee's father, and thus the brother-in-law of A. W. Lee, whose sister, Anna, Mahin married in 1864. He tutored A. W. Lee during the latter's apprenticeship at the *Muscatine Journal*.

John's brother, James, went into partnership with him as the Mahin Brothers until James's death in 1877. In 1889, John's son, John Lee Mahin, joined the *Journal* and served as business manager until 1891 when he went to Chicago to pursue a career in journalism and advertising. He became one of the successful pioneers in the advertising agency field and it was reported that his firm, the Mahin Advertising Agency, ranked with Lord & Thomas and N. W. Ayer & Son in prestige and stature of clients.

In 1900, a second son, Harold J. Mahin, took over the duties of business manager of the *Journal*. In 1902, Harold also left for Chicago, and in 1903, the Mahin stock in the Journal Printing Company was sold to A. W. Lee, W. L. Lane, and H. M. Sheppard and became part of the Lee newspaper group.

John Mahin had two daughters, Mabel and Florence. Florence married a man named Alford in 1900. John had a brother, Frank, who moved to England and became the United States consul in Nottingham. It was in Frank's home that A. W. Lee died following his heart attack while on a trip abroad in July, 1907.

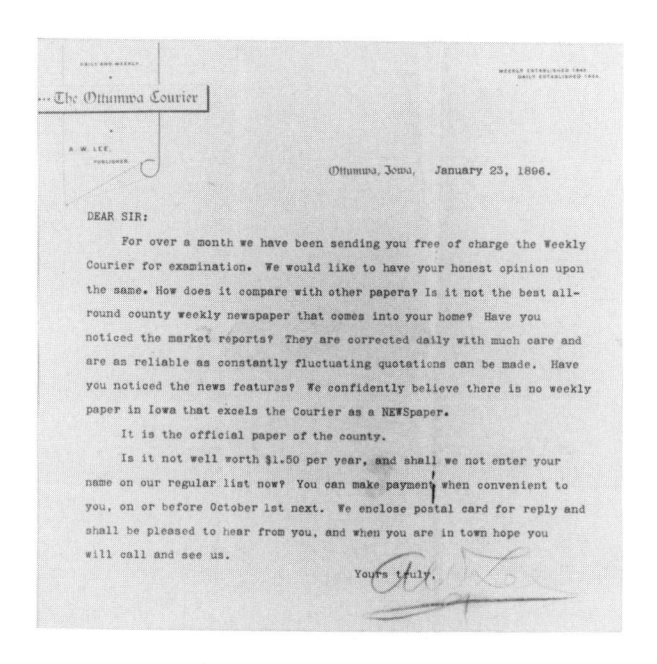

In this 1896 letter, A. W. Lee personally solicited a subscription from a citizen who had been receiving complimentary copies of the paper. The cost: $1.50 per year. The terms: the subscription was to start immediately; payment was not due for nine months!

When he became a reporter under Lee, wrote Adler later, "something in me changed my whole line of thinking." As a printer, he had always quit work the minute the whistle blew. Now, however, he found himself involved in a career that was more challenging to him. Working for Lee, a man whose whole life was devoted to the demands of his profession and the good of the community, gave direction and focus to his newly chosen career. Soon Adler was working evenings and Sundays, but found out for the first time that work — no matter how hard or how exacting — could be immensely rewarding, satisfying, and refreshing to the spirit.

It was this sense of regeneration and accomplishment that led people to work hard and commit themselves personally to accomplish the goals established by A. W. Lee. "Mr. Lee was a kindly man and the finest Christian gentleman I ever knew," wrote Adler. "He believed in the hopes and aspirations of young men and always tried to help them whenever he could." He had some unique styles of communication, one of which was to leave personal notes to people where they were sure to see them. Sometimes these were suggestions or leads, occasionally the solicitation of solutions to common problems. Quite often, they were complimentary remarks about a job well done or an editorial well written.

These qualities and factors gave A. W. Lee an unusual touch and attracted more professional talent and experience to Ottumwa than any small-town newspaper had a right to in those days. Aaron M. Brayton, founder of the *La Crosse Tribune* in 1904 and a distinguished figure in American journalism, has referred to Lee as "a methodical and open-minded man who wanted to respect journalism as he respected himself.... He was one of the pioneers who showed the capacity which, during at least one-quarter of a century, transformed the rural-city newspaper from the status of parasite and mendicant to a sturdy and self-respecting and profoundly useful factor in the development of America." By the time E. P. Adler had established himself as a working journalist, wrote Brayton, Lee had made the *Ottumwa Daily Courier* into "one of the first self-supporting and vigorously independent newspapers in the Mississippi Basin."

Lee's vigorous policy of letting his editors pursue independent roles, take risks, and assume responsibilities beyond the conventional helped the *Courier* to grow and prosper beyond what was achieved by most newspapers of its size and in its kind of environment. Brayton said, "Lee saw his own prudence and orderly management develop in Ottumwa a newspaper that in its class had no peer either in financial independence or in the functions which justify journalism — solid news reporting and clear, courageous editorial positions."

For more than 85 years, La Crosse, Wisconsin, has been a key location on the map of Lee newspapers. This picture, taken in the early 1900's, shows Main Street, facing west toward the river.

La Crosse, the seat of La Crosse County, was the site of a French fur-trading post in the late 18th century, well situated at the foot of high bluffs on the Mississippi where the La Crosse and Black Rivers meet. After becoming a center for lumbering operations, the town was incorporated in 1856.

Today, with a population of almost 50,000, the city is a center of industry and agriculture and is ranked as the largest metro market between Minneapolis and Madison. It is the site of three institutions of higher learning: the University of Wisconsin-La Crosse, Viterbo College, and Western Wisconsin Technical College.

Significantly, Lee's policies of independence, risk-taking, and delegation of authority were to become part of the Lee company tradition.

E. P. Adler liked to tell a story which says a great deal about Lee's courage as a publisher and the individual responsibility he entrusted to his staff members. Adler, a reporter at the time, had researched and written an article that had the potential of blowing the lid off the wheeling and dealing of a prominent and popular politician who was allegedly embezzling money from the federal department he administered in Iowa.

"I talked to Mr. Lee after reviewing the wording of the article a dozen times," recalled Adler, "and asked him what I should do. I told him that its publication would either make or break the *Courier*. In his usual cheerful manner, he ended the conversation by saying to me, 'You will have to use your own judgment. I cannot advise you.' We ran the story."

"Publication of the exposé caused more havoc than if the levee had burst," wrote a colleague many years later. However, the paper survived an outburst of hate mail from the political supporters of the man whose integrity had been damned and successfully resisted threats to close the paper down for slander.

Other newspapers in the state wrote strong editorials the next day, lambasting the *Courier* and supporting the politician. But Adler and Lee had the satisfaction of seeing them obliged to publish the follow-up story when the official in question was summarily removed from office by the United States government.

No matter what the outcome might have been or how risky it was to wave red flags in the faces of influential officeholders, it was characteristic of A. W. Lee that he would rather have seen the paper go under than to kill a valid story because of political clout, and he trusted his staff members to make sound judgments about validity. As the editors of the 1947 history, *The Lee Papers*, wrote, "It was this recognition that newspapers not only must print the news but must be maintained in a position where, if necessary, they could look any man or corporation or institution in the face and tell that man or corporation or institution to go to hell, that early became a distinguishing mark of a Lee newspaper operation."

From the very beginning of his journalistic career, A. W. Lee made certain that he was never placed in a compromising position. So sensitive was he on the subject of editorial integrity that, shortly after he purchased the *Courier*, he resigned an appointment as local postmaster even though it was customary in those days for the publisher to hold that position if he was politically acceptable. Lee felt that he could not serve two masters — the public and the government — at the same time. It was said to be the first time in the history of the postal service that such a midterm resignation had been made, short of ill health, death, or moving out of the state.

Mary and A. W. Lee had three children, only one of whom survived past childhood. Laura Anna Lee, pictured here with her mother, lived to be 83.

William died in 1890, shortly before his third birthday. Alfred was stricken with appendicitis and died in Ottumwa at the age of nine.

After the death of her father in 1907, Laura Lee inherited controlling stock in the five newspapers then in the Lee Group. Although she was at all times wholly informed about the papers and actively interested in their progress and development, she did not attempt to manage them or become directly involved with corporate administration. Rather, she sought the advice of officers and directors and then played a strong role in selecting the publishers and top editors.

Over the years, Laura Lee became less and less active in the company. In fact, she later moved from Iowa to Washington, D.C., and began spending her summers in New England from the week before Memorial Day until the beginning of October. She enjoyed relatively good health most of her life until she fell and broke her hip in Washington. She came through an operation with no apparent problems but then suddenly had an embolism and died at the age of 83.

The deaths of Lee's sons were his greatest tragedy. Those closest to him later said that his passionate determination to help young men find jobs and be successful was a result of losing his own sons and his dreams of their bright future.

Lee's approach to newspaper publishing included a willingness to experiment with all aspects of the paper, not just the editorial functions. In the 1890's, for example, it was customary for businesses to run daily advertisements in the paper without any changes in text, format, or position for weeks on end. Only for very special occasions did an advertiser, such as a large department store, run a special ad, and then it was usually to alert readers to a special sale or to announce a store-wide event. Because most ads were carbon copies of the previous ones, no one paid much attention.

The picture changed abruptly and significantly when Lee purchased the *Courier*. Examining the advertising columns of the paper, he asked his business manager, David M. Conroy, why ads couldn't be just as compelling as editorials. He thought the dull, unappealing nature of most ads defeated the whole purpose of their being: to attract the attention of readers and motivate them to go to the store.

Lee introduced a plan that demonstrates the innovativeness he brought to newspaper publishing. As he said then, "I'd like to see the time when our paper will contain display ads that are changed every day." This is a common practice now, but was revolutionary then.

"Mr. Lee believed that there was just as much news in what a store had to sell as in an item of actual happenings or doings of people," commented Conroy many years later. This practice later became a norm in the industry.

At first, Lee had his work cut out for him trying to get advertisers to write new advertisements regularly and pay the additional — though very modest — cost of composition. But he persisted in his goal and was rewarded by improved circulation and readership — and a boost in advertising from pleased merchants whose sales increased.

As a result of A. W. Lee's foresight, and the addition of the *Davenport Times*, the *Courier-Post* in Hannibal, Missouri, and the *La Crosse Tribune* in La Crosse, Wisconsin, the five newspapers he published prior to his sudden death in 1907 gained in circulation and earned recognition as catalysts for community growth. The company — thanks to A. W. Lee's leadership — was acquiring a rich editorial and management legacy that exists to this day.

Newspapers have always been an inexpensive source of news. This receipt, dated February 29, 1896, is for a full year's subscription to the Muscatine Journal.

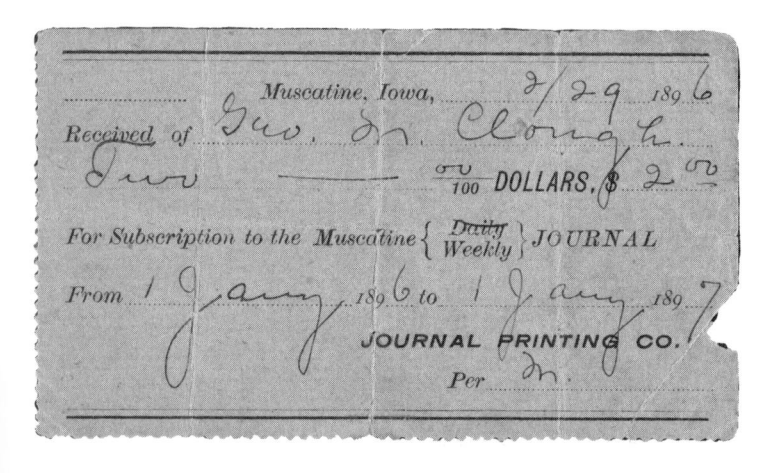

Advertising at the turn of the century (opposite page) mainly took the form of repetitive announcements. The Lee newspapers were among the first to encourage advertisers to put "sell" into advertising copy when A. W. Lee decided that there was news value in the products and services that local merchants and household firms were offering to the public. He convinced advertisers that they would attract more customers if they varied their messages and keyed them to seasonal events and special community needs.

THE OTTUMWA DAILY COURIER, TUESDAY EVENING, APRIL 14, 1891.

| We Are In It! | Everything Selling at | Next to Nothing. |

G. H. SHEFFER,

Will Today inaugurate the Greatest Sale in the History of Ottumwa. Remember this is a Sale of the Best Goods which the Market Produces and You Don't Want to Miss it.

I QUOTE BUT A FEW OF THE LEADERS.

40-inch All-Wool Henrietta Suits in all Colors and Black with Silk or Braid Trimmings at $4.50.
An Elegant Faille Francaise at 75c.
First-Class Satin Rhadame at 75c.
Tennis Flannels at 6¼c.
Good Prints at 4c.
Chevoit Plaids at 5c.

Ladies' India Lisle Thread Vests at 5c each.
L. L. Unbleached Muslin at 4c.
3-inch Umbrellas, Silver Handles, at 65c.
Full-Size Crochet Bed Spreads at 75c.
Apron Checked Ginghams at 5c.
Ladies' Fast Black Hose at 6¼c.
Peerless Corsets at 23c.
Best Grades Summer Corsets very Cheap.

OTHER BARGAINS TOO NUMEROUS TO MENTION AT

We are giving away to cash buyers an Elegant Folding Table. Ask to see it.

HER CLAIM DISCREDITED.

"Artemus Ward's" Executor at Waterford, Me., Says the Humorist Never Married.

WATERFORD, Me., April 13.—The claim of the Illinois woman to be the widow of "Artemus Ward" excites much interest in this, his native town. The American executor of Charles F. Browne is Mr. Horace Maxfield, who lives here and who knows more about the famous Artemus than any one else. Browne's alleged marriage is a thing never before heard of or suspected here, and nobody here credits it. All that is left of Artemus Ward's property is the Yonkers house and say $5,000, and this by his will goes to the five children of the late John C. Gerry of South Waterford, Ward's cousins. All that could be attained by a widow of Ward's would be her third of the income from the Yonkers house—about $100 interest or rental. That Browne was born here April 26, 1834, hardly admits of a question.

THE PAYNE COURT MARTIAL.

Second Trial of the Sons of Veterans Commander-in-Chief Concluded.

INDIANAPOLIS, Ind., April 13.—The second trial by court martial of Walter S. Payne of Fostoria, O., ex-commander-in-chief of the Sons of Veterans, was concluded here. When Payne turned the office of commander-in-chief over to his successor, George B. Abbott of Chicago he was unable to produce funds amounting to $1,800, committed to his custody. Formal charges were preferred against him, and at the trial held at Dayton he was convicted. At the national encampment, Payne's defense is that the $1,800 alleged to have been taken by him was invested in real estate within the expectation that the profits, which were expected to be large, would accrue to the order. The debt has long since been made good.

The Utopia Survivors.

NEW YORK, April 13.—The Italian immigrants saved from the wreck of the Utopia, who were brought to this city, were landed at the barge office. Many of them mourned the loss of some friend or relative, and some instances one member of a whole family was all that was left. Of one family of eight, only the father and one son reached here—mother, brother and four children having been lost. One sad case was that of a little Italian boy about 9 years old, who was alone, his parents having been drowned. When the accident happened he jumped overboard and got astride of a plank to which he clung until picked up by the rescuing boats. He was taken care of by the Italian Home society. Capt. Marr, of the Anglia, the steamer which brought the rescued immigrants here, stood by the registry clerk's desk as the immigrants passed by to be registered, and to each he gave $12. It was the division of the fund that had been subscribed for their relief.

The Cherokee Strip Gold Fields.

ARKANSAS CITY, Kan., April 13.—This city is considerably excited by the report of E. T. Buchanan. He returned to the city from a several weeks' visit in the Cherokee Strip a short time since. He had been there prospecting for minerals, and brought home with him samples of ore. He had some of the samples assayed, and the report which he received was to the effect that his find would run from $300 to $1,000 gold to the ton of quartz. Mr. Buchanan is highly elated, and says his find is within fifty miles of this city. He is organizing a company of 500 men, and they will take thirty days' supply of provisions and go to the gold field. Mr. Buchanan has samples of his ore on exhibition in this city. He claims his gold find is bona fide, and if it is the Cherokee Strip will soon be overrun with settlers and miners.

Peaches Uninjured.

COLUMBUS, Ind., April 11—Advices from the great peach kings of Indiana, Dean Brothers, and other growers at Henryville, Otto, New Providence and Memphis, Ind., state that no injury to peaches can be perceived, and the only harm appears to be the checking of the blossoming for a few days.

The Western Lines Refuse to Withdraw the Alton Tickets.

CHICAGO, April 13.—The opinion is generally expressed that the eastern board of ruling exceeded its power when it requested the western connections of the Alton to boycott that road, or in other words, to stop ticketing business over that road. From present indications not one of the western roads will comply with the request. General Passenger Agent Charlton of the Alton wired to every western road asking it to inform him whether it intended to submit to the dictation of the eastern roads and turn the Alton tickets to the wall. About twenty replies were received and one assured the Alton that it was not in the boycotting business and would continue to sell tickets over the Alton as usual.

Blown to Pieces by Nitro-Glycerine.

WASHINGTON, Pa., April 13.—About four miles from this place a two quart nitro-glycerine can exploded, instantly killing Tom Mounts Jr., aged 18 and probably fatally injuring his younger brother William, aged 12. The boys had found the can, which they supposed was empty, and struck it against a fence post, causing a terrible explosion. Parts of the body of the oldest boy were found two hundred feet from the scene of the accident. The younger boy was blown about one hundred and fifty feet through the air and was found in an adjoining orchard. He is internally injured.

Republican Elected All.

PROVIDENCE, R. I., April 11—At the Bye election for senator and twelve representatives the Republicans elected all their candidates. The Republicans have a large majority in both houses.

Anna Dickinson Under Treatment.

NEW YORK, April 11—Miss Anna Dickinson, the talented reader, accompanied by her maid, left at 9 a. m. for Goshen, N. Y., to undergo medical treatment.

TELEGRAPHIC BRIEFS.

John G. Carlisle says that he is not a presidential candidate.

Attorney General Miller has recovered from illness and resumed his duties.

Gen. J. R. Cooke, a native of Missouri, died at Richmond, Va.

Ex-Governor Thomas C. Fletcher of Missouri, is ill of pneumonia at Washington.

The Oklahoma City election resulted in the election of a straight Democratic ticket.

A report from Philadelphia outlines the formation of a copper trust greater than the sugar combine.

J. M. Shoemaker has been appointed receiver of the Columbia Iron and Steel company at Pittsburg.

D. Augustus Straker, colored, is a candidate for the judicial bench at Detroit. Bench and bar indorse him.

Elizabeth, N. J., is much excited over the discovery of a case of spotted or typhus fever. The patient is a Pole.

A tramp at Ashland, Pa., stole Jacob Weduock's coat from the attic. In it had been hidden $10,000 in currency.

Patrick Murray, stabbed by Moses T. Walker, colored catcher of the Stars at Syracuse, N. Y., died.

W. S Skaggs, a Lebanon, Mo. government prisoner on the way to Columbus, Mo., escaped by jumping from the rapidly moving train.

The Hon. Jeff Orr of Springfield, Ills., is in Wichita as volunteer counsel for J. C. Adams, sentenced to death for slaying Capt. Couch.

Mrs. Caroline Witbelm, owner of the Witbelm brewery, Pittsburg, has confessed judgment for $10,000, for the benefit of her creditors.

The priests of the diocese of Concordia banqueted Bishop Scannell at Concordia in honor of his appointment to the vacant see at Omaha.

The recent heavy influx of coal caused the failure of Frank Barnerd, coal dealer, San Francisco. The assets will pay 15 per cent of the $82,000 liabilities.

Secretary Blaine has fixed Monday, Oct. 5, as the date for the reciprocity conference with Canadian government officials. The arrangement is satisfactory.

The Iowa Homestead, a prominent agricultural paper published at Des Moines, is fighting the southern Farmers' Alliance, and says the people should have nothing to do with it.

Alphonse J. Stephanie, who was convicted of murder in the second degree for the shooting of a rascal spotted on typhus sentenced in New York to state prison for life.

Ex-Senator Ingalls made much of his time on his way back home near Atchison, Kansas riding in the engineer's cab on replies. The train man said he was delighted. The engineer was a Populist.

My Stock of Spring Goods

Is Unequaled and I defy competition in regard to Quality, Price and Workmanship. I am one of the oldest established Merchant Tailors in the city and my statements are always backed with facts.

I am always Pleased to show Goods whether you Buy or not.

FRED SWENSON, Merchant Tailor.
513 EAST MAIN STREET.

DON'T FAIL TO SEE

THE NEW ATTRACTIONS IN

SPRING JACKETS

AT LOW PRICES, AT

FRED. ROSEN & BRO'S.

The Golden Eagle Clothing house,

229-231 East Main Street.

OUR - FURNISHING - GOODS DEPARTMENT.

LOOK OUT FOR THE DATE.

FRIDAY AND SATURDAY, APRIL 17-18.

WE WILL HAVE A SPECIAL SALE OF THE FOLLOWING GOODS

Two Hundred Dozen Unlaundried Shirts made of New York Mills Muslin and 2,40) Linen Bossoms, the best $1.00 Shirt ever sold in the United States

At 49 CTS.

Only 3 shirts to Each Customer. 25 Dozen Silk Ties worth 50 cents,

At 24 CTS.

Be sure and call and see these goods, for there is some money to be saved.

THE GOLDEN EAGLE.

Men's Suits.

We offer this week 500 Men's All-Wool Suits cut in Sack and Frock. Materials: Black Cheviot, Mixed Cassimeres, Fancy Worsted Corkscrews, English Melton and Imported Worsteds.

Regular Value, $20 and $18.5

YOUR CHOICE.

$15.00

CHILDREN'S SUITS.

Our former efforts to sell Children's Suits cheap will be excelled the coming week. We propose to sell 500 Suits in one week. To do it we have concluded to sell all

$6, $5.50, $5, $4.75 and $4.50

Suits at

$4.00.

These suits are made of Fine Casimeres, Worsteds, Flannels, Cheviot and Imported Goods.

OTHER SUITS AT $1.50

Among the most significant philosophies were integrity in news reporting, delegation of authority to independent publishers, the encouragement of risk-taking in pioneering new ventures or procedures, motivating employees to improve their skills and performance, encouraging more interesting advertising, and a tradition of service to the public and the community.

Lee is best recognized for his foresight in developing the premise that, no matter how many newspapers were to come into the fold, each publisher should be his own boss. As such, it was his essential responsibility to ensure that the paper would pay its own way and yet not be subservient to any outside group, political or commercial. Making a profit was important, said Lee, because it assured independence. But, he added, there were times when responsibility to the newspaper craft and to the community would be equally vital.

The newspapers owned by A. W. Lee before his death included:
Ottumwa Daily Courier, *April, 1890*
Davenport Times, *July, 1899*
Muscatine Journal, *January, 1903*
Hannibal Courier-Post, *February, 1907*
La Crosse Tribune, *February, 1907*

Appearing in this photograph (left to right) are: John F. Powell (Ottumwa), Frank Burgess (La Crosse), A. W. Lee, Frank D. Throop (Muscatine), E. P. Adler (Davenport), and W. J. Hill (Hannibal).

A. W. Lee had vision. Moreover, as one tribute to him expressed it, he had above all "the genius to gather together men upon whom he could rely to give substance to his dream."

Milestones during the A. W. Lee administration

- April, 1890 — A. W. Lee purchases the *Ottumwa Daily Courier* for $16,000 and becomes its publisher.
- July 1, 1899 — Acquisition of the *Davenport Times*, the beginning of a newspaper syndicate. The paper is renamed the *Daily Times*.
- January 20, 1901 — Charles D. Reimers, then managing editor of the *Courier*, is named publisher of the *Times*. E. P. Adler is named business manager, then succeeds Reimers (who retired) as publisher.
- January 1, 1903 — Lee takes over the *Muscatine Journal* from his brother-in-law, John Mahin. Walter Lane, of the *Courier*, is sent to Muscatine as business manager, followed by Frank D. Throop, Lee P. Loomis, and Clyde R. Radedeaux.
- February 1, 1907 — Lee acquires the Hannibal *Courier-Post* and names W. J. Hill (ad manager of the *Muscatine Journal*) publisher.
- February, 1907 — The *La Crosse Tribune* is purchased. Frank H. Burgess, from circulation at the *Daily Times*, becomes its publisher. Founder A. M. Brayton continues as editor.
- July 15, 1907 — A. W. Lee dies while abroad, in Nottingham, England. E. P. Adler becomes publisher and president.

The growth of The Lee Syndicate 1890-1907

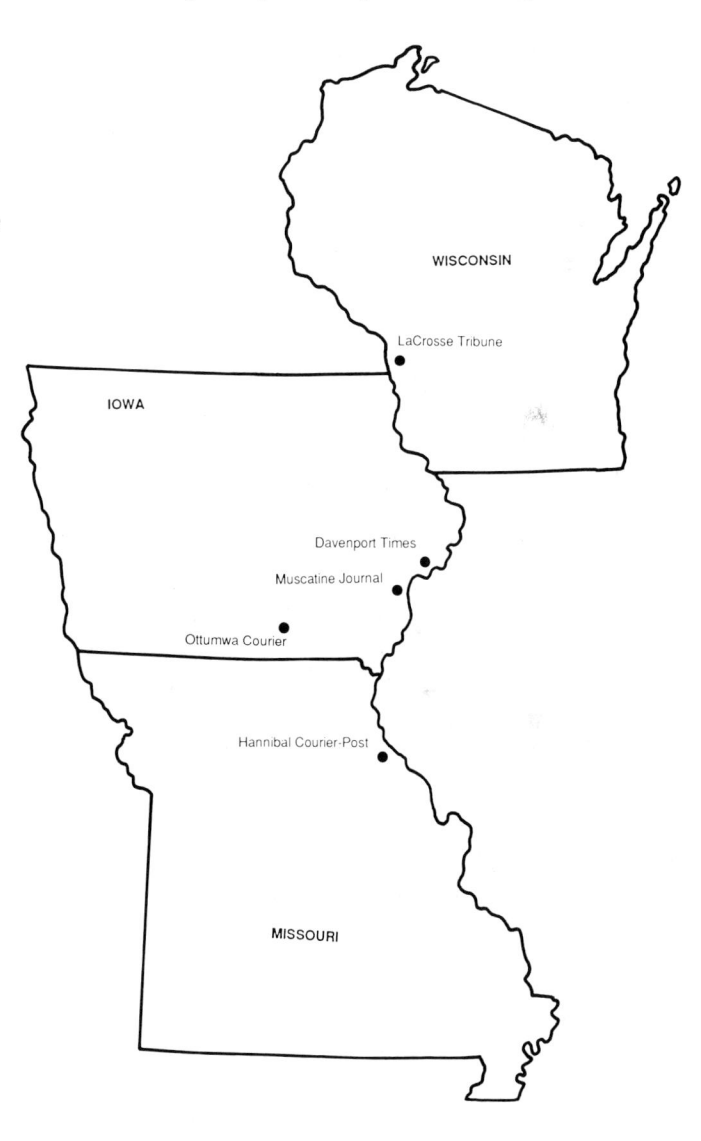

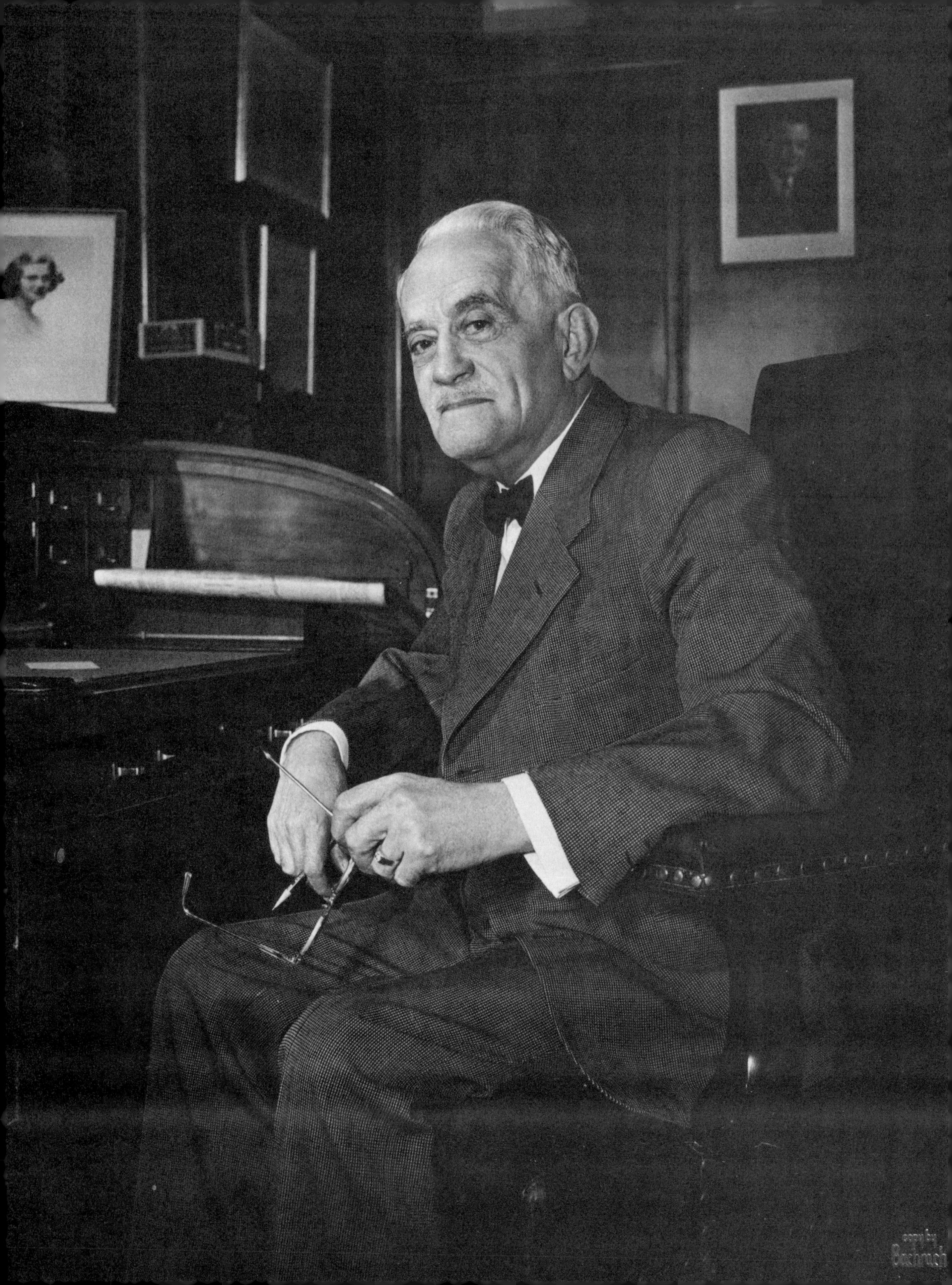
copy by
Bachrach

Chapter Two
an Instinct to Build

1907-1949   *Emanuel Philip Adler*

Born September 30, 1872, in Chicago. Son of Philip Emanuel Adler and Bertha Blade Adler; brother of Betty Adler.

Attended public school in Ottumwa, Iowa, with schooling ended in the eighth grade.

Worked as a printer's devil on German language weekly, 1885, and later as an apprentice printer for *Saturday Press*, in mid-1880's.

Worked as a printer in the composing room of the *Ottumwa Daily Courier* under A. W. Lee in late 1880's, becoming a reporter in 1893, and in succession thereafter city editor, managing editor, and business manager.

Transferred to the *Davenport Times* in 1899, and promoted to publisher in 1901.

Married Lena Rothschild, February 4, 1902.

Father of one son, Philip David Adler, born November 5, 1902.

Appointed president of Lee, August 12, 1907, following death of A. W. Lee.

Elected president of the Davenport Bank and Trust Company, June 7, 1932.

Active in professional associations, including tenures as vice president of the Associated Press, president of the Inland Press Association, 1917-18, and committee chairman with the American Newspaper Publishers Association, 1918-20.

Served on many boards, including the American Red Cross, YMCA, the Community Chest, United Jewish Appeal, Mississippi Valley Fair and Exposition, the Davenport Museum, the Davenport Municipal Art Gallery, St. Luke's Hospital, and numerous civic, religious, and political organizations in Iowa from 1910 until his death in 1949.

Died March 2, 1949.

After the *Ottumwa Daily Courier* became recognized as a leading daily newspaper in its region, A. W. Lee began to look for a second newspaper he could acquire and develop. It would be this purchase that would give young E. P. Adler an opportunity to demonstrate his managerial and editorial skills.

Lee considered many alternatives, but the focus of his attention was Davenport, Iowa. Although the town had fewer than 15,000 people, it was the home of five daily newspapers, two of them in German to cater to one of the predominant national stocks in the Scott County region. The *Davenport Times*, which had been founded in 1858 and had managed to survive while other dailies came and went, became the focus of his interest. It was described as having "a goodly amount of reading matter but a rather meager amount of advertising."

Evaluating the *Times* as a daily with a solid readership but with untapped circulation and marketing potential, Lee purchased the paper on July 1, 1899. He named the *Courier's* managing editor, Charles D. Reimers, as publisher of the new acquisition and also sent E. P. Adler, who had recently been elevated to business manager, to Davenport to serve in the same position for Reimers. At the time of the transfer, Adler was seriously considering leaving the newspaper business and beginning a new career in advertising in St. Louis. Lee convinced him that his skills were needed in Davenport. In recognition of the opportunities Lee had already given him, Adler agreed to accept the position. Adler soon learned how valuable his skills really were.

Davenport began as a trading post on the Mississippi River, at the site of the signing of the treaty ending the Black Hawk Indian War in 1832. It prospered with the arrival of the first railroad to bridge the Mississippi in 1856 and the increase in commercial traffic along the river during the last half of the 19th century. The early settlement was named after Colonel George Davenport, fur trader, landowner, and an army officer who served as a quartermaster general during the Indian War.

The drawing is from an original "in the possession of Geo. L. Davenport." Its legend indicates a population growth from 60 people in 1836, to 11,000 in 1856.

Known to associates as E. P. during his entire career (or as Mannie — short for Emanuel — to his closest friends), he had been in Davenport only a short time when there were rumblings that the printers might strike over certain grievances voiced by the "czar of the back room," Tom Kelley. Kelley, who saw the fledgling labor union movement of the day as a key to personal power, thought he could take advantage of this new business manager and bluff him into giving in to certain concessions. But E. P., who at this point had 14 years of newspapering under his belt, had plenty of experience to draw upon. He knew Kelley's demands were excessive and he was sure Kelley also knew they were.

Why E. P. was called Mannie

"We always called Emanuel Philip Adler 'Mannie,'" says Selma Waterman, who was 17 years younger than Adler but knew him well from her youth. "That distinguished him from his father, whose first names were just the reverse, Philip Emanuel, and who was called Emanuel by relatives and friends alike."

The nickname clung to him during his boyhood and teens and was used in family circles throughout his life. In the business world, however, he became "E. P." and was seldom referred to as "Mannie" by his associates.

The "I&I Interurban" making a stop at Davenport's Brady Street depot in the early 1900's. The popular trolley offered fast, economical transportation to Muscatine and suburban communities. The Ionic columns on the Democrat Building can be seen in the background.

Without becoming ruffled or losing his attitude of friendliness, Adler stood firm. Kelley had to back down on his strike threat, but he remained glum and uncooperative. His leverage was gone and, perhaps more importantly, he felt he had lost face.

E. P. knew the importance of maintaining a comfortable relationship and was determined to establish one with Kelley. He purposely stayed out of the composing room, knowing that this was the domain of the printers and that staff members from the front office were not welcome unless it was to dispense paychecks. But a few days later he poked his head in the door and waved to Tom. "Hello, sweetheart!" he said, to the amazement of everyone present, and quickly shut the door. From that time on, they got along just fine.

The labor problems in Davenport had not escaped the vigilance of A. W. Lee, who was understandably concerned about this potentially explosive situation. He asked E. P. what could be done about the strike threat.

"Oh, that's all settled," said E. P. calmly. "You don't have to worry about any labor problem."

After several similar demonstrations of Adler's ability to manage things by winning people over, it was no wonder Lee appointed E. P. publisher of the *Times* when Reimers retired in January, 1901.

From his earliest days, E. P. was a man of predictable habits, one of which was to arise with the sun each morning and be at his desk by 6:45, before any of his employees were expected to appear. He devoted his spare time to learning about every phase of the newspaper industry in general and his own company in particular. So it was not surprising that he was ready to meet the emergency when an unexpected tragedy threatened the future of the Lee newspapers.

In early June, 1907, A. W. Lee sailed with his wife, Mary, her mother, and their daughter, Laura, for a four-month tour of Europe. When they arrived in Liverpool, England, a heart condition reappeared that had troubled Lee for several years.

They immediately travelled some 100 miles east to Nottingham, where a boyhood friend of Lee's, Frank Mahin, was the American consul. Mahin was also the brother of Lee's sister's husband, John Mahin, from whom Lee had purchased the *Muscatine Journal* five years earlier.

A full-page announcement greeted the citizens of the "Tri-Cities" (Davenport, Rock Island and Moline) on February 9, 1904, as the Daily Times *told of the purchase of a new press. According to the text of the ad, the new machine is completely electric and "does away with all the levers, belting and shafting" that ran earlier presses. It promises to be the "finest printing office equipment in the states of Iowa or Illinois, outside of Chicago." The press cost $20,000 and produced 25,000 papers per hour.*

E. P.'s habits

According to Isadore Katz, an attorney who knew the Adler family well, E. P. Adler was a man of predictable habits. He was an early riser and was invariably in the office by 6:45 — sometimes much sooner — each morning. He always walked to and from work, rain or shine, a distance of about 50 blocks; he was an inveterate cigar smoker and had a decided preference for Blackstones.

Whenever possible, he refreshed himself during workdays with a brief nap after lunch. "I remember," says Katz, "there was a certain chair where he would sit after he had eaten his lunch and take a short nap. He liked to go to bed early, and even when he was giving a party at his home, he'd say goodnight to his guests and go to bed at 9:30. But you know, nobody ever took offense. That was just E. P. He took good care of himself physically. Even his own doctor said that he was very smart about his health."

Those who worked with him remember the silent manner in which he indicated that enough discussion had taken place and that a meeting was over. E. P. would simply pick up the always-present copy of one of his newspapers and start to read it.

A. W. Lee, President of the Lee Newspaper Syndicate Succumbs to Illness Abroad

Was Editor for Years of the Ottumwa Courier, President of the Commercial Club and Leading Citizen

HEAD OF SYNDICATE OF FIVE PUBLICATIONS

Late Mr. Lee Went Abroad Several Weeks Ago to Spend Summer—Stricken With Heart Failure

Readers of the Ottumwa Daily Courier on July 15, 1907, were shocked to see this front-page obituary of a man who had meant so much to Ottumwa, Davenport, and other communities throughout the region. He was affectionately referred to as "the guiding light" of the five daily newspapers under his personal administration. While we may think communications in that day were crude, it is interesting to note that the news was published in Ottumwa on the same day that he died in Nottingham, England.

After two weeks of care at the hands of the best available physicians, Lee seemed to be recovering enough to continue his journey. However, he suffered a setback and died on July 15, seven days after his 49th birthday.

Back home, while Lee's associates experienced shock and intense feelings of personal bereavement, there was no panic at the newspapers. They had been left in competent hands, with complete plans for continuing operations during their owner's extended absence, even though two of the papers, the Hannibal *Courier-Post* and the *La Crosse Tribune*, had been acquired barely six months earlier.

Shortly before his death, aware that his illness could be fatal, Lee advised his wife that he had full confidence in Adler and Jim Powell to run the papers. Powell was the print shop foreman who had encouraged E. P. to become a reporter. Recognizing Powell's many strengths, Adler had encouraged A. W. Lee to bring him into the business office, as well. Powell quickly earned A. W. Lee's respect as a solid newspaperman and was named business manager of the *Courier* when Adler was sent to Davenport.

Thus it was that E. P., once described as "a fire-eating and adventurous but resourceful pioneer" was selected to head up what was then becoming known as the Lee Syndicate. And Powell, "an essential and cautious conservative," was appointed second-in-command, in charge of the company's business management.

Lee's widow, Mary (or Minnie, as she liked to be called), saw her choice validated as the company strengthened its position in the newspaper field by acquiring other dailies. But Adler's reasons for these acquisitions were different from those of most other publishers. The purchase of the Lincoln (Nebraska) *Star* in June, 1930, was a characteristic example.

"When Mr. Adler purchased the *Star* at a substantial figure," recalled one of his business managers, "I learned something about him that I had never known before.

"'The paper has been well handled and is popular,' Mr. Adler told me. 'But that isn't really what you buy when you buy a newspaper. In Lincoln we have bought a chance to be part of one of the finest cities and most progressive communities in America.'

Lincoln, Nebraska, was founded in 1864 and quickly became a grain and livestock trading center. Originally called Lancaster, it was renamed after Abraham Lincoln. It became the state capital in 1867. Gradually it assumed new stature as an educational as well as a commercial center in the state.

The state capitol building was completed in 1926 and symbolized the wide and fertile plains of Nebraska. It is topped with a statue of a sower in the act of scattering seeds. It was thought to be the third most magnificent building in the country, topped only by the Lincoln Monument in Washington, D.C., and the Empire State Building in New York City.

This caricature of E. P. Adler appeared in a directory of the many businesses in the Quad Cities area around the turn of the century. A caricature of each president appeared in the locally published book, which promoted the region.

> **E. P. Adler's early newspaper acquisitions**
> Following in the footsteps of the leader he emulated and admired, E. P. Adler continued the Lee policy of acquiring newspapers whose potential he felt had not yet been tapped. Among those purchased prior to the company's 50th anniversary were:
> Davenport *Democrat*, November, 1915
> *Wisconsin State Journal*, July, 1919
> Mason City *Globe-Gazette*, April, 1925
> Kewanee *Star Courier*, June, 1926
> Lincoln *Star*, June, 1930

"I saw the point.... What Mr. Adler had seen in Lincoln was a beautiful city, a great political and educational center, a citizenry of the finest type. If he could make the newspaper part and parcel of such a community, its success would be assured. He wanted to be part of Lincoln, to participate in its problems and its opportunities, to help with its community work, both civic and social, and so to deserve the success that would come to the *Star* as a natural by-product."

Such was Adler's doctrine and the way he interpreted Lee's vision of newspapers as instruments of civic responsibility. He carried the idea of accountability a step or two farther than Lee had done, making it clear that managers at all levels should participate in programs and activities whose objectives were to improve the towns and cities reached by the newspapers. Over the years, he pursued his policies of community involvement avidly and in a very personal manner.

In Davenport, for example, he helped to form the Greater Davenport Committee in 1911, and later the Davenport Industrial Commission, both of which focused their attention on attracting new businesses to the community. Such was his farsightedness and perception that, reportedly, no important civic projects were ever planned without his being consulted.

One of his most memorable civic achievements was staving off a devastating bank failure in Davenport at the beginning of the Depression. A young bank examiner, V. O. Figge, later to become a major figure in banking as well as one of E. P.'s closest friends and advisers, found himself in the thick of the battle in the fall of 1931.

"There I was," Figge recalls, "a young bank examiner with little experience, in an unfamiliar town, trying to cope with a financial crisis of historic proportions. Then I met E. P. and everything changed. He was a director of the Union Bank and had been called back from a business trip in New York because of the emergency. The other bank in Davenport and the largest in Iowa, the American Trust, was in imminent danger of collapse. Yet E. P. agreed to head a citizen's committee that took over the bank and serve as its president without pay while trying to reorganize it and raise sufficient capital to keep it in business."

His commitment to American Trust didn't preclude his continuing involvement with the other bank. This was a city-wide crisis and E. P. was determined to solve it.

There was one dramatic scene in which E. P. went to the Union Bank when long lines of panicky depositors were waiting nervously to withdraw their funds. He convinced many to change their minds by announcing to the milling crowd that the accounts of the Lee newspapers were not being withdrawn. He also told them he had prevailed upon the State of Iowa to transfer more than $400,000 in state funds to the bank as a gesture of confidence. He explained that he also knew about poverty, having come from a very poor family. This compassionate understanding of the fear that gripped these depositors had a calming influence. The crowd began to dissipate.

Then, to demonstrate further his commitment to the bank, he walked along the cages of the tellers and persuaded the remaining depositors to go home by writing in their passbooks that he would personally guarantee their funds if the bank were to fail. E. P. was not a rich man by today's measurement, but he lived modestly, saved diligently, and invested wisely so that he was a man of considerable means. Had the bank failed, however, he might well have been wiped out financially.

"The bank crisis," recalls Isadore Katz, a prominent attorney in Rock Island, Illinois, across the river from Lee headquarters in Davenport, "was an example of the kind of action he could — and did — take to help the community. In effect, he put his entire net worth and his financial future on the line. He could have lost it all. I can't think of anyone else who was ever willing to give everything he had."

Following the Crash of 1929, many banks all across America were on the verge of financial collapse. Davenport, Iowa, which had never known a bank failure, was thrown into near-panic when its major banks began running out of cash. On September 29, 1931, depositors began lining up, four abreast, in a run on the Union Bank that was to last two days. E. P. Adler and members of the Board prevented chaos. Today, its successor, Davenport Bank and Trust Company, is the largest in Iowa and has the highest return on assets in the nation. It is now a $1.6 billion bank and has never had a year in which it didn't outperform the previous year.

During a critical nine-month period, E. P. oversaw the closing of both Davenport banks, became the first president of a new one, the Davenport Bank and Trust Company, for which he raised more than a million dollars in new capital and motivated the federal government to provide further guarantees of monetary support. He personally contacted President Herbert Hoover, an Iowan himself, who later stopped by Davenport while making a whistle stop on his campaign trail. After speaking from the platform of the rear car, Hoover is said to have spied Adler, said, "There's my good friend, Mannie Adler," and invited him up for a photograph.

This occasion was one of the few instances in which E. P. Adler was ever seen playing a public role. For the most part, he was always behind the scenes, providing counsel if not actually planning events and strategies, and oftentimes contributing substantial funds to public-service ventures. He was a consummate philanthropist who not only helped to finance cultural institutions but gave direct support to young people who otherwise could never have educated themselves in their

E. P. was very close to his sister, Betty Adler Waterman, who also enjoyed a notable career with the Lee papers. She joined the Ottumwa Daily Courier staff as a proofreader in the late 1890's, when her brother was its city editor. After E. P. became publisher of the Daily Times, he brought Betty to Davenport to strengthen its women's department. Betty's popular columns sometimes appeared under the pen name of "Betsy Bolivar." She later wrote a book, Within the Year After, *that chronicled her experiences as a foreign correspondent covering the Versailles Conference for the Lee newspapers. She had the opportunity to know General John Pershing and had several extensive interviews with him which she incorporated into her book.*

President Herbert Hoover was well known to Davenport citizens, having been born and raised in West Branch, 40 miles west of the city. It is said that he and E. P. were friendly enough so that Adler could reach him on the telephone to discuss matters of importance to the Davenport area.

chosen careers. Isadore Katz was one such recipient. He recently described his experiences, pointing out that they typified those of dozens — perhaps hundreds — of other people whose lives and careers were enhanced by Adler's never-ending generosity.

"I first met E. P. at Temple Emanuel while I was enrolled at Augustana College," Katz recalls. "E. P. was a devout attendant and could be counted on to be in the third row on the right side by the pulpit on Friday evenings. I didn't have a sou to my name and somehow it came to E. P.'s attention that I might need funds to stay in college, and he told me that if I ever got in a tough spot he would tide me over.

"Mr. Adler asked what I needed and gave me $200. He was a delightful man. He said, 'Isadore, now whatever you need, let me know.' He did this for a number of young men, and I don't think any of them ever paid him back. I paid him $25 at a time, even in the 1930's when I had no extra money. I don't think he expected to be paid back.

"Once when I came home for the holidays, I took the pulpit and gave a sermon about the history of religion. E. P. was in the congregation, as usual. He sent me the most wonderful letter saying, 'I heard your sermon and I was so impressed with it that I want you to give me your manuscript to read.' When I told him I didn't have a manuscript, but had given the sermon extemporaneously, he asked me to try to remember what I'd said and write it all down."

It took Katz 16 hours that weekend, but he recaptured most of his speech. After receiving the sermon, Adler said to Katz, "Any debt you still owe me is now paid in full." He had the sermon reproduced and gave copies to friends.

The great Chicago fire of 1871 caused unimaginable damage to that unfortunate city. Looking across the ruins of the Field, Leiter & Co. store, one can see the still-standing wall of the First National Bank at the corner of State and Washington Streets. Devastating though the fire was, its aftermath was to benefit small towns to the west as Chicagoans decided to move rather than rebuild.

Thus it was that, some five years after the fire, Philip Emanuel Adler left his long-time home on Milwaukee Avenue and moved his family to Ottumwa, Iowa. He left behind what had been his modestly successful tobacco factory and liquor business and, with a partner, established the saloon of Rosenauer & Adler.

E. P. Adler, already known as Mannie, was only four at the time.

Adler's satisfaction came from seeing the end result of the help he provided to so many. His largess came from the heart, not from a ledger book, and he was insistent about not being considered a lender. "With E. P. it was a *passion* to be charitable," recounts Katz. "Despite the extent of his philanthropy, he did not want recognition for what he did. He had no desire to be acknowledged. I've heard him forswear being lauded for any of his efforts. After he died in 1949, I remember reading a passage that had been written into his will in which he recalled coming to Davenport as a poor young man, to a strange community, and starting to work for Mr. Lee. He felt he owed an immense debt to the community. His outlook was that a man should pay back to the community everything he could in proportion to what the community had given to him."

Adler, who had been born in Chicago on September 30, 1872, was the son of German immigrants who had come to America seeking freedom. From them he inherited a deep sense of appreciation for that freedom and a determination to see it preserved. He carried it with him when the family fled Chicago in the aftermath of the great fire of 1871 and settled in Ottumwa, Iowa, where the economy was based heavily on meat packing and coal mining.

Life was always an uphill battle in the Adler family, which was why E. P. had to go to work as soon as he finished the eighth grade. But he was eager, ambitious, and curious — traits that made self-education successful. He learned everything that he might have through formal schooling — and much more. By the age of 13, he had already learned the printing trade and was familiar with the requirements of getting a daily newspaper to press.

Although E. P. grew up in a family that was close-knit and caring, circumstances were to dictate that he would be on his own for much of his life. His mother died when he was 26, and his father the following year. He enjoyed a solid and

On February 5, 1902, E. P. married Lena Rothschild, the youngest daughter of a wealthy and well-known Davenport family that had prospered in the grain business. Many a family gathering was held at the Rothschild family residence, a large, well-appointed Victorian at 13th and Main Streets.

Lena became seriously ill while their son, Phil, was in his senior year at the University of Iowa. With the help of a nurse, she was present to watch him graduate but died the following October, in 1926.

happy marriage, but it was all too brief. His wife, Lena Rothschild, a relative of the German branch of the Rothschild family, died unexpectedly in 1926 when their only child, Philip, was still in college. E. P.'s beloved sister, Betty, had passed away just a year earlier. The sadness he felt might have turned many a lesser man into a cynic, but E. P. persevered in his lifelong philosophy that he owed a strong debt to society.

D. N. Richardson was one of the founders of the Democrat *in Davenport in 1855. He was also the paper's first editor.*

Mrs. D. N. Richardson inspecting the Democrat's *old hand press in 1924. With her are George Nelson and Vince Dougan.*

According to those who knew him intimately, E. P. could be brusque and tough on occasion, especially when business demanded firmness. While admittedly feisty, he was always regarded as fair, compassionate, and warm. His chauffeur-driven car was loaned to many a bride and groom for their wedding day.

He was a staunch Republican, which was interesting because one of the papers he acquired in 1915 from the Richardson family in Davenport was the *Democrat*, a paper that lived up to its name in its editorial loyalties. But he could live with both viewpoints and never penalized anyone for having an opposing opinion.

The causes to which he donated money were never prejudiced for or against any religion or political viewpoint or economic group. Yet when he believed in a cause that needed monetary support, he had a bulldog tenacity as a fund-raiser. He never shied away from soliciting, even if doing so might antagonize people. That was why he was so effective when he faced the milling crowd during the run on the bank and all but demanded that they refrain from withdrawing their money.

As Katz summed it up, "E. P. had *guts!*"

Another of E. P. Adler's strongest attributes was his capacity for discovering and remembering essential biographical information about his employees. "When I first came to know E. P.," recalls Henry Hook, a longtime employee and former publisher of the *Democrat*, "I was constantly amazed at the man's talent for remembering everyone in the company. Not just names, but strengths and weaknesses on the job, peoples' involvement in their communities, and even the attributes of close family members. He was thoroughly conversant with the situations of 150 or so people who worked for him."

This photo, taken in the late 1800's, shows hopeful workers lining up at the Democrat's employment office.

Hook describes E. P. as a man who could be stern and tough when need be but who did not flare up or become ruffled under pressure. "I never saw him lose control. He was on top of things and never left it up to his managers to do his homework for him. That was one reason why, when his publishers gathered around him to discuss plans or strategies, they always listened diligently to what he had to say.

"When he voiced an opinion, they knew there was no arguing unless they had done a great deal more research than he had on the subject. Yet on the few occasions when he made an error in judgment, he was the first to admit that he had been wrong — no matter how strong a conviction he might have had."

Credible evidence that he made few miscalculations in business was the financial record over the years. "The significant thing," reported Hook, "is that, going way back, our investments in the Lee Syndicate kept increasing in value, even when some years were not so good and especially during the Depression and its aftermath. E. P. took the stand that when people invested their money, they deserved a dividend.

"I remember one year when a couple of the Lee dailies didn't have any excess funds for dividends. Adler announced, 'As long as I'm living, this paper is going to pay a dividend.' And he reached into capital and paid a five-percent dividend.

"Owning Lee stock has made many people very wealthy. Any number of them became millionaires without ever having seen a copy of the *Wall Street Journal*, without ever having consulted an investment adviser, and without ever lying awake nights wondering how to invest their money. They bought, or were given, Lee stock, left it alone, and now they're millionaires," says Hook. Lee's financial strength continues to this day, with dividends raised every year since the company went public in 1969.

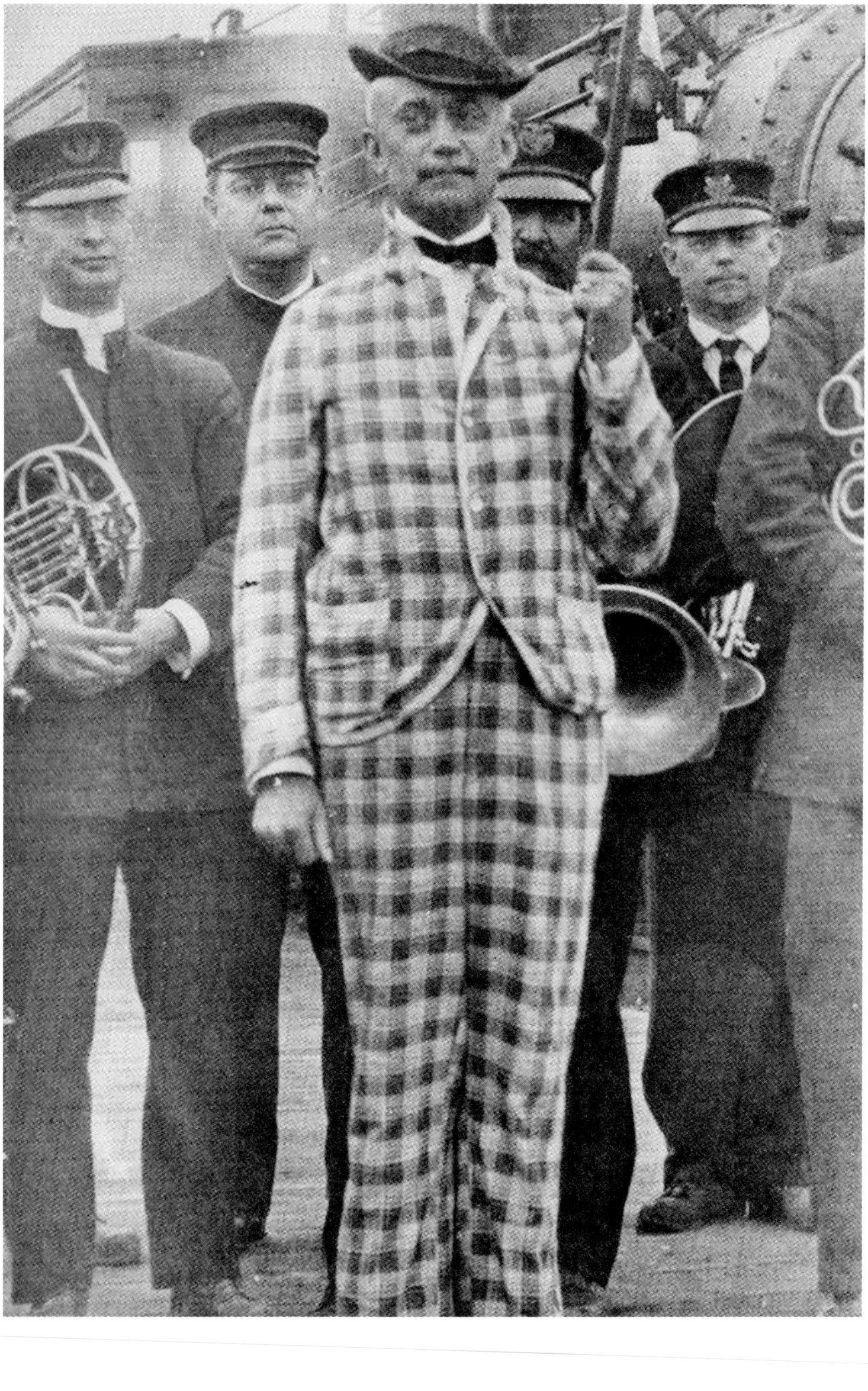

Max Blade

Bertha Blade Adler (E. P. Adler's mother) had a brother named Max. The Blades had immigrated from a picturesque little town in the German province of Hesse. Max was described as "a tall gangling lad" in his youth.

As an affectionate and caring uncle, he played an important role in the life of the young E. P. Adler. In his teens, E. P. went to Colorado to seek his fortune but ended up broke and hungry instead. For a while, he worked as a pressman in Denver but still couldn't make ends meet. It was Uncle Max who sent him $25 for his train fare back to Ottumwa. Characteristic of the wise uncle he was, he never mentioned this fine bit of philanthropy to E. P.'s parents.

"My father, Max Blade, had a very fine business mind," says his daughter, Selma Waterman. "He stepped in several times when the going was difficult financially for one or another of the papers. Most importantly, though, as Uncle Max, he took over as head of the family, helping Betty and E. P. when their mother died in November, 1898, and their father in the following spring. Like E. P., he never sought credit for things he did for people. I think that is where E. P. got his own deep sense of modesty and reserve."

E. P. Adler was one of Davenport's greatest boosters. He not only spent countless hours in community service but also donated untold sums to public works and needy citizens. However, he was notorious for hiding his light under a bushel, keeping the extent of his philanthropy to himself and seldom making public appearances even on behalf of causes that he supported strongly.

The notable exception to this occurred in late May, 1915, when he was asked to lead the parade in a "Booster Mission" for Davenport at a time when he headed a group developing the city's port and commercial facilities. He not only agreed to lead the band but showed up in a rumpled and ill-fitting checkered suit, cockeyed bow tie, and a hat that was at least two sizes too small. From the expression on his face, he looked like a small boy who had been caught snitching apples from a cart.

"From the standpoint of the public, it was one of his greatest moments," recalls Selma Waterman, one of his relatives, who was 27 at the time. "But I don't recall that he ever again appeared out of character in his whole lifetime. And, of course, he never showed anyone a print of the picture taken by one of his own newspaper photographers!"

The Davenport Democrat first occupied this building at 407-411 Brady Street in 1924. Later, all operations were moved to the Times Building.

The benefits of association with Lee were not limited to those who owned and profited from its stock. In the days when company benefit programs were still nonexistent, many an employee found himself snatched from the brink of personal disaster when Adler stepped in to offer assistance. "The Old Man" (many used this term affectionately when referring to E. P., including his son, Phil) "used to give charity in a way that nobody knows," recalls Judge Nathan Grant, who served as an attorney for the Adler family before going on the bench. "There was no company insurance in those days to help protect employees in times of distress. But E. P. used to provide assistance when there was a financial problem. In several instances, when employees who were the breadwinners died, he took care of their families for the rest of their lives, if necessary. No one really knows, but we estimate that he gave about $750,000 to the art gallery in Davenport and before he died probably gave away at least half of his own personal fortune to one cause or another."

His daughter-in-law, Henrietta Adler, remembers him saying many times, "The only purpose of money is what good you can do with it."

When asked why he always shied away from recognition as a donor, he used to say, "The only way to give is through the heart."

His longtime friend and associate, A. M. Brayton, paid tribute to E. P. in an informal profile in which he wrote, "The steps by which Mr. Adler climbed to personal prominence in his own business were buttressed by a sense of fellowship with those who stood in the trenches with him. Out of this came an affectionate regard for his business associates, an instinct to build them as he built himself. And then came the broader aspects, the economic welfare of the community, the value to civilization of civic and social forces. And it is almost a paradox that the higher his own problems and the absorption of his own business mounted, the greater the effort, the more generous the spirit, and the keener the intelligence which he gave to things that were for community, state, and nation."

Years later, Davenport's former postmaster, Rolla Chalupa, summed up how E. P.'s fellow citizens felt about him. "To me, he was, and always will be, the premier citizen of this community. There never was, nor ever will be, anyone like him."

Much of what E. P. Adler contributed to the development of the company during his long period of leadership, from 1907 until his death in 1949, has become legendary. In addition to strengthening the business concepts established by A. W. Lee, Adler gave special emphasis to the purchase of each newspaper as a rare opportunity to embark on community service. He enhanced

> **E. P.'s major community projects**
> E. P. Adler served on the boards of many community, civic, and religious organizations, including the American Red Cross, YMCA, the Community Chest, United Jewish Appeal, the Davenport Museum, the Municipal Art Gallery, St. Luke's Hospital, the Chamber of Commerce, Friendly House, and the Greater Davenport Committee. Because he seldom revealed the real extent of his philanthropic work, even to his family, no one will ever know the hundreds of individuals he also helped during the course of his lifetime.

this concept not only through his own participation but through his continuing generosity in providing financial support for projects for the public good.

He also ingrained in Lee managers the idea that they must be unstinting in doing their homework for two reasons: to get to know everything they could about the strengths and weaknesses of employees under their supervision and to be so knowledgeable about the facilities and operations for which they were responsible that they would always be on top of day-to-day operations and able to make clear decisions in times of crisis.

Two years before Adler's death, A. W. Lee's daughter, Laura, expressed what E. P. had brought to the company when she said, "He has not only kept my father's ideas and ideals fresh in his own memory, but he has been able to imbue even the youngest men under him with the wisdom of these same methods... the invisible links which have drawn the Lee family so closely together and which have helped to make it such a successful organization. Truly, E. P. Adler is the guiding spirit, the essence of the Lee company."

E. P. Adler aborted kidnap attempt

E. P. Adler was active in the Inland Daily Press Association, serving as its president in 1917 and 1918. Later, he was chairman of its Newsprint Committee, a post he held for a score of years. It was in that capacity that he traveled to Chicago by sleeper for a meeting of the association February 20, 1934, little dreaming that he himself was about to make unexpected headlines 24 hours later.

En route to the station at Davenport, a friend who had accompanied him there cautioned E. P. that he thought he was being followed by a shadowy figure in a brown suit he had seen lurking in the railroad depot. E. P. sensed no cause for alarm and seemed not at all disturbed. He arrived safely at the Morrison Hotel in Chicago, selected because it was the site of the meeting to be held the next day.

Early in the morning of February 21, E. P. left his hotel room on the fifth floor to go down for breakfast. In the corridor, he was suddenly jumped by two men who had been hiding in the adjoining room. One of them slugged him so viciously that blood spurted from his left ear. But E. P. was physically much stronger than the two anticipated and managed to race down the hall to an elevator, screaming so loudly that his attackers fled.

House detectives rushed to his assistance and he was, at least momentarily, safe. They then broke into the adjoining room where they saw an astonishing sight: a huge steamer trunk, perforated with tiny holes and containing revolvers, sponges, adhesive tape, and other items that were clearly accouterments for a kidnap plot.

A few minutes later, glancing down the corridor, E. P. spotted the man in the brown suit whom his friend had warned him against at the Davenport depot and whom he now thought he recognized as one of his attackers.

"Get that man!" shouted Adler to the detectives.

The fellow was captured and identified as Charles W. Mayo, 28, of Birmingham, Alabama, who confessed his part in the plot but shortly thereafter hanged himself in the cell where he had been temporarily jailed. Three other men were arrested and ultimately convicted. The four had visions of ransoming Adler for $40,000 after knocking him out, transporting him to a South Side hideaway, and negotiating for his release.

What they had not counted on was that the "little man" with habits so punctilious that he was easy to follow and anticipate, was strong, muscular, and feisty in any kind of contest, physical or otherwise.

Not until the trial was it realized how close to death E. P. had been. According to the testimony of a physician called in by the prosecution, he probably would have suffocated in the trunk before he ever arrived at the intended hide-out. Photographs of E. P. with bandaged head and the infamous kidnap trunk made the front pages of newspapers across the United States. Yet it was characteristic of the man that he minimized his injuries and pooh-poohed the possibilities of any future kidnap attempts. The only concession he ever made was to agree not to travel alone.

Right after the event, knowing that publicity would be widespread, he did send off a radiogram to son, Philip, and daughter-in-law, Henrietta, then on a West Indies cruise. It read:

HAVE SUDDENLY BECOME FAMOUS. SLIGHTLY INJURED. NOTHING SERIOUS. HOME TONIGHT. DON'T WORRY. — DAD.

Milestones during the E. P. Adler administration

- August 12, 1907 — E. P. Adler becomes president of the Lee Syndicate immediately following the unexpected death of A. W. Lee.
- July, 1911 — Adler continues the Lee tradition of community service by serving as one of 30 charter members of the Greater Davenport Committee to build levee improvements, finance new enterprises, and attract new businesses to Davenport.
- November, 1915 — The *Democrat* is purchased from the Richardson family. Frank Throop arrives from Muscatine as business manager.
- July 1, 1919 — *Wisconsin State Journal*, at Madison, is taken over and A. M. Brayton (formerly editor of the *La Crosse Tribune*) is named publisher.
- April 1, 1925 — Mason City (Iowa) *Globe-Gazette* is acquired and Lee P. Loomis (formerly of Muscatine) is appointed business manager. Former owner, Will F. Muse, continues as editor.
- June, 1926 — The Kewanee (Illinois) *Star Courier* is purchased from Leo H. Lowe. Philip D. Adler becomes editor and publisher.
- 1928 — The Lee Syndicate Company, a holding company in name only, is organized with $100,000 capital as a banking reserve for any emergency.
- June 5, 1930 — The Lincoln *Star* is purchased by the Lee syndicate. Frank Throop, of the *Democrat*, is selected as publisher (remaining until his death in 1943), with J. E. Lawrence as editor.
- May 10, 1931 — Lee P. Loomis is named publisher of the Mason City *Globe-Gazette* upon the death of Will F. Muse.
- August 30, 1931 — The Lincoln *Star* and the *Nebraska State Journal* are consolidated. J. C. Seacrest and his sons, Fred S. and Joe W., continue in control of State Journal Publications. Throop continues as publisher of the *Star*.
- July 11, 1936 — The Davenport *Times* publishes a 172-page 50th Anniversary issue, which features an article by E. P. Adler, "Looking Back Over a Half Century."
- January 7, 1937 — The first permanent Lee broadcasting unit, KGLO, at Mason City, Iowa, begins radio broadcasting full time, at 100 watts power.
- 1941 — The two Lincoln newspaper companies purchase about 25% interest in radio station KFAB, Omaha.
- December 9, 1944 — Station WTAD, Quincy, Illinois, is purchased by Lee.
- 1948 — Station WTAD expanded to include WTAD-FM.
- December, 1948 — The Wisconsin State Journal and the Capital Times companies of Madison, Wisconsin, are consolidated into a new corporation, Madison Newspapers, Inc., and both newspaper operations are housed in the enlarged Wisconsin State Journal building.
- February 1, 1949 — The *Wisconsin State Journal* is converted to morning and Sunday issues, and the *Capital Times* remains in the afternoon field six weekdays.
- March 2, 1949 — E. P. Adler dies and Lee Loomis is named president.

An Instinct to Build 43

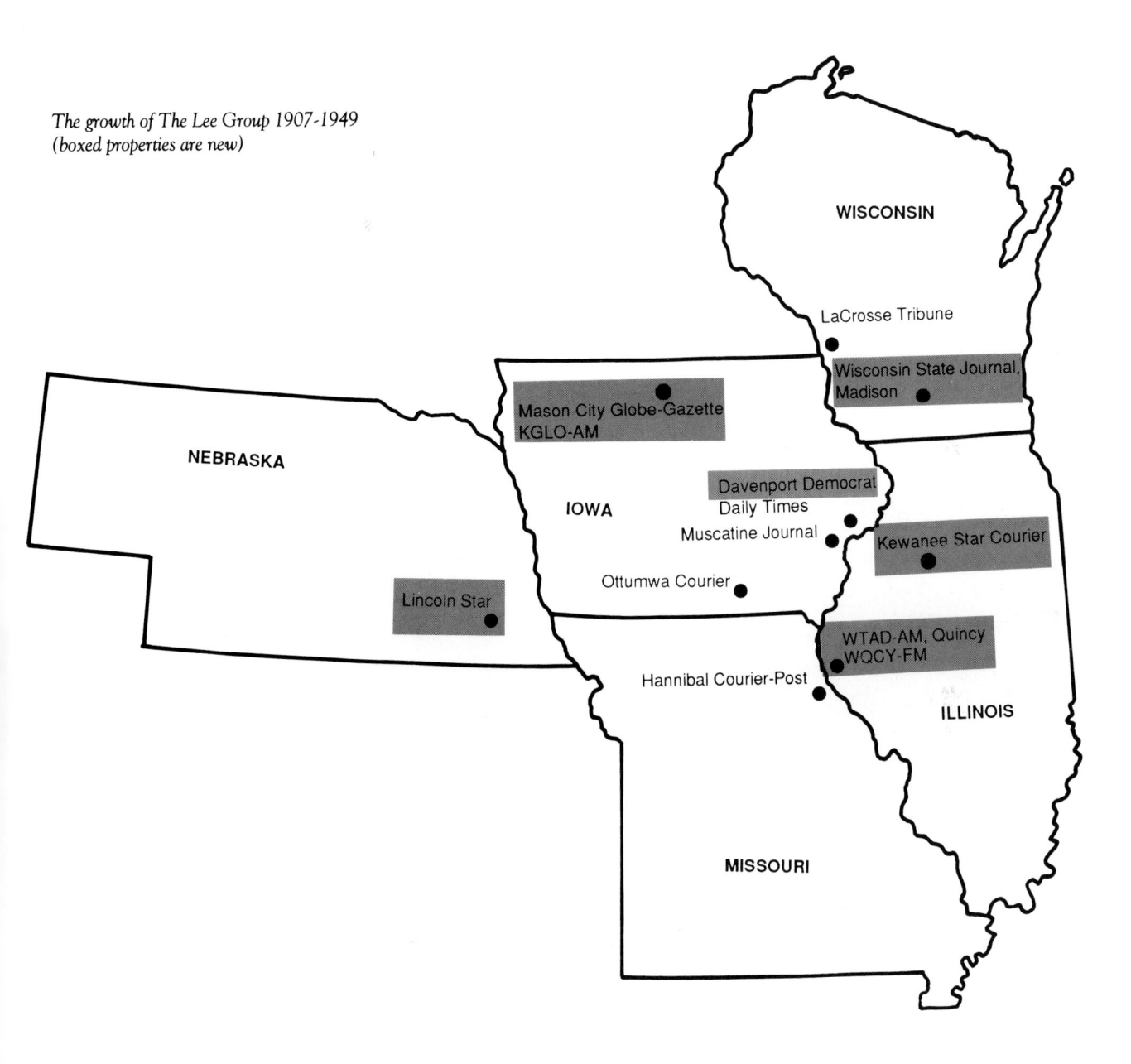

The growth of The Lee Group 1907-1949
(boxed properties are new)

- LaCrosse Tribune
- Wisconsin State Journal, Madison
- Mason City Globe-Gazette KGLO-AM
- Davenport Democrat Daily Times
- Muscatine Journal
- Kewanee Star Courier
- Ottumwa Courier
- Lincoln Star
- WTAD-AM, Quincy WQCY-FM
- Hannibal Courier-Post

WISCONSIN
NEBRASKA
IOWA
ILLINOIS
MISSOURI

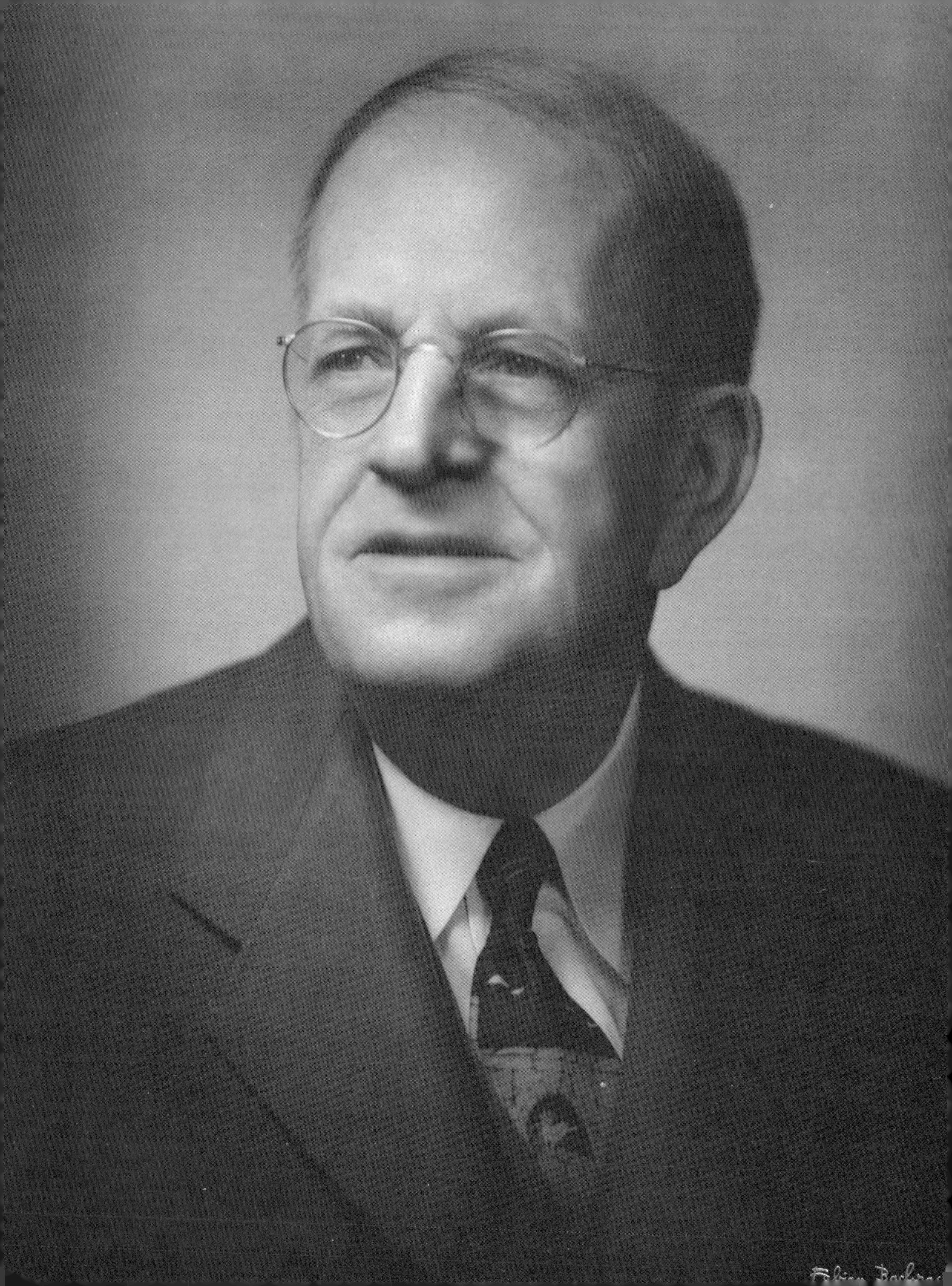

Chapter Three

A Believer in Broadcasting

1949-1960   *Lee P. Loomis*

Born September 28, 1884, in Hannibal, Missouri.

Son of Lewis J. Loomis and Mildred Anna Lee Loomis.

Attended private and public schools in Bevier, Missouri, military school at Kirkwood, Missouri, and Oberlin College in Ohio, which he left during his freshman year to support his mother.

As a youth, worked on a Mississippi river boat and also in his father's coal mine.

Married in Muscatine on June 17, 1915, to Margaret Anna Hakes, a teacher who later actively joined him in community service.

Father of one daughter, Elizabeth Hakes Harrer.

Started with Lee in 1902, at the age of 18, as a farm-to-farm subscription solicitor for the *Ottumwa Daily Courier*, where he later served as bookkeeper, reporter, and city editor.

Joined the *Muscatine Journal* as managing editor (1907) and later publisher (1915).

Appointed business manager of the Mason City *Globe-Gazette* (1925) and publisher (1931).

Pioneered, founded, and developed Lee interests in broadcasting beginning in 1937 with KGLO Radio.

Appointed president of Lee Radio, Mason City, and Lee Broadcasting, Quincy, Illinois.

Appointed vice president of Lee Group in 1943 and president in 1949.

Active in professional associations, including Director of Bureau of Advertising, Inland Daily Press Association, Northwest Daily Press Association, and Iowa Daily Press Association, which he served for two years as president.

Served on numerous civic and community boards, including the North Iowa Fair Association, was active in religious and fraternal organizations, and was in great demand as a public speaker because of his talents as a storyteller.

Retired as president of the Lee Group, 1960.

Died of a stroke at 79 on February 10, 1964.

E. P. Adler did not always see eye to eye with Lee P. Loomis, the young publisher of the Mason City *Globe-Gazette* and nephew of A. W. Lee. In 1937, Loomis suggested to a skeptical E. P. Adler that the Lee Group, newspaper publishers for 47 years, should expand into radio. Historically, newspapers and broadcasting stations had been jealous and suspicious of each other. Furthermore, Adler's own experiences with "electronic communications" had been less than rewarding, notably in the case of a misadventure in the early 1920's. His *Wisconsin State Journal* had sold $100,000 worth of stock to organize a radio broadcasting company in Madison, but the enterprise had been torpedoed by a court decision that would have put the station off the air eventually. So Lee sold the property to the University of Wisconsin to avoid a legal conflict of interest.

In 1893, two small Iowa settlements known as Shiboleth and Masonic Grove, agreed to join together and form one town. Founding fathers chose the name Masonville, perhaps because several residents were believed to have been Masons. When postal authorities received notification of the name change, they quickly pointed out that a "Masonville" already existed in Iowa, so the name Mason City was adopted.

Mason City is the heart of huge deposits of clay, shale and limestone, making it a center for the brick and tile industry. In the early 1900's, nine plants produced enough of these products to fill 300 rail cars each week.

The building in the foreground of this picture, which was taken about 1900, shows the Masonic Temple Building at what is now the intersection of South Federal and Second Streets. The Mason City Globe-Gazette offices were on the first floor from 1900 to 1912.

Loomis could appreciate Adler's hesitation. Since joining Lee as a subscription solicitor in 1902, he had known and admired E. P., who had earned a reputation as an accomplished manager of people and operations alike. As Adler's junior in years, service, and position, he would hardly have lost face had he yielded to E. P.'s opinion that broadcasting and newspaper publishing in Mason City would be a sorry combination.

But Loomis was known for having "a special mix of humility and business aggressiveness." In this instance, aggressiveness triumphed over humility and Loomis took full advantage of the company's policy of encouraging its publishers to function independently when it came to matters of community betterment. As his daughter, Betty Harrer, recounts the circumstances, "My father was farsighted enough to realize that the purchase of broadcasting stations would be beneficial to the company. He had to fight hard since newspapermen in general, and his own colleagues in particular, were dead set against the idea. Radio stations were considered to be stiff competitors that were not worthy of any kind of compromise. But my father took the viewpoint that his company could develop both types of communications profitably.

"As he used to say, 'After all, why shouldn't we be getting some of the advertising dollars that are now going to radio stations?'"

It was as characteristic of E. P. that he gave Lee Loomis his blessing to proceed as it was that he also made it clear he expected to see a profit within two years. Thus it was that radio station KGLO went on the air as an affiliate of the *Globe-Gazette* in January, 1937. Loomis was so convinced the station would succeed that he invested an undisclosed amount of his own money to help fund the venture. Furthermore, he also had to undergo an extensive battle with the Federal Communications Commission in Washington before he could obtain a construction permit to start Mason City's first broadcasting station. The FCC's position was that a newspaper and a radio station in the same market couldn't

On January 17, 1937, when KGLO began broadcasting to the citizens of Mason City and the surrounding area, this tiny building housed the transmitter. The 290-foot Truscon tower can be seen next to the building. Both were familiar sights to travelers on Highway 18 a mile outside of town and served the station until 1941 when new transmitters and towers were added.

FCC regulations and restrictions

Lee Loomis was determined to build a radio station as part of the *Globe-Gazette* operations. However, he almost failed because many of his own people — as newspapermen — objected to the idea of being associated with radio. To complicate matters, a number of prominent citizens in Mason City also applied to the FCC for licenses to build radio stations.

Loomis finally won out, but eventually had to form two different companies, one to run the newspaper and the other to operate KGLO. According to Henry Hook, the FCC originally permitted newspapers to own or acquire broadcasting facilities but later changed the rules so that the two could not be combined. Newspaper/broadcasting combinations that existed before the ruling was changed could continue joint operations because of a "grandfather" clause that protected existing arrangements. But once a station was sold or moved, the new rules applied and the functions had to be kept separate.

have the same ownership — a policy that would vacillate over the years and which would ultimately cause Lee's divestiture of this fine broadcasting property.

Loomis and his associates saw the promise of broadcasting and looked for similar markets where their expertise could bring new profits, stature, and strength to the company. Over a number of years, he purchased radio station WTAD in Quincy, Illinois, added both television and FM to the Mason City and Quincy stations, and built KEYC-TV and FM in Mankato, Minnesota. One trusted lieutenant who helped manage the growth with a keen eye for profitability was his son-in-law, Don Harrer. Harrer started in the traffic department in Mason City, managed KEYC in Mankato, and finally returned to direct the Mason City television station, KGLO-TV. He helped it grow from a tiny station serving a single community to one of 5,000 watts serving 36 Iowa and Minnesota counties in one of the richest farm markets in the country.

"The philosophy of Lee management at the time," says current Vice President-Broadcasting Gary Schmedding, "was to concentrate radio station purchases in towns where existing Lee newspapers could create a comfortable working relationship. It's interesting that there was networking even in those days. Although the newspapers and TV stations protected their turf fairly carefully, they competed effectively." The stations were all in towns that were medium sized, rural, and served an agriculture-based economy. This policy would continue until 1970, when WSAZ-TV in Huntington-Charleston West Virginia, was purchased.

This page from the book, The Lee Group: Mid-America to the Mountains, *shows the growth of KGLO from a local station of 100 watts in 1937, to a regional station broadcasting to the entire region with 5,000 watts reaching 122,270 homes by the year 1960. The photo shows the original facility as it appeared in 1937 with the stations's roving promotional vehicles parked in front.*

A Believer in Broadcasting 49

This studio was built in 1954 to house the new KGLO-TV, along with its sister radio stations, KGLO-AM and KGLO-FM. Local residents were invited to a series of open houses where they could see themselves on television. KGLO-TV became the tenth television station in the state of Iowa.

With cumbersome, box-like DuMont cameras, KGLO-TV began broadcasting at 7:30 pm on Saturday, May 15, 1954. It was a DuMont and Columbia Broadcasting System affiliate with a signal that reached most of northern Iowa and southern Minnesota, but extended into Wisconsin, as well.

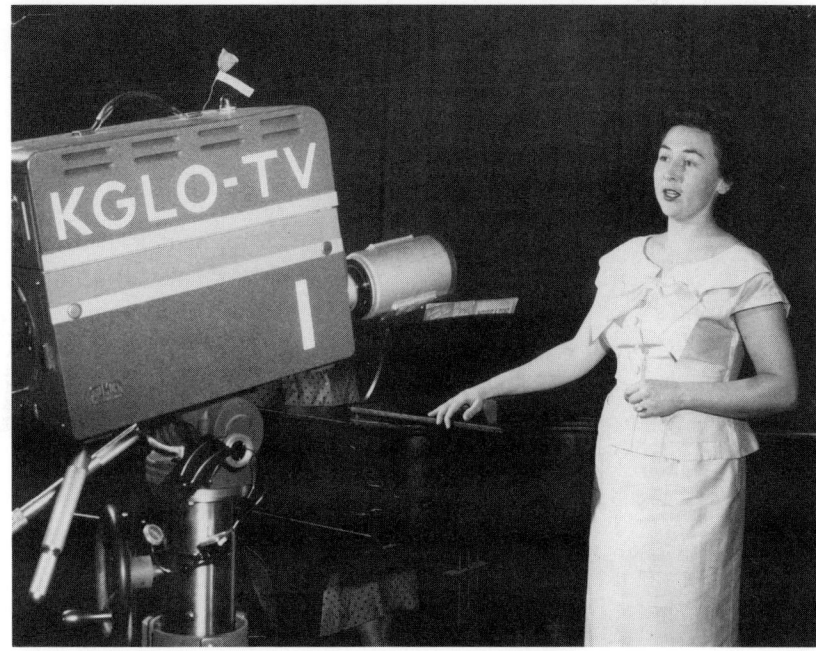

Convincing national advertisers to purchase air time on the Mason City and Quincy radio stations wasn't easy in those days, as advertisers believed they could effectively reach listeners through the powerful, clear-channel stations in Chicago and St. Louis which claimed to blanket the Midwest. Walter Rothschild, who later became vice president of broadcasting, had a novel idea: he recorded the Chicago and St. Louis stations to demonstrate how poorly they sounded to local listeners in the small towns of the Midwest. Then he took the heavy recordings to New York and trudged up and down Madison Avenue visiting advertising agencies and demonstrating the poor signal quality of the big-city stations in the outlying areas. The strategy worked, and the stations prospered.

Before becoming president of what was then called the Lee Syndicate upon the death of E. P. Adler in 1949, Lee Loomis had consistently given evidence that he was qualified to follow in the footsteps of Adler and A. W. Lee.

Born on September 28, 1884, in Hannibal, Missouri, Loomis attended public and private schools, then entered Oberlin College in Ohio.

The American newsboy, delivering papers in small towns and rural neighborhoods, became a symbol of youthful dedication and ambition. Long after they had achieved fame — and usually fortune — as publishers and chief executives, men like Lee Loomis, A. W. Lee, and the Adlers liked to relate how they had learned the business from the bottom up.

This 1941 photograph shows Lee Loomis talking with one of the Globe-Gazette's newsboys, Bob Douglas, now the owner of Mason City's Douglas Insurance Agency. Note the radio on Loomis's desk.

While still in his freshman year, he was forced to leave because his father's coal-mining business was failing. It was right after the turn of the century that he went to Ottumwa to take his first permanent position in the newspaper business, working for his uncle, A. W. Lee, then publisher of the *Ottumwa Daily Courier*. He strove all the harder to make a name for himself on his own because he felt being related to the publisher was a disadvantage.

He served as a bookkeeper until the day when A. W. Lee walked into the office, looked over his shoulder and commented, "Lee, you'd make a good bookkeeper if you could only write," and promptly transferred Loomis to the editorial department. As a cub reporter, he was so anxious to prove his competence that he frequently slept on a bench in the police station in order not to miss a story.

Loomis was a born versifier and sometimes even wrote crime reports in verse, though his reporting was anything but soothing. Despite a welcome lack of criminal activity in town, Loomis was ingenious enough at locating breaches of the law so that his reporting — both in language and in content — soon attained a reputation for being spicy. "Some days," reported one of his associates later, "it was so spicy that Loomis and his city editor would deliberately make it a point to be out of the building when the copy reached Mr. Lee's desk for review."

This wonderful picture, taken in St. Louis at the F.W. Guerin Studio, shows Lee Loomis when he was seven. The painted background and props were typical of studio photographs taken in the late 1800's.

Relationship to A. W. Lee

Lee P. Loomis was born in Hannibal, Missouri, on September 28, 1884. He was the son of Lewis J. Loomis and Mildred Anna Lee Loomis, A. W. Lee's sister. A. W. Lee was, therefore, his uncle.

Loomis had one daughter, Elizabeth, who married Donald Harrer, former manager of the Lee broadcasting station at Mankato, Minnesota.

As a result of his diligence and ability to develop a good news story, he quickly advanced to the position of city editor. Shortly before A. W. Lee's death, Lee received a phone call from Frank Throop, publisher of the *Muscatine Journal*, saying the paper needed a managing editor.

"Whom shall I send?" asked Lee.

"Send anyone you want," replied Throop, "so long as it isn't that upstart nephew of yours, Lee Loomis." Throop was a conservative individual, with a record of dedicated community service. He did not want anyone on his staff who might unduly rock the boat. Furthermore, he knew that Loomis had acquired a knack for salty language, largely as a result of his crime reporting.

A. W. Lee recognized the disparity but was unable to find any other suitable candidate. So he proposed that Loomis be sent to Muscatine on a temporary basis until a young man more suited to Throop's taste could be recruited. Loomis arrived at the *Journal* in 1907, so convinced that this was merely a short-term arrangement that he kept his room in Ottumwa, thinking he'd return soon.

After nearly a month on the new job, Loomis went to his boss one day and asked, "Frank, when are you going to get a managing editor?"

"I've got one," replied Throop.

"When is he coming?"

"He's already here."

"Well, where the hell is he?"

"You darned fool," Throop laughed. "Go look in the mirror and you'll see him!"

Loomis proved his worth to a man who was one of the most productive and demanding managers in the Lee organization. In 1915, at the age of 31, Loomis became publisher of the *Muscatine Journal* when Throop was named publisher of the *Democrat* in Davenport. After ten successful years in Muscatine, Loomis was transferred to Mason City as business manager of the *Globe-Gazette*. The move came on April 1, prompting Loomis to comment, "What a hell of an April Fool's joke to play on good, unsuspecting Mason City people!"

Loomis was known for his brisk sense of humor and throughout his lifetime always knew how to laugh at himself.

As it turned out, everyone was happy with the new arrangement and he became the *Globe-Gazette's* publisher on the death of William F. Muse in 1931.

Although he had a completely different personality from that of E. P. Adler, Loomis possessed many of Adler's best attributes. He was almost compulsive about being in the office

> **Lee Loomis's personality**
>
> "Lee Loomis knew all of his employees personally," says his daughter, Betty Harrer, whose husband is the former manager of several Lee broadcasting stations. "He was very people-oriented. At home, he used to speak about various employees often, telling about their accomplishments and families and sometimes a problem or two he was trying to resolve. He had an old-world idea of politeness, imparted from his Quaker grandmother, and always tipped his hat when he met a lady on the street, no matter how slightly he knew her."

whenever the press was running, even when it meant being up at the crack of dawn or giving up a Sunday evening's relaxation. He also managed to devote more than his full measure of time to civic affairs. At the time he arrived in Mason City, for example, bank failures were plaguing Iowa, and he played a leading role in trying to prevent them or at least to soften their effect.

Like Adler, he was not only a philanthropist who gave generously to local causes, but a catalyst when it came to motivating others to do likewise. He would donate a check for, say, $100 and comment "I'm giving $100 toward the first $1,000. Now you people go out and get the $900 balance." They almost always did.

During the Depression, recalls his daughter, "he was the first person in the *Globe-Gazette* to take a

Mason City's interest in aviation dates back to the early days of flight, and the Globe-Gazette was involved in the development of its airport from the very beginning. The town's first community airport was dedicated in August, 1927, with a gala celebration that included a visit from Charles Lindbergh, who had completed his historic solo flight across the Atlantic earlier that year.

W. Earl Hall, then editor of the Globe-Gazette, played a part in the airport's construction through his behind-the-scenes effort to persuade the American Legion and the Chamber of Commerce to support it. He was also instrumental in arranging Lindbergh's visit.

Today's airport has been much improved since its beginning, partly due to the work of Lee Loomis in preparing a detailed proposal that resulted in a federal grant for further construction.

cut in salary, thus setting an example for all of the other staff members."

Being a good newspaperman was not enough for Lee Loomis. He insisted that he had to be an equally dedicated community participant and civic booster. He led the way in church, civic, and charity causes, and he expected others in "the Lee family" to follow suit. Sometimes this prompted him to have a "visit" with those who might be a little slow about falling in line. Yet he was able to handle such sensitive matters adroitly and tactfully.

"When Lee talked us into contributing our time and efforts to a cause," said one of his editors, "we never had the feeling that we were being pressured. Quite the contrary, we felt grateful to him for having moved us off our butts into an involvement with something positive."

There seemed to be few limits to the scope of Loomis's voluntarism. He took the lead, for example, in raising a special fund of $3,000 that sent emissaries to Washington to request a grant for the construction of a municipal airport at Mason City. He worked out the details of the proposal so skillfully and convincingly that the emissaries returned not only with government approval but with a federal grant in hand. At the end of World War II, when housing became a critical problem in Cerro Gordo County, he subscribed the first $1,000 for the *Globe-Gazette* and the second $1,000 for KGLO to organize the Mason City Development Association, adding more when needed. He loved county fairs and was particularly proud of serving as a director of the North Iowa Fair Association, propitiously at a time when it was having financial difficulties and he could help with a needed reorganization. Similarly, he was generous with his church, St. John's Episcopal, as well as the Episcopal Diocese of Iowa.

It was characteristic of him — as it had always been with E. P. Adler — that he was seldom the chairman of the groups he supported, preferring to remain behind the scenes and never receiving, or wanting to receive credit. He attributed this attitude and his outlook to his Quaker grandmother. "She instilled in me a sense of personal duty that was natural and healthy," he once recalled. "Every night at bedtime, she would look at me with her piercing eyes and inquire sternly, 'Hast thee done anything this day of which thee might be ashamed?' I have only to ask myself the same question to keep my life in balance."

> **"North Iowa's Leading Newspaper"**
> When Lee Loomis was publisher of the Mason City *Globe-Gazette*, he instituted a tradition of giving the paper a positive, upbeat image, both visually and textually. He discouraged front-page stories that might be an affront to any individual, organization, or cause. Today, "North Iowa's Leading Newspaper" has honored Lee's heritage and is known for its clean, uncluttered image and its fair, forthright coverage of the news.

This picture, taken in 1957, 30 years after Lindbergh's visit, shows how Lee Loomis's foresight paid off. With the help of other civil leaders, Loomis prepared detailed proposals that resulted in a federal grant to improve the airfield.

Even before he became president of Lee, it was Loomis's habit to read all of the company's newspapers from front to back — ten of them by the time he had assumed command. Although he maintained the same policy as A. W. Lee and E. P. Adler of letting individual publishers run their own show, he did not hesitate to call attention to errors, misprints, and especially any omissions that suggested sloppy news coverage. He never liked to see what he called "horror stories" about anyone on the front page, though he was often forced to accept these — reports about otherwise decent citizens who had succumbed to temptation, passion, or greed.

When Lee Loomis turned 70 on September 28, 1954, the town turned out to help him celebrate. His daughter, Betty, and her husband, Don Harrer, join him here with Betty Harper of Kewanee to view his birthday cake.

Mason City Development Association

The Mason City Development Association was another product of Lee Loomis's foresight and determination. He not only helped to plan the organization and recruit people during the late 1940's, but was one of its chief fund-raisers. To the initial $2,000 donated by the Mason City *Globe-Gazette* to establish MCDA, he added many thousands more. It was characteristic of Loomis that he was not the chairman or front man but always functioned behind the scenes, never wanting, or getting, the credit he deserved.

Today, Mason City is recognized as a leader in Iowa's industrial development, with a diversified economic base that has stabilized the community.

EAT HERE
When You Attend the Gala Celebration

HOT DOGS

Buy 'Em By the Dozen

5c each

Delicious HAMBURGERS

10c

GOOD COFFEE 5c

at the

BLACK and WHITE LUNCH

120 North Federal Ave.

Moose Old-Time DANCE
Paul Lockie Orch.
SATURDAY, JUNE 18

Only 25c

A Pre-Anniversary Celebration Dance Saturday night. Bring your Queen . . . she and you will have a glorious time.

Buy COAL this Summer and SAVE

Dixie Block Lump . . $6.50
Special Prepared
  Lump $6.25
Furnace Egg $6.00
Call for Eastern Coal Prices

DIXIE BLOCK COAL CO.
526 2nd St. N. W. Ph. 715

BUY FOR LESS
OUR PRICE

15c Barbecue Sauce,
8 oz. bottle **10c**
Sweet Corn,
3 cans for **19c**
Half and Half
Tobacco, can **10c**
Dixie Dog Food,
Pound Can **5c**
Omega Cake Flour
and Cake Pan ... **29c**
Libby's Crushed Pineapple,
No. 10 can **69c**
15c Can Black
Pepper **9c**
Marshmallows,
lb. Package,
in Cellophane ... **10c**

Prices good until Sunday.
We reserve the right to limit quantities.

Morris Food Store
"WHOLESALE and RETAIL"
221 6th Street S. W.

SPECIAL CHILDREN'S
5c — MATINEE — 5c
SATURDAY AFTERNOON
Fairly and Little Shows

Any Child Under 16 Years of Age
Admitted to Any Show or Ride **5c**

Admission to Grounds FREE

One of the criteria for being a good newspaper publisher was not only to seek out and report the daily news but to support advertisers to the hilt by purchasing goods promoted in ads like these.

His daughter, Betty, says that she was never allowed to read papers delivered to the house until after her father had looked them over carefully. "He wanted always to know at what hour they arrived and what condition they were in when they were delivered. These matters were vital to him because they were important to the subscribers. He was also compulsively curious about the editorial positioning and treatment of news stories because he was strongly in favor of emphasizing local coverage, focusing on stories the townspeople were familiar with or wanted to know about. He knew full well the success of the papers depended upon their audiences and that neglecting them was a sure way to failure."

In keeping with a policy that had long been prevalent at Lee, Loomis insisted that families of employees should patronize as much as possible the businesses that advertised in the local newspapers. "In our household," Betty recalls, "my mother and I felt that we went a little beyond the call of duty. We were so committed to buying advertised products that I still feel a little queasy thinking about some of the new kinds of breakfast foods we ate because they ran ads in the *Globe-Gazette*."

With his Quaker heritage and innate sense of modesty, Loomis felt that money and material things were not important beyond providing a comfortable and dignified lifestyle. In the long run, what really mattered was people and how they related to each other.

Paradoxically, when Loomis became head of the Lee Syndicate he once again became a "bookkeeper," the job from which his uncle, A. W. Lee, had judiciously removed him when he first started work. But by now he was so accomplished in mathematics that, with a few key entries in what he labelled his "little black book," he was always precisely aware of the financial health of each of the newspapers and broadcasting properties under his command. He never overlooked the smallest detail, even to the point where his wife once complained he was wearing himself out with inconsequential data.

He explained his attention to specifics with a comment that he often made when pointing out grammatical errors or minor deviations from fact in a paper, "Let the little things get away from you and you're in trouble." He encouraged communication from employees at all levels,

Lee Loomis, songwriter

No Mason City Chamber of Commerce party would be complete without song parodies written by Lee Loomis. Many exhibited his love for his community, such as this one, from a 1946 Christmas party at Mason City's Hotel Hanford. Sung to the chorus of "Oklahoma!" the tribute to Mason City sounded like this:

Mason City,
Where the corn grows towering round about.
Where men work and play,
With a lust for living like a shout.
Mason City,
Every day we're milling out cement.
Making brick and tile,
Our pork's the style,
Happy, busy, yes and so content.
We know we belong to our state.
And the state we belong to is great.
And when we say,
Yeeow — I-o-w-a — I-o-way,
We're only saying,
You're mighty fine, Mason City.
Mason City, OK!

Bureau of Advertising

The Bureau of Advertising of the American Newspaper Publisher's Association was one of Lee Loomis's pet projects. He served on its Governing Board for many years and was recognized as one of the key figures in building that organization, as well as being a pioneer in newspaper advertising. He was awarded numerous honors for distinguished service, including a Distinguished Service Award from the Bureau of Advertising, the Iowa Master Editor and Publishers Award, and the Minnesota Award for Distinguished Service in Journalism.

but his greatest satisfactions came from the performance of the task at hand each day."

During the 11 years he served as president, from his election to the post in 1949 until he retired in 1960 because of failing health, Loomis continued to strengthen the heritage established by A. W. Lee and E. P. Adler. To these he added new dimensions, most notably an expanded media outlook that positioned Lee as a serious player in the world of broadcasting, and a broadened geographical horizon that breached the traditional confines of the Midwest and added valuable new franchises to the company's newspaper operations. He exemplified a willingness to take risks in order to foster corporate growth. He avidly pursued the concept that scrupulous loyalty to advertisers would reap benefits for newspeople and broadcasters who supported those who supplied their incomes. He also served his profession through national associations. For many years, Loomis was on the Committee In Charge (later called the Governing Board) of the Newspaper Advertising Bureau, which today is the industry's marketing arm, with 900 member newspapers.

As the obituary in the *Congressional Record* concluded, "Lee Loomis stood tall."

Milestones during the Lee Loomis administration

- 1949 — Lee Loomis is named president of Lee following the death of E. P. Adler.
- 1949 — Philip Adler becomes publisher of the *Davenport Times* and a vice president of Lee Newspapers.
- 1950 — The first corporate plan to link all Lee properties is formed when Lee Enterprises is organized to buy the newspaper stocks of A. W. Lee's daughter, Laura Lee.
- September 22, 1950 — Lee Enterprises, Incorporated is created.
- December 20, 1950 — The State Journal Company and the Star Publishing Co. of Lincoln, Nebraska, are merged into the single Journal-Star Printing Company.
- January 8, 1951 — The *Star* begins morning publication, while the *State Journal* remains as an afternoon paper. A combined Sunday edition is continued. Later, all Lincoln papers are published in the remodeled Journal building.
- October 2, 1951 — The Davenport Times and The Democrat publishing companies are merged into Davenport Newspapers, Inc., and the *Democrat* staff moves into the remodeled Times building on Second Street. The *Democrat* is published in the mornings, the *Davenport Times* in the afternoons.
- September 23, 1953 — KHQA-TV, Hannibal, Missouri-Quincy, Illinois, begins telecasting as the first Lee TV station.
- May 15, 1954 — KGLO-TV, Mason City, Iowa, begins telecasting.
- June 1, 1959 — The Lee Group acquires the six Anaconda Company daily newspapers in Montana — in Anaconda, Billings, Butte, Helena, Livingston, and Missoula, for $6 million. The parent company is Lee Newspapers of Montana, Inc.
- February, 1960 — Lee Enterprises becomes the corporate owner of all the Lee newspapers and the majority owner of the subsidiary radio and television properties.
- October 1, 1960 — Separate publishing companies merged into Lee Enterprises.
- 1960 — Lee Loomis retires because of illness and Philip Adler becomes president of Lee Enterprises.

The growth of Lee Enterprises 1949-1960
(boxed properties are new)

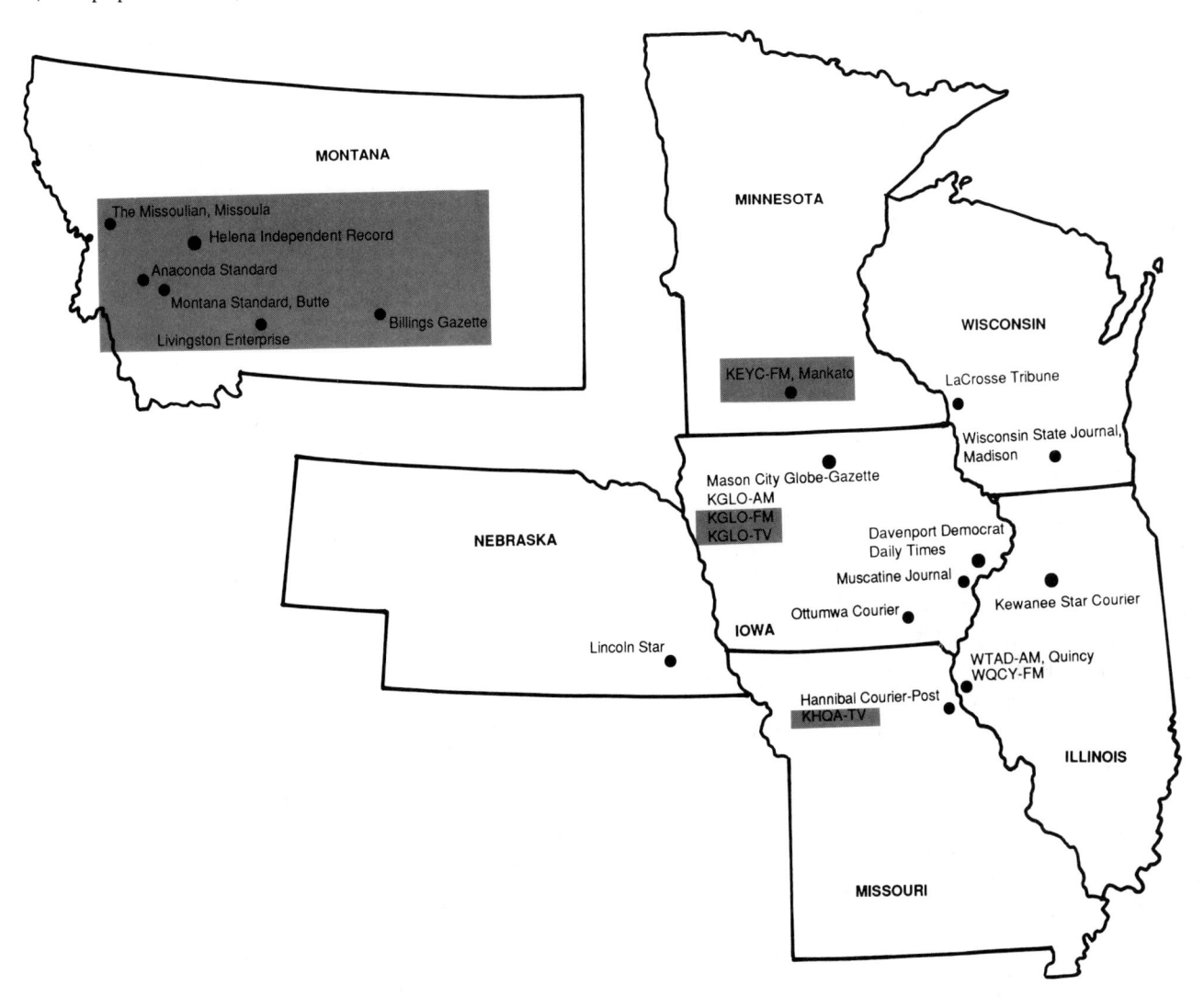

MONTANA
- The Missoulian, Missoula
- Helena Independent Record
- Anaconda Standard
- Montana Standard, Butte
- Livingston Enterprise
- Billings Gazette

MINNESOTA
- KEYC-FM, Mankato

WISCONSIN
- LaCrosse Tribune
- Wisconsin State Journal, Madison

IOWA
- Mason City Globe-Gazette
- KGLO-AM
- KGLO-FM
- KGLO-TV
- Davenport Democrat Daily Times
- Muscatine Journal
- Ottumwa Courier

NEBRASKA
- Lincoln Star

ILLINOIS
- Kewanee Star Courier
- WTAD-AM, Quincy
- WQCY-FM

MISSOURI
- Hannibal Courier-Post
- KHQA-TV

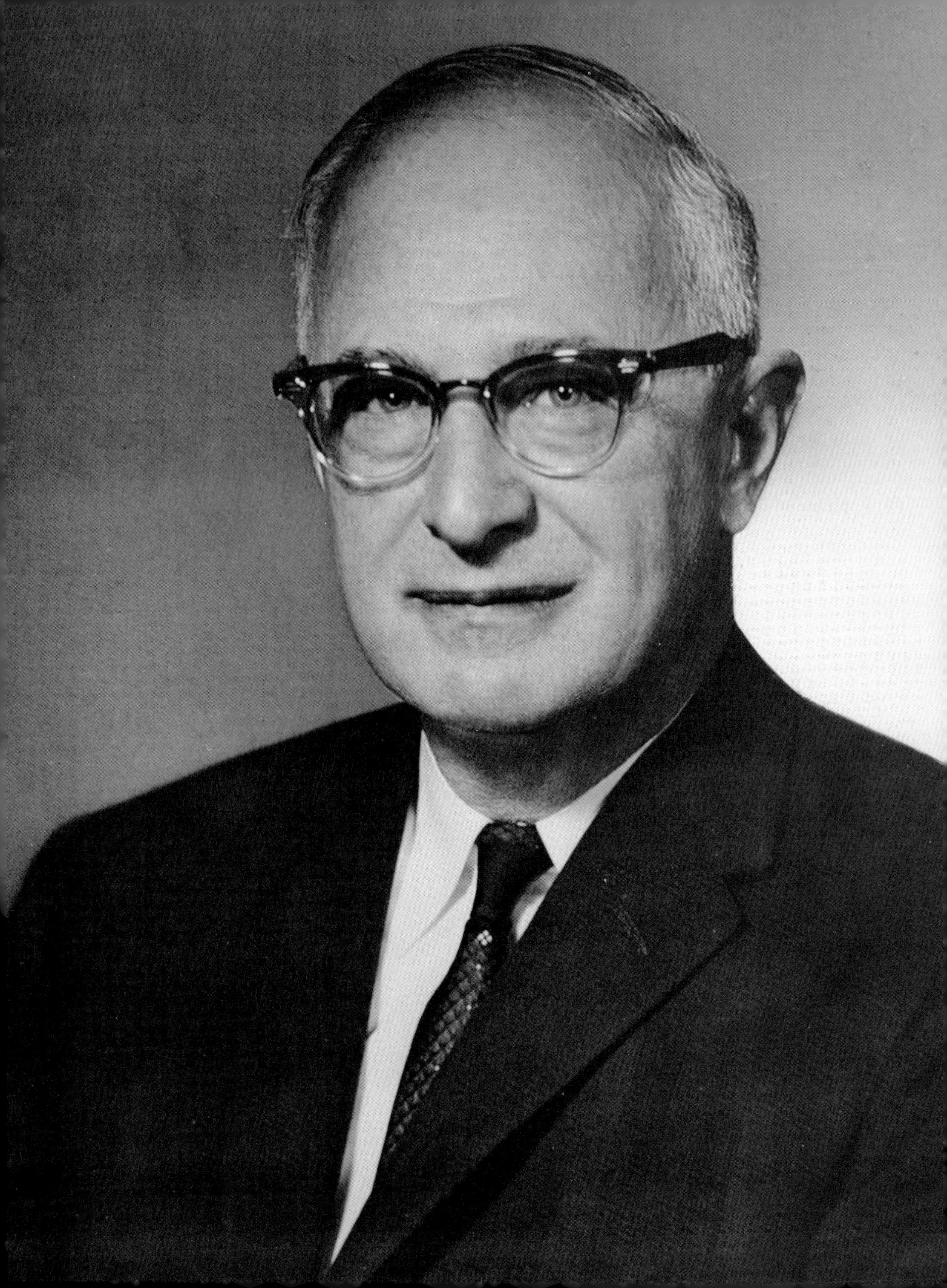

Chapter Four
the Compassionate Consolidator

1960-1970   *Philip D. Adler*

Born November 5, 1902.
Son of Emanuel Philip Adler and Lena Rothschild Adler.
Worked summers as a printer's devil, 1918-20.
Editor of high school newspaper and annual, 1921.
Graduated from Davenport High School and entered University of Iowa, 1922.
Editor of college newspaper, the *Daily Iowan*, 1925.
Served in the ROTC, 1924-25.
Graduated from the University of Iowa, 1926.
Joined Lee as editor and publisher of the Kewanee *Star Courier*, 1926.
Married Henrietta Carol Bondi in Galesburg, Illinois, 1928.
Father of one daughter, Betty, May 1, 1929.
Served in the Office of Censorship in Washington, D.C., during World War II, 1944-45.
Appointed publisher of the Davenport *Daily Times*, 1949.
Elected vice president of Lee newspapers, 1949.
Appointed president of Lee Enterprises, 1960.
Retired as publisher of the Davenport *Times-Democrat*, 1969.
Retired as president of Lee Enterprises, 1970.
Served on many boards, including hospitals, colleges, religious bodies, community public-service organizations, fraternal societies, and professional associations, 1929-84.
Won numerous awards for both publishing attainments and public service, 1964-70.
Died May 29, 1984.

E. P. Adler made a considered decision. His son, Philip, with whom he was very close, had shown great interest in the newspaper business. He had always been captivated by stories of his father's journalistic experiences and read and studied everything he could lay hands on about the business of print communications. Throughout his youth, he worked hard after school and during vacations at a variety of newspaper jobs, ranging from delivering newspapers to setting type, cleaning the press room, selling advertising space, and later composing copy for the editorial columns. He came to know the trade and proved to be a fine writer and an astute editor.

At the University of Iowa, Phil worked his way up the organization of the *Daily Iowan*, becoming editor and receiving an award from the university for his outstanding contributions.

Now E. P. took a step that many an educator or psychologist might have shuddered to hear: he purchased a newspaper for his son and appointed him editor and publisher, positions the young man would assume upon graduation from the University of Iowa. Thus it was that Phil Adler received his diploma on a hot Friday in June, 1926, and his unique graduation gift on the following Monday.

The newspaper was the Kewanee *Star Courier*, which its editor and owner, Leo Lowe, decided to sell because of failing eyesight. His price: $300,000, a tidy sum in that pre-Depression year, yet one that E. P. felt was worth the cost for a potentially valuable asset for the Lee Syndicate. He also recruited an experienced and able managing editor, Chris Ketridge, knowing that his talents and capabilities were complementary to Phil's and that together they would make a productive and well-balanced team.

His first day, June 14th, was Flag Day. In a bold step, Phil started running a new masthead he had earlier asked to have designed. The new masthead eliminated the American flag, a symbol

As a child, Phil was intelligent and naturally inquisitive. He attended Davenport's public schools. One incident from his primary-grade days at the Tyler School was long remembered by his family. E. P. received a call from the principal one day requesting that he come to school and take Phil home. When he got to school, he found Phil with two sprained ankles, the result of a fight with a schoolmate, Bix Beiderbecke, who later became one of the great trumpet players of the Dixieland era.

In high school, Phil was editor of both the school newspaper and the high school annual and found time for numerous other school activities, as well. He was a good student and easily won a place in the University of Iowa's freshman class of 1922.

Although he showed strong evidence of his journalistic abilities in college, particularly as editor of the undergraduate newspaper, he was well rounded in his interests and activities, enlisting in the ROTC and participating actively in programs in the fine arts and the performing arts.

Later in his life, he headed up the drive to finance and build the university art museum, one of many activities in the arts for which he received special recognition.

found on many newspaper mastheads of the day which Phil thought was too common. He took this action to dramatize the many changes he planned in upgrading the paper editorially and modernizing its appearance.

Kewanee, set amidst the rolling hills of west central Illinois, was founded in 1854 as a farm and livestock center. It was named in honor of the Sac and Fox Indian tribes that made central Illinois their home. The name Kewanee means "prairie chicken" in Winnebago.

Since its incorporation in 1872, it has served as the marketing, financial, and industrial hub of Henry, Stark, and Bureau counties. Its citizens hold an annual festival to mark the area's distinction as the "Hog Capital of the World."

This 1896 photograph shows William McKinley (with photographs of him hanging overhead) riding through the intersection of North Fremont and West Third Street during his presidential campaign.

Today, the brick building at the corner is Kewanee's town hall.

Henry County was solid Republican and one of only a handful that voted against Roosevelt in 1932. Predictably, many startled readers complained but soon saw the new publisher bringing a higher quality of journalism to their paper and accepted the changes as beneficial to all.

The young Adler began his indoctrination as a publisher by learning everything he possibly could about his adopted hometown. He quickly introduced a new perspective to the *Star Courier*. He put an end to his writers' and editors' practice of using syndicated and ready-to-print copy

Phil Adler, a dedicated family man, is seen here with his wife, Henrietta, and daughter, Betty Adler II, who was named after E. P. Adler's sister.

When he was in Washington, D.C., during World War II, Phil wrote letters to Henrietta every day. He also wrote daily to Betty whenever she was away from Davenport — while she was in college and later when she and husband Lloyd Schermer moved to Missoula, Montana.

"He was truly a gentleman's gentleman," says Murph Wolman, a close friend and associate who knew him well for many years.

known as "boiler plate." He instructed them to ignore press releases and other handouts from public relations sources that were slanted in favor of their clients. He told his reporters to get the "real" story. At the same time, he encouraged them to uncover community news that was compelling and meaningful, then urged his photographers to be more creative in finding human-interest subjects with local significance. He motivated his circulation crews to range farther and farther afield, attracting new subscribers by giving away teaspoons, atlases, and other useful premiums. And he inspired his advertising staff to be more competitive by introducing a new bonus program.

About four months after Phil Adler had assumed his role as publisher of the Kewanee *Star Courier*, his new-found experience was put to its first big test. He heard about a local boilermaker, John Cooper, who claimed to be in the process of inheriting a million-dollar Virginia estate. Since Cooper had worked in the community for years and had no record of dishonesty, he was so thoroughly believed and trusted that he was able to borrow considerable sums of money from people who bought his story. He furthered his cause by making substantial commitments to his church and a nearby hospital. His purchasing habits — such as buying new cars three at a time — also attested to his wealth.

Adler prompted his reporters to ask probing questions to get the complete story. Since some of the answers raised even more questions, the paper voiced doubts about the credibility of Cooper's statements. Adler was rebuffed by members of the community who warned him that he was making enemies, especially among those destined to benefit from Cooper's benevolence.

Even when he and his managing editor persevered and discovered the Virginia "estate" was nonexistent, they were publicly accused of

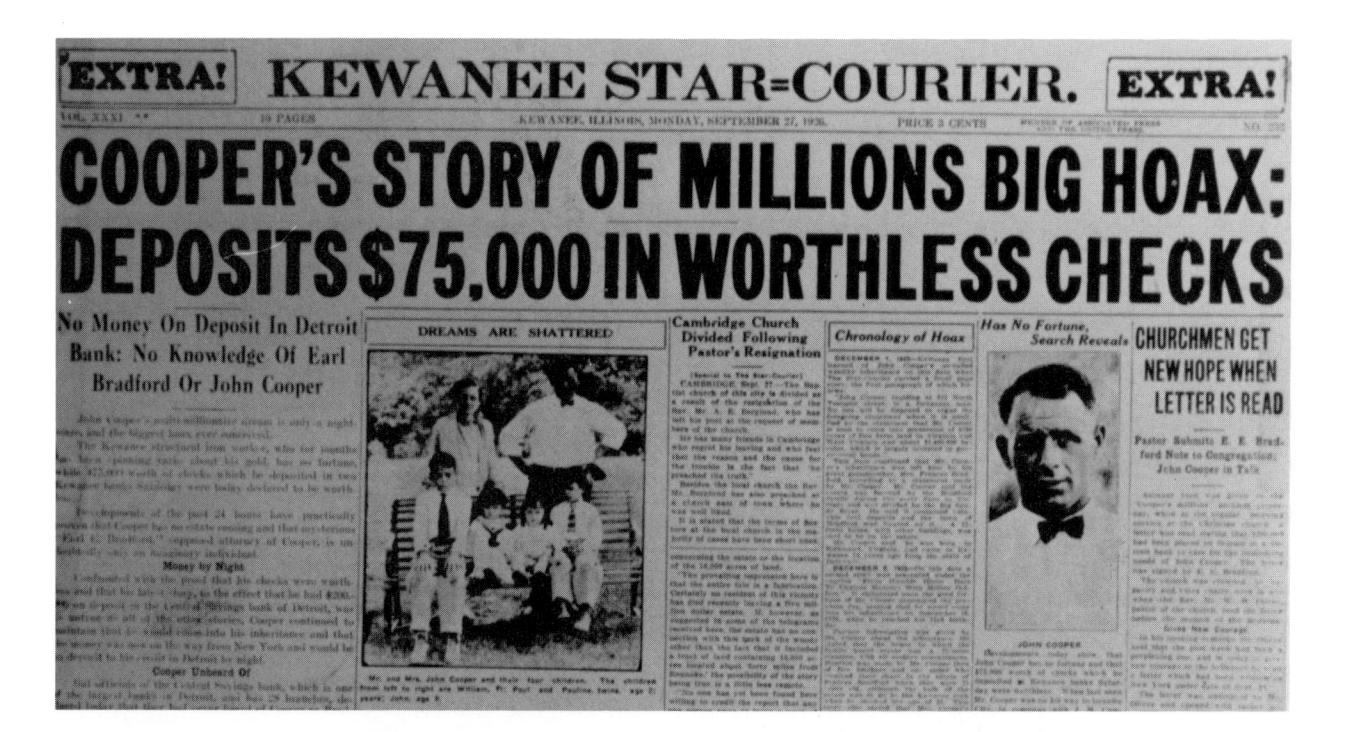

The front page of the Kewanee Star Courier *on September 27, 1926, attested to Philip Adler's doggedness in pursuing story leads, despite strong public opposition and indignant outcries that he was on the wrong track. As long as he knew his research was solid and the facts were straight, there was no deterring Phil from getting a story, or for telling the entire story.*

using tabloid tactics to boost circulation. At one point, with Adler running daily reports on the paper's findings in the case, several hundred indignant supporters of Cooper announced they were immediately cancelling their subscriptions.

Adler continued publishing his stories, convinced that his approach was professional and his research was reliable. He was rewarded for his persistence when the bubble burst. Cooper vanished abruptly, leaving behind bundles of outstanding debts, $75,000 in bad checks, and an uncounted number of irate merchants who had been bilked. The *Star Courier* triumphed with banner headlines about the "Big Hoax" and not only won back its lost subscribers but many more to boot.

During the Cooper affair, Phil Adler acted independently, never running to E. P. for advice, thus justifying his father's confidence in him. With increased circulation in hand, he was on the way toward repaying the $300,000 price tag that had brought the newspaper into the Lee fold. Other sources of income helped, too.

During the Depression, Phil's advertising manager was Harry Harper, a friend from University of Iowa days and a person the current chairman of Lee remembers well. "He was a wonderful man; a crusty old son-of-a-gun who always wore a bow tie," says Lloyd Schermer, now Chairman and CEO of Lee Enterprises.

Harper saw the Chicago-based district manager of Montgomery Ward in town and approached him with an idea. "I want to try something with you," he said. "Let's print a four-page broadside (advertisement) and have the U. S. Post Office carriers and route drivers distribute it in Henry County."

"Give it a try," was the response. Soon the store was swamped with customers.

"This was the birth of the insert business," says Schermer. "It started in Henry County with Harry Harper, Phil Adler and the *Star Courier*. They began to print the circulars for Montgomery Ward covering Illinois, first, then Missouri, Indiana, Wisconsin, Iowa and finally the 20-state Midwest region. They were printing millions of circulars, running them on that old press in Kewanee. Phil's wife, Henrietta, his daughter, Betty, printers, the business office people, pressmen, and all the spouses of the folks who worked there would help with these circulars."

This project let the Kewanee *Star Courier* pay an enormous dividend that kept several of the other Lee Syndicate papers floating during the Depression. "Phil was fit to be tied because they had huge accounts receivable and warehouses full of newsprint and circulars. Printing them almost made the wheels fall off the old press," says Lloyd. "Eventually Harry built a separate company called Mail-O-Graph and became the largest circular printer in the country with seven presses going around the clock. He was printing millions of them for Sears, Montgomery Ward's, Goldblatt's, and others. Who would have imagined this multi-million dollar pre-print industry was started by Lee in Kewanee? That's where it all began."

Phil Adler was the publisher of the Kewanee Star Courier *from 1926 to 1949, when he moved to Davenport and became publisher of the* Daily Times. *This photo shows Phil during the Kewanee years.*

W. H. "Harry" Harper and Mail-O-Graph

In 1932, the Kewanee *Star Courier*, like every other newspaper in the country, faced large losses as advertising linage dropped off drastically. The result might have been disastrous had it not been for W. H. "Harry" Harper, the newspaper's ingenious advertising manager.

Harper sold Montgomery Ward on the idea to print large quantities of inexpensive advertising circulars to help move its inventory at a time when customers simply were not making many purchases. Harper knew the *Star Courier* had plenty of press capacity. So he submitted a quote for 75,000 circulars, more printing than the plant had ever attempted before that time. Ward accepted the offer.

Before he knew it, Harper found that Ward's demands had increased fivefold, as more and more Ward stores requested circulars. Rather than cut back on the orders, he recruited everyone at the plant, as well as their families, to assist with the overload. Even editors and composing room foremen joined in the effort, working around the clock to take circulars off the press, bundle, and handle them as needed.

In the end, Ward was so impressed that this "little newspaper plant in Illinois" had delivered the goods that orders rose to more than a million. As Harper said later, "This Depression-born experiment blossomed into a small industry."

Teamwork and quick thinking on the part of Star Courier *staff members at 2:00 a.m. on April 13, 1942, led to an orderly evacuation of the newspaper's circulation files, records, and key editorial documents before the mid-town fire reached and devastated vital parts of the* Star Courier *building.*

Despite the staff's dislocation as a result of the catastrophe and a great deal of inconvenience while offices were being restored and damaged equipment replaced, the paper continued its daily reporting without interruption.

Phil's cousin, Selma Waterman, whose mind is sharp and memory clear at the age of 101, knew Phil most of his life. She points out that one of the things that contributed to Phil's success was the unusually close relationship he had with his father. "It was an ideal father/son relationship," she recalls. "Phil and E. P. cared a great deal about each other and had a strong communication.

"They were also in the habit of writing letters to each other almost every day, expressing their goals and discussing their problems very openly. This was one reason why both Adlers enjoyed a wide reputation for being communicative, honest, and open in their dealings with employees, who came to be part of the larger 'family' that the two men — being only children — had not enjoyed in their early years at home. It was also one of the reasons why they both reached out to the community so well and so often to take on projects that made their towns better places in which to live."

In the early 1940's, Phil guided the *Star Courier* into the support of many good works that were well beyond the responsibility accepted by the average newspaper in America. He fought hard for improved school facilities and better equipped and staffed hospitals, and was active in recruiting manpower to help with the war effort.

One of the greatest challenges he and the *Star Courier* faced came when a major fire in Kewanee devastated three city blocks in 1942, causing almost $3 million in losses. Although the newspaper plant survived because of an effective sprinkler system, flooding of the basement press room forced Adler to move his staff and equipment to temporary quarters for a week. There they published a disaster extra and continued to keep the public informed.

Adler took the lead in urging the community to disregard the costs and rebuild the damaged zone as quickly as possible. His editorials and actions helped to secure emergency priorities, and by the end of the year, reconstruction was well on its way.

It was during these World War II days that Phil moved to Washington, D.C., to assist the government's Office of Censorship in keeping critical information from the enemy. Ironically for a newsman, his major responsibility was to make sure certain matters were kept *out* of the press. He was involved in the censorship of news about the Manhattan Project, which produced the first atomic bomb. Another of his assignments was to determine the extent and significance of a Japanese attempt to fire-bomb parts of the northwestern U.S. using wind-carried balloons containing thermite bombs. The fact that so few people know of this sinister tactic is a testimony to Adler's diligence in keeping stories out of the press, thus discouraging the Japanese from

Fu-Go Balloons from Japan

During World War II, after a surprise raid on Tokyo by American bombers on April 18, 1942, the Japanese decided to devise a way to retaliate. Their ingenious plan, developed over the next two years, was to manufacture large balloons capable of carrying incendiaries or anti-personnel bombs that would be detonated within moments after an airborne balloon touched earth. The plan was to saturate the West Coast of the United States with these bombs whenever high-level winds were favorable and flowing strongly from west to east across the Pacific.

Eventually, in November, 1944, the first of some 9,300 fire-bomb balloons, called "Fu-Go," were launched. It was determined by the Japanese, through the release of radio-equipped balloons that relayed back information on speed, altitude, and distance, that it required from 50 to 70 hours for a balloon to proceed 5,965 miles across the ocean to the West Coast. The balloons, made of three or four layers of silk tissue paper glued together, were about 33 feet in diameter and filled with hydrogen.

When the first balloons landed in Montana, Wyoming, and Oregon (one drifted as far east as Ohio), causing small fires in dry forest areas, the United States undertook an investigation of what at first seemed like a very puzzling phenomenon.

It was at this time that Philip Adler, who had volunteered for duty in Washington, D.C., to aid the war effort, was assigned to the fire-bomb project. He and his associates in the Defense Department decided that the only real threat was to American forests, with relatively little danger to buildings or civilians.

For this reason, they requested — and got — the American press to abstain from reporting evidence of balloon landings. This code of secrecy was expected to frustrate Japanese intelligence and deter any further attempts at mass fire bombing.

The silence was broken, however, after May 5, 1945, when a woman and five children were killed near Lakeview, Oregon. While on an outing in the woods, they saw a balloon land and went to pull it from a grove of trees just as it exploded. It was then decided to warn the public about this little-known danger, even if the publicity would bring comfort to the enemy. Ironically, the Japanese had already decided to abandon the project about a month before the Lakeview tragedy.

Henrietta Bondi Adler, wife of Philip and mother of Betty, as she looked in her Red Cross Motor Corps uniform.

During World War II, she volunteered her services in Washington, D.C., where she worked for the Motor Corps in addition to other duties. Henrietta continued her interest in the Red Cross and worked with the Davenport chapter for many years. She received several high awards and recognition for her work for that organization.

pursuing the plan. In a strange twist of fate, some material used in these balloons was supplied by Nippon Paint Co., Ltd., a company that would later become a joint venture partner with Lee in a company called NAPP Systems Inc.

During his stay in Washington, Adler kept in direct communication with the newspaper, to which he returned on many weekends, and continued effectively as its publisher.

"For a while," recalls Mrs. Waterman, "Phil was tempted to stay in Washington because it offered him a chance to broaden his horizons. But he was much too loyal to his father. You see, E. P. was in his seventies and was very lonely because of the death of his beloved sister, Betty, in 1925, his wife, Lena, in 1926, and the loss of a succession of close newspaper associates." The ties of family and tradition were strong, and Phil returned to Kewanee. E. P.'s intentions for his son became clear several years later, immediately after E. P.'s death, when Phil opened a letter his father had left him. It contained the request that Phil move to Davenport to succeed him as publisher of the *Times.* Actually, throughout E. P.'s last illness, Phil commuted between Davenport and Kewanee, effectively running both papers.

"Phil went through a tremendous struggle with himself at that time," Mrs. Waterman continues, "because he revered his father and was not at all certain that he could really follow in his footsteps. Phil was a fine writer — much better than his father — and was able to express himself clearly and forcefully."

In this respect, Lloyd Schermer remembers the time when he was working at the *Daily Times* in Davenport that he submitted copy to Phil to review prior to sending it to the editors.

"I thought this particular piece was a real gem and would easily pass muster," recalls Schermer. "But Phil called me into his office, and I was astounded to see all the improvements he made with his blue pencil to something I thought was so good. He gave me new insight into concise writing."

Phil was as good a manager as he was an editor. He frequently made constructive criticisms that improved articles and editorials without hurting the feelings of the reporters and editors who prepared them. He had the ability to motivate people to think more clearly and write better than they thought they could.

"I think he was able to do this," explains Mrs. Waterman, "because he always gave the impression that his actions were based on the improvement of the paper and never on his own personal tastes and preferences. He could be in a very ticklish and sensitive situation and come out of it without ruffling feathers or making enemies."

Because his personality was so different from that of his more autocratic father, many thought of Phil as a gentle manager. But however gentlemanly and solicitous of the feelings of others Phil appeared, he was anything but a pushover, as those who tested him soon learned. He had a bar of iron in his backbone and a reputation for making firm decisions and sticking to them. "Phil Adler was one of the most decent men I ever knew," recalled Arthur B. "Tim" Hanson, a former Marine major general who became a Washington, D.C., attorney and represented A. W. Lee's wife and daughter for many years. "A thorough-going gentleman and about as nice a guy as you'd ever want to meet. He hated to hurt people's feelings, but if he had to make a hard decision, he would do it."

Phil's innate toughness when the chips were down was apparent during the 1952 printers' strike against the Davenport *Times*. One of the major issues in the strike was the printers' refusal to accept wire stores which were sent to the *Times* on punched tape.

When the Lee Board of Directors met in the early 60's, it was quite an affair. Members of the "Expansion Board" (which authorized Lee's growth into Montana) included (from left): David Gottlieb, general manager of Lee Enterprises; Walter White, Lincoln publisher; Lloyd Schermer, Missoula publisher; Charles White, Kewanee publisher; Phil Adler, president of Lee and co-publisher, Quad City Times-Democrat; *Ray Rorick, Mason City publisher; Strand Hilleboe, Billings publisher; Dick Morrison, Butte publisher; Harry Harper, Mail-o-graph; Henry Hook, co-publisher, Quad City* Times-Democrat; *"Luke" Nelson, Muscatine publisher; Lloyd Bunker, Ottumwa publisher; Bill Burgess, LaCrosse publisher; Don Anderson, Madison publisher; and E.L. Sparks Jr., Hannibal publisher.*

By comparison, today's board consists of just eight members — three Lee officers and five independent outsiders who are in a position to evaluate and judge the performance of the CEO and his management team.

The strike was one of the American newspaper industry's first confrontations with organized labor over the issue of automation, and Phil's handling of the situation blazed a trail for other newspapers. Dave Gottlieb, the paper's business manager at the time, had been negotiating with the union. When it turned into a strike, he took charge of the production effort and managed to get the paper out every day without the participation of the union printers. The *Times* never missed an issue. Gradually, strikers were replaced with nonunion people and the union eventually gave up the effort.

When Phil and Dave decided to take the strike, it was not an easy decision, and it was not based on any antiunion philosophy. Phil had worked with many of the union members as an apprentice in the composing room, and both men knew these workers as friends, colleagues, and, in some cases, stockholders. Hostility to unions was not a part of the Adler family tradition: Phil's father had carried his card in the International Typographical Union until the day he died.

Although taken a few years prior to the incident, this photo shows the awnings at the Daily Times *building which Phil asked to have lowered to protect striking workers from the rain.*

Because of their heritage of public service during more than half a century since the company's founding, Lee newspapers and radio stations adapted quickly and exhaustively to the immediate needs of American communities during the critical days of World War II.

Adler and other Lee managers not only communicated the goals, such as the collection of scrap for wartime production, but made it clear that their own employees were expected to join them in helping whenever and wherever needed.

Even in the midst of the conflict, Phil treated his adversaries with consideration. Selma Waterman remembers, "There were lines of strikers marching slowly around the building. Everything was quite orderly. It had always been the Lee company policy to be honest and forthright when dealing with labor and their leaders.

"Well, in this particular instance, it had begun to rain. Phil was sitting in his office and he looked out and saw that the strikers were getting wet. Many an executive might have said, 'It serves them right.' But not Phil. He called one of his employees and asked him to lower the awnings around the building to provide protection. That's the kind of man he was."

Advances in production technology — and the strike experience — caught the attention of many newspaper executives, most of them from papers far larger in size. Some sent people to Davenport to see how Dave Gottlieb got the paper out despite the strike and to learn how to train executives to publish under strike conditions.

"The real significance of the strike was that it set a pattern for the rest of the country," says Lloyd Schermer. "Once we demonstrated how punched tape improved productivity, it was pretty hard for a union somewhere else to say it wouldn't work or that it wasn't more productive. Anyone who did was clearly arguing to slow down production."

Phil, more the intellectual than his father, was nevertheless always willing to follow E. P.'s example and roll up his sleeves when the occasion demanded. Once he organized a Victory Drive at the start of World War II to collect scrap metal. He set an ambitious goal of 250 tons and encouraged all townspeople, including Lee reporters, editors, advertising salespeople, and other staff members, to lend a hand.

On July 14, 1988, President Reagan returned to Davenport where he had worked as a radio announcer. John Gardner, then publisher of the Quad-City Times, presented the President with a commemorative front page on behalf of the Davenport Chamber of Commerce.

Henrietta Adler recalls Ronald Reagan working in Kewanee for the Star Courier, announcing sports scores from the balcony to people assembled below. He then moved to Davenport where he was well known long before his Hollywood days or his political career began.

Known in those days as "Dutch," Reagan intended to become a radio announcer and worked at station WOC in Davenport. The station was at the top of a building that housed a Buddhist shrine and the Palmer School of Chiropractic, which owned the station. Reagan walked down through the school many times after signing off the air to eat with students in the cafeteria. Reagan soon moved to Des Moines to join radio station WHO, an NBC affiliate, when WOC merged with that station.

The former president certainly knew some of the Lee employees and others associated with Lee, in part because his brother, Neal, was with the Davenport Chamber of Commerce.

"When I was going to go to California one time, after Ronald Reagan had become an actor," recalls Judge Nathan Grant, "I wrote a letter to him and was invited to stop by his studio and meet him. This was on the set for King's Row, a popular movie of the day. I waited outside the dressing rooms at Warner Brothers, and pretty soon, in came this tall, good-looking guy. He greeted me like a brother and asked about some of his friends in Davenport.

"Then he surprised me by asking if I'd like to meet a gorgeous movie actress and I replied that of course I would. He called and out came Ann Sheridan. She was the most beautiful redhead I had ever seen.

"Ronald Reagan had the greatest personality and I got a tremendous kick out of coming back to Davenport and telling my friends about my experience."

A few days later, a disgruntled young reporter was rooting through the basement of an Iowa barn, loading rusty, greasy parts of a dismantled plow on one of the trucks loaned by the newspaper. After an hour of strenuous work, he announced that he was going to hitchhike back to the newsroom and "finish the reporting assignment the guys in the head office are paying me to do. This is for the birds."

An unrecognizable man down below him in the cellar, clad in torn overalls and filthy gloves, removed his equally smudgy cap and looked up at him. "O.K., if you're that tired, young man, go ahead and leave. But please tell my secretary that I have a couple more hours to go — this is too important to all of us."

"Sure, sure. What's your name?"

"Phil Adler," came the response.

The reporter changed his mind and went back to the scrap-metal pile.

Tim Hanson held special admiration for Phil Adler's devotion to duty and loyalty to Lee newspapers. Various large publishing syndicates repeatedly tried to lure him to join big urban newspapers. In at least one instance, such offers also involved a completely new daily, which he would be free to mold from the start. But Phil would have none of it and made it clear that his life was with Lee.

Phil Adler had a mind for detail and a memory to go with it. Years after an event had taken place, he could recount the circumstances in their entirety. Henry Hook, who had been at Lee for many years in broadcasting and was publisher of the *Morning Democrat* and co-publisher of the *Times-Democrat* with Phil Adler when the two Davenport papers combined, remembers. "When I retired," Hook says, "Phil sent me a letter in which he expressed his apologies for specific disagreements we had at one time or another — and which I had long since forgotten. He was always the first to admit it if he made a decision that later proved wrong."

Hook remembers him as an extremely neat person who felt tidiness was an integral part of a successful business. "He liked to have things cleaned up around the building, but he made his point in a humorous way — like telling the ad manager that his reps were not hitting their wastebaskets very well. He was concerned with efficiency as much as neatness.

"Phil kept his finger on the pulse of the business in every way, even to the extent that he would go over the bills and the paychecks when he was publisher. All the bills would be stacked up and he'd go over every single entry. If he felt the company was spending too much for any particular item, he would set aside the bill for later discussion with the business manager."

Phil kept his eye on operations in every corner of the growing Lee operation. Gary Benshoof, then a 22-year-old engraver who had turned down a $100-per-week job for the opportunity to work in the *Davenport Times*' new color lab at $55 weekly, remembers how Phil used to walk around and greet employees. "The way Phil remembered my name and always had something nice to say made me feel like a real man." Benshoof, typical of many Lee employees, has risen through the ranks in his 30 years with Lee from the engraving room to quality control manager, then project manager during the NAPP development period, and now directs NAPP's international sales and technical development.

Isadore Katz, a friend and attorney who served the company on occasion for many years, attributes Phil Adler's success to his natural gifts as a leader. "Like his father," says Katz, "he had the ability to lead the way and at the same time treat those under him with respect and understanding. With Phil, it was always clear to employees where their duties and responsibilities lay. When he became president of Lee Enterprises in 1960, he inaugurated an attitude of understanding which has become ingrained in Lee and is prevalent today. It all started with the fact that he was an avid communicator as a young man and that it was almost an obsession with him to get the facts straight, present them clearly, and follow up when necessary."

As the fourth man in the succession of leaders who have brought Lee Enterprises to what it is today, Philip D. Adler enhanced the best of the company's heritage and at the same time opened up new opportunities for future growth.

He was responsible for expanding Lee's geographic range even before he officially took the helm of the company. In 1958, Don Anderson, publisher of the *Wisconsin State Journal*, came to him with the suggestion that Lee consider purchasing a group of six Montana newspapers in Anaconda, Billings, Butte, Helena, Livingston and Missoula which were owned by the Anaconda Mining Company. At the time, Phil was co-publisher of the *Times* and vice-president of Lee, but was virtually in charge of the company because of Loomis's serious illness. (It was the custom in those days for the men who ran the company to stay in office until they died.

"That's the way it was done," recalls Lloyd Schermer. "They died with their boots on even if they were too sick to really function as CEO. Phil, in his own gracious way, respected Loomis's title although he was really running the company. To insure that future leaders did not suffer similarly, Phil instituted a mandatory retirement while he was CEO.")

When Anderson came to Phil with the concept of expanding into Montana, Phil listened attentively because he knew Don had literally grown up in the saddle on his folks' ranch in Montana. Later, he moved to Wisconsin to become a cub reporter and quickly climbed the ladder to the position of managing editor and then publisher. During visits to his home state, he anguished over the sorry state of journalism there.

Taken about 1950 on one of her trips to New York, this picture of Betty was one of her parent's favorites.

The Anaconda papers were weak because the company's main business was mining, not journalism. There was political bias in reporting, and censorship existed merely by omitting objectionable stories.

"They were forbidden," Don explained, "even to print the word 'silicosis,'" referring to the lung disease prevalent in the mining community. The editors were permitted to take a stand on foreign or distant issues, but they risked their jobs if they ran negative editorials about the mining industry.

"We had a name for how Anaconda controlled the news," remembers Randy Jacobs, a banker whose family owned the state's oldest bank, the First National Bank of Missoula. "It was called the 'copper collar.'"

Phil gave Anderson freedom to explore this unusual opportunity for Lee to grow, and the company acquired the Montana papers for $5.7 million despite competition from some 30 newspaper chains and other would-be buyers, a dozen of which offered a considerably higher price for the papers. What clinched the deal was Lee's demonstrated involvement in the communities Lee papers serve. Anaconda was also impressed with the quality of the company's journalistic product as well as the promise that the six papers would remain in the company (other bidders wanted to sell off the unprofitable papers in Butte and Helena).

Immediately upon acquisition, Anderson and Adler made one fact clear: each paper would be independent — publishers and editors would be free to set their own policies as long as they reported the news without bias. Many staff members from the Anaconda days elected to remain on the job, relieved that, as professional journalists, they would now be able to bring some dignity to the term, "freedom of the press."

Some were skeptical at first, despite Lee management's first order of the day, "Print the news!" But they soon realized that there were no strings — they had this journalistic freedom, with no "ifs," "ands," or "buts."

Lee's chief negotiator for the purchase of the Montana papers from the Anaconda Company was Don Anderson, Lloyd Schermer's mentor and publisher of the Wisconsin State Journal. *Anderson was a natural choice for the job because his parents had homesteaded in Montana and Don was originally from Bozeman. A tall, mustachioed, jovial and well-liked man, Anderson was known as a gifted writer, a great editor and a wonderful human being.*

Anaconda agreed to sell to Lee despite higher bids from other interested parties. "The Anaconda folks believed in Don and knew he was sincere in not wanting to dismantle the papers," says Lloyd. "In the end, Anaconda really did care that their newspapers went to a company committed to providing readers with a high level of journalism."

The Compassionate Consolidator 79

The Daily Missoulian

Missoula, Montana, Tuesday Morning, June 2, 1959   Price: Five Cents

Hello Missoula!

The Lee Newspaper Group of the Middle West has acquired the Anaconda Co.'s newspaper interests in Missoula, Helena, Butte, Anaconda, Livingston and Billings.

We are understandably proud that, after months of careful consideration, we have the opportunity to carry on the publishing responsibilities of these Montana newspapers.

We know the role these papers have played in American frontier history, and we recognize their stake in the future of a great state.

Of major concern to Missoula is our desire to make The Missoulian and The Sentinel the best possible home town newspapers.

Our staff, in the main, will be people you already know, who have lived here for years, and have dedicated their lives to this community. They will make the decisions, set the policies, with whatever help we can give them.

We understand the character and needs of cities like Missoula, because we, too, successfully publish newspapers in great university and agricultural centers.

A newspaper prospers only as a community thrives. We take pride in publishing good newspapers, and we want the economy of Missoula and western Montana to flourish. We will do all we can to promote that prosperity.

• • •

The name "Lee" is new to many in Montana, yet there have been business ties between our newspapers for years. Our representatives in the national advertising field, Jann & Kelley, have been associated with your Montana newspapers for some thirty years. Through them we have known the operating heads of your newspapers for a long time and they have known us.

The new publishing company is being headed by Don Anderson, who was born and reared in Bozeman. Mrs. Anderson also was born and educated in Montana.

Although publisher of one of our major newspapers, the Wisconsin State Journal at Madison, Don Anderson has taken time each year to relive his Montana experiences with pack trips and canyon expeditions, so we approach this task not as strangers, but as friends.

As Montana comes to know us better you will realize that each newspaper has a policy of independence and individuality just as our newspapers have shown in Iowa, Nebraska, Wisconsin, Illinois and Missouri.

Publishers and editors call the turns as they see them; there is no such thing as dictated editorial policy. We serve only one interest—the public.

There were no strings attached to the sale of these newspapers. Our only obligations are to our subscribers and our communities.

In the Midwest our newspapers are variously Democratic and Republican, but mostly independent in politics. The only policy each follows is to help improve its community. We are proud of a record of fair play to all readers, regardless of race, creed or faith.

• • •   • • •

The Lee Group started in 1890 as a family enterprise and it still is, essentially. A. W. Lee's family came from a Quaker homestead in Philadelphia to the West Branch settlement, which was Herbert Hoover's boyhood home, soon after Iowa became a state.

Three of our papers are well over 100 years old. We have 10 newspapers in the Midwest, in addition to a number of TV and radio affiliates. No Lee paper once acquired has ever been sold.

As newspapering goes, we are a medium-sized group, but we share the same pride in good publishing plants the Montana newspapers have demonstrated.

As you know us better, you will realize that we value employe loyalty. The men and women who have worked conscientiously to develop your newspapers are competent and devoted to their tasks. We have met many of them, and we plan to build on with this team.

Through our continued confidence, we hope to reach new goals. Publishing newspapers, we believe, is a public trust. In the years which lie ahead, we will work hard to merit this trust in Montana.

The Lee Newspapers of Montana

The center column story in the June 2, 1959, Missoulian is how most Montana citizens learned of Lee's purchase of the paper. The column highlights Lee's attitude towards their readers and promises the new owners will work hard to earn readers' trust.

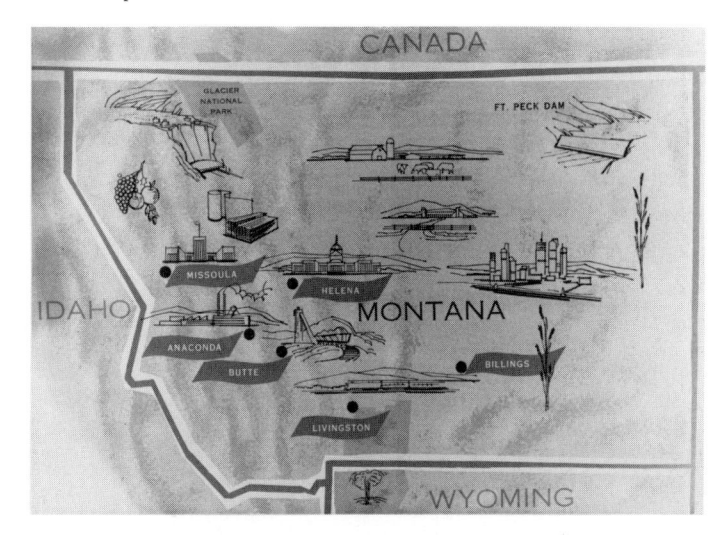

Map showing the locations of the six newspapers in Montana purchased from the Anaconda Company. The paper in Anaconda was discontinued and the one in Livingston was later sold and became a weekly paper. But the other four have flourished, making Montana one of the most active states in the Lee Enterprises newspaper network, with a combined circulation of more than 150,000.

A major turning point came when the editor at the Butte *Montana Standard* asked Anderson what restrictions the paper would have on reporting a strike at the nearby Anaconda mines.

"Why are you asking me this question?" said Anderson, puzzled.

"Because the paper has never printed news of any kind about the strike, although it's been going on for some time."

"Nonsense!" said Anderson. "Print the news and try to get both sides of the story."

That night, Anderson was writing letters, seated out of sight in a corner of the newsroom.

LEE ENTERPRISES
INCORPORATED

Chairman of the Board, LEE P. LOOMIS, The Globe Gazette, Mason City, Iowa
President, PHILIP D. ADLER, The Daily Times, Davenport, Iowa
Executive Vice President, WALTER W. WHITE, The Lincoln Star, Lincoln, Nebraska
Vice President, DON ANDERSON, The State Journal, Madison, Wisconsin
Secretary, WILLIAM BURGESS, The Tribune, La Crosse, Wisconsin

October 1, 1960

211 BRADY ST., DAVENPORT, IOWA   DAVID K. GOTTLIEB, GENERAL MANAGER AND TREASURER

Dear Stockholder:

Enclosed is your certificate for stock of Lee Enterprises, Incorporated. The number of shares (and cash for a fractional share) to which you are entitled has been computed as follows:

Company	No. of Shares	Conversion Basis	Shares of Lee Enterprises
The Star Publishing Company		X 3.2753	
Wisconsin State Journal Company		X 7.5979	
Davenport Newspapers, Inc.		X 4.3462	
The LaCrosse Tribune Company	10	X 5.1043	51.0430
Globe Gazette Publishing Company		X 5.2411	
Courier Printing Company		X 2.9703	
The Star-Courier Company		X 2.1055	
Journal Printing Company		X 3.5316	
The Courier-Post Publishing Company		X 2.9899	

Total 51.0430
Shares Issued 51 –
Cash Per Fractional Share $4.30

Our attorneys have advised us that in their opinion the exchange of stock of the Newspaper Companies for stock of Lee Enterprises is a tax-free transaction _except_ as to the amount of cash issued for a fractional share. You should report the entire amount of the cash payment as long term capital gain for income tax purposes.

Very truly yours,

LEE ENTERPRISES, INCORPORATED

By *Dave K Gottlieb*
Treasurer

When Lee Enterprises, Incorporated, was formed from the nine existing newspapers, letters like this were used to compute the number of new shares each holder of old stock received.

In 1946, when the 10 shares of The La Crosse Publishing Company were first purchased, their value was $1,000. These shares converted into 51 shares of Lee Enterprises in 1960. As of November 15, 1988, those shares had multiplied into 8,262 shares as a result of numerous splits. Their value on November 15, 1988: $223,074.00!

One of the veteran newsmen came in from covering a story. He slapped a colleague on the back and pronounced emphatically, "Bill, we're not whores any more — we're newspapermen!"

Phil was at the forefront of the program to move Lee from the group of individual companies it had been at mid-century to the time in the summer of 1967 when all of the divisions, newspapers, and broadcasting were consolidated. The catalyst had been the purchase of the Montana papers in 1959.

At the time, the company was known as the Lee Group. The "Syndicate" name fell out of favor because ever since Prohibition the word had generally referred to criminal organizations. There was no central management structure (E. P. Adler had been the titular head only out of love and respect), nor a bank account. It was a loose affiliation by anyone's standards. Each publisher had his own paper in which he owned stock. Some publishers owned stock in other papers, creating interlocking arrangements. Out of mutual trust and the force of E. P.'s personality, the arrangement had worked. "If Bill Burgess needed a new press in La Crosse, each of the other publishers went to their local banks, borrowed what was needed, and sent it to La Crosse," says Lloyd Schermer. "Of course, it was always paid back. That's how business was done."

When Phil Adler and Dave Gottlieb approached the Northern Trust Company of Chicago for financing the Montana purchase, the loan officer would have none of this informality. He wanted all the assets of the group of papers brought together and would loan funds only to that combined organization.

Phil Adler was elected president of the newly reorganized Lee Enterprises, Incorporated, and Dave Gottlieb became treasurer. In his book on Phil Adler, John Newhouse explains that the merger was a tricky assignment for them. "The task of bringing eleven corporations with many stockholders into one compact unit began. It required evaluating the stock of each corporation and relating it to shares in the new company. It involved selling a new idea to shareholders, most of whom had owned and cherished their stock for many years."

Through diligent canvassing, Phil learned of possible problems with the publishers of the Lincoln *Star* and the *Wisconsin State Journal*. "We thought we were a hell of a lot more important than the Kewanees, Ottumwas and the like, says Martin "Murph" Wolman, then general manager of Madison Newspapers, Inc., and later publisher

Lee shares were first traded publicly in March, 1969, when over-the-counter trading began. Trading began on the American Exchange in March, 1970, and on the New York Stock Exchange in April, 1978.

of the *Wisconsin State Journal*. "Phil doubled our valuations so there were no problems when the merger came along." When the final vote was taken, there was only one dissenting stockholder. The ease of completing the reorganization into Lee Enterprises was a testimony to the stockholders' trust in and loyalty to Phil Adler and their respect for Dave Gottlieb's business acumen.

Another of Phil's significant contributions was the way he guided Lee from a private to a public company during the late 1960's. In 1969, Lee Enterprises offered a block of stock for sale to the general public for the first time in over-the-counter trading. A year later, Lee stock was admitted to trading on the American Exchange.

Phil's decade of leadership brought Lee the greatest period of growth and transformation it had yet experienced. The man who implemented so many changes, however, has been described as one whose guiding values revolved around tradition and loyalty. He was deeply conscious of the ideals and integrity that had driven the growth of the Lee papers from the beginning and picked up the torch of civic and community service that had been carried by his predecessors in the company.

His loyalties began with his wife, Henrietta, and daughter, Betty. Brought together with the help of his Aunt Betty, Phil and Henrietta were married in 1928 and honeymooned in Europe. Always adventuresome, Henrietta finally let Phil (with E. P.'s help) persuade her to give up her hobby — flying her own airplane! Their family was completed with the birth of their daughter, Betty, whose life would become deeply entwined with the company over the years.

John Newhouse tells the story that Henrietta often had to carry the suitcases on their frequent travels because of Phil's tricky back and sees that as a symbol of the supportive role she played. "Henrietta Adler," he writes, "lifts other weights for the publisher, as do the wives of most successful executives. She presides over a serene and well-ordered home. She fends off many of the blows that come a publisher's way. She is his most enthusiastic cheering section. The result is a strong team that presents a united and happy front to the world outside."

86 Lee's Legacy of Leadership

Shortly after the new corporate headquarters building was completed, the board met in the new building for the first time. In this photograph, taken on October 12, 1967, seated from left are: Lloyd Schermer, publisher of the Missoulian; *Alfred Magnusson, legal counsel, of Lane and Waterman, Davenport; Philip D. Adler, of the* Times-Democrat, *Davenport, president; and David K. Gottlieb, vice president, treasurer and general manager of Lee Enterprises, Davenport.*

Standing from left are: Walter W. White, executive vice president, publisher of the Lincoln Star; *Charles W. White, assistant publisher of the Lincoln* Star; *Don Anderson, vice president, publisher of the* Wisconsin State Journal; *Walter Rothschild, vice president and general manager, electronics division, Quincy; and William T. Burgess, secretary, publisher of the* La Crosse Tribune.

about the use of money, Phil wrote, "Dad expressed this best to us in a letter with his will when he said, 'I should like you to feel about these things as I have always felt and that is, that money that may come to you through your own efforts or any other way is not to be construed as belonging to you alone so that you should have sole use of it. I firmly believe we are only elected stewards of what we get and a goodly portion of it should be distributed by us to others.'"

A reserved man, Phil sought no recognition, even objecting to the inclusion of his name in *Who's Who in America.* Yet his contributions inevitably brought recognition. One in particular moved him visibly. In 1966, the University of Iowa named him the recipient of their first Distinguished Service Award. The citation was a glowing tribute to a lifetime of service.

"If the qualities of a man might be likened to those of a river," it read, "Philip D. Adler is like the great river beside which he was born and near which he lives and works: quiet and calm, a constant force to be admired and respected — and sometimes to be reckoned with....

"As a citizen, Philip Adler was born with a deep sense of humanity in his soul.

"To community challenges without number through the years, he has been a wellspring of leadership and inspiration. His service has embraced whatever causes might strengthen his community — its young and elderly, its health and education, its commerce and arts, its beauty and spirit.

"The generosity of his service has known no boundary set by race, or class, or creed."

Philip Adler's generosity

"Philip Adler had a habit that endeared him to many people," recalls Judge Nathan Grant, an old friend of all the Adlers. "Many people will read a book and if they come across a passage they think might be of interest to someone they know, will call that person's attention to the title and chapter. But not Phil Adler. He would mark the passage and send the whole book to a friend or a business associate.

"Frequently, he would deliberately go out and buy books that he thought friends should read and send them as gifts. I have a number of these in my own library. Because Phil was so interested in all of the creative arts and because he was such an avid reader himself, he was a natural source of information and motivated others to be more aware and more perceptive."

Name changes in the Davenport papers

A.W. Lee and Charles Reimers, the managing editor of Lee's Ottumwa paper, bought the *Davenport Times* from the Brady family on July 1, 1899. The purchase price was $20,000. It was a daily paper published in the afternoon and had begun as the *Blue Ribbon News* in 1878.

As E.P. Adler considered ways to compete with the four older, well-established newspapers in Davenport at that time, he saw an opportunity to incorporate the 100,000 population of the entire tri-cities area (Moline, Rock Island and Davenport) as part of his paper's market, so quickly dropped the "Davenport" and renamed the paper the *Daily Times*.

The *Democrat*, which began publishing in 1855, was purchased from the Richardson family in 1915. Most papers of that era had the name of the political affiliation of the paper as part of its name. At the time E.P. Adler purchased the *Davenport Times*, one of the city's other papers was the *Republican*.

The *Daily Times* and the *Democrat* were both afternoon papers. In the days before television, it was accepted that the afternoon was the best time to publish in order to reach the most readers. The two papers competed for the same audience.

On October 2, 1951, the Times and the Democrat publishing companies merged into Davenport Newspapers, Inc. The *Democrat* executives and staff moved into the remodeled Times building on Second Street. The paper went into the morning field and was renamed the *Morning Democrat*. The *Times* continued as an afternoon paper.

On June 1, 1964, The *Democrat* and the *Times* were merged into one paper, the *Times-Democrat*, publishing one edition in the morning and another in the afternoon.

In 1975, the papers became the *Quad-City Times* in recognition of the importance of Bettendorf, Iowa, the fourth of the "quad" cities, as well as an interest in omitting any suggestion of an editorial affiliation with a particular political party. The paper continues to publish both morning and afternoon editions.

Major General Arthur B. "Tim" Hanson, USMC

Arthur B. "Tim" Hanson studied law and received his degree at the Marshall-Wythe School of Law, associated with the College of William and Mary in Williamsburg, Virginia. His father was a lawyer and for many years had served as the attorney for the Lee Company, working with E. P. Adler on corporate matters and also handling the affairs of Laura Anna Lee, the daughter of A. W. Lee. Tim was temporarily sidetracked from law when he enlisted in the marines, serving with great honor during World War II.

With the war over, and three days after returning from his assignment in Japan, Tim was taken by his father — then 60 — to meet Laura Lee. "Miss Lee," said the older Hanson, "This is my son, Arthur. He's going to take care of you in the future since I'm getting too much on in years."

"I met Miss Lee, then," recalled Tim, "and I'll never forget the dear old soul. She was in her late 40's. She looked me up and down — I was all of 29 — and she said, 'Well, I think you'll do.' And that was the way we met. I handled her affairs from then on. And it was always 'Miss Lee' and 'Mr. Hanson,' never any 'Laura' or 'Tim' or even 'Arthur.' She was a very fine person."

Tim Hanson continued from that day on to handle the affairs of Laura Anna Lee and represented his firm as Washington counsel for Lee Enterprises until the time he died of cancer, just short of his 73rd birthday in December, 1989. For many years, and particularly after his father died in 1961, he was very close to Philip Adler, whom he described as "a very fine person and just about the nicest guy you'd ever want to meet." As his father had done before him, Tim was also general counsel to the American Newspaper Publishers Association.

Gregory Schermer, Betty and Lloyd's son, went to work for Hanson after graduating from law school. He remained with Hanson's firm in Washington, D.C., for eight years and returned to Davenport in 1989 as Lee's internal counsel.

Milestones during the Adler administration

- October 1, 1960 — Philip Adler becomes president of Lee following the retirement of Lee Loomis.
- October 5, 1960 — KEYC-TV, Mankato, Minnesota, begins telecasts.
- October 1, 1962 — Lee establishes its employee savings plan.
- June, 1963 — Lee headquarters moves to Davenport Bank Building.
- June 1, 1964 — Davenport, newspapers become the *Times-Democrat* and begin 24-hour publication under a single title, though publishing different editions for morning and afternoon.
- September 30, 1966 — Lee Newspapers of Montana is liquidated and merged into Lee Enterprises.
- January, 1966 — The year is proclaimed a "Landmark Year" for Lee with the formation of a planning committee, headed by Dave Gottlieb and Lloyd Schermer, to direct projects for future growth.
- January, 1967 — Lee acquires remaining one-third minority interest in the Billings Gazette Printing Company for approximately $775,000 of Lee stock.
- June 30, 1967 — Broadcast merger specifies 1.0734 shares of Lee Enterprises for each share of Lee Broadcasting. All of the divisions, newspapers, and broadcasting are consolidated.
- July, 1967 — The new Lee headquarters building in Davenport is completed.
- September 23, 1968 — The decision to "go public" is reached following two prior years of discussions by the board of directors.
- March 19, 1969 — Lee stock becomes available to the public for the first time when it is offered over-the-counter at the price of $20.50 per share.
- July 5, 1969 — Lee purchases 73 percent of the Journal-Times Company, Racine, Wisconsin, for $4,050,000 from J. D. McMurray, publisher of the *Journal Times*.
- October 1, 1969 — Lee purchases *Corvallis Gazette-Times*, Corvallis, Oregon, for $2 million.
- December, 1969 — Lee purchases the remaining 27 percent of the *Journal Times* in Racine for $1,200,000.
- January, 1970 — Philip Adler retires and David Gottlieb is named president.

The Compassionate Consolidator 89

The growth of Lee Enterprises 1960-1970
(boxed properties are new)

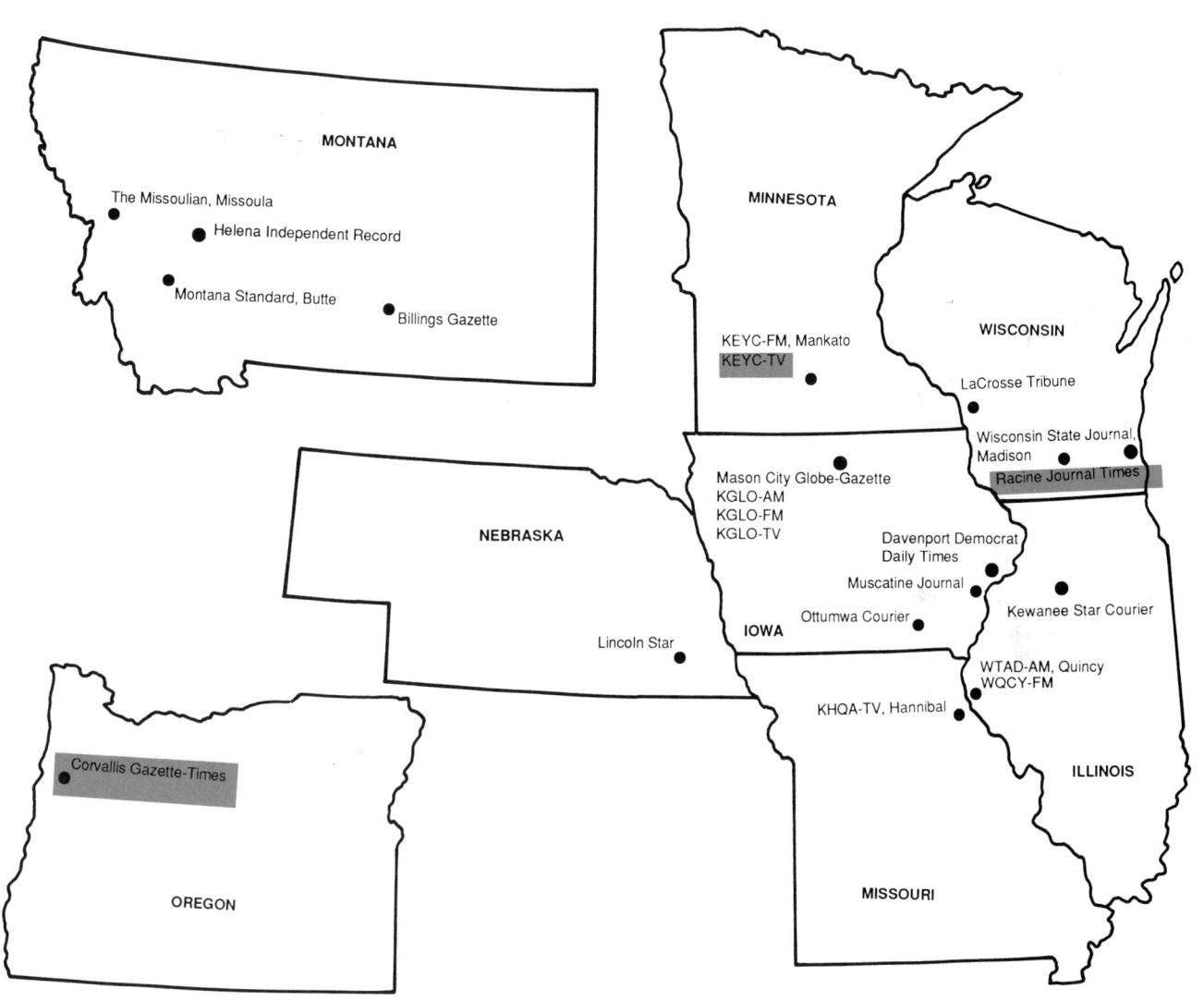

MONTANA
- The Missoulian, Missoula
- Helena Independent Record
- Montana Standard, Butte
- Billings Gazette

MINNESOTA
- KEYC-FM, Mankato
- KEYC-TV

WISCONSIN
- LaCrosse Tribune
- Wisconsin State Journal, Madison
- Racine Journal Times

IOWA
- Mason City Globe-Gazette
  KGLO-AM
  KGLO-FM
  KGLO-TV
- Davenport Democrat Daily Times
- Muscatine Journal
- Ottumwa Courier

NEBRASKA
- Lincoln Star

ILLINOIS
- Kewanee Star Courier
- WTAD-AM, Quincy
- WQCY-FM

MISSOURI
- KHQA-TV, Hannibal

OREGON
- Corvallis Gazette-Times

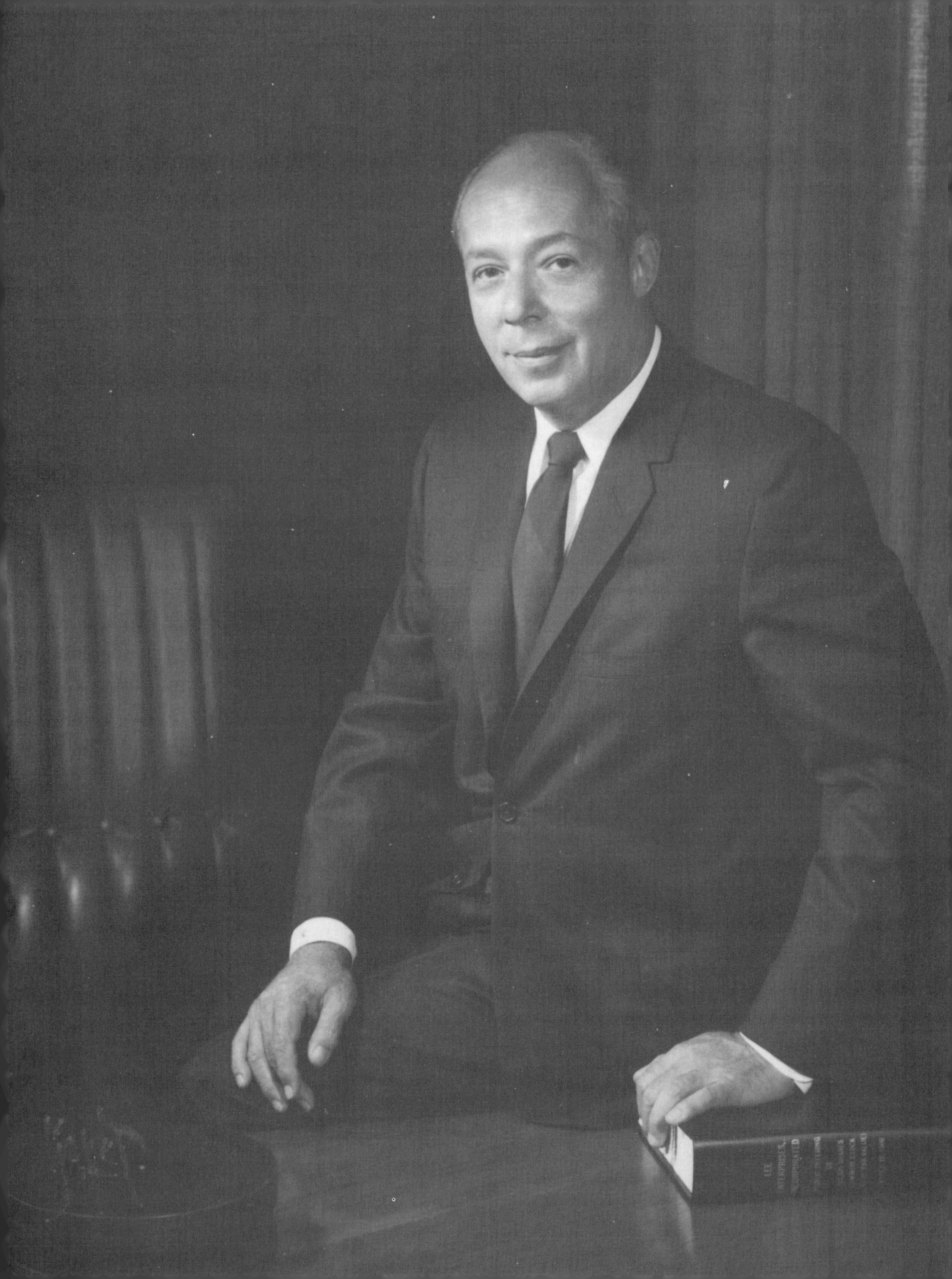

Chapter Five

Seeing Beyond the Horizon

1970-1973   *David K. Gottlieb*

Born June 26, 1914, in Tiffin, Ohio.

Son of David S. and Helen Kohn Gottlieb.

Graduated from Ohio State University where he was business manager of the student newspaper.

Worked part-time during summers for newspapers, including the *Davenport Times*.

Married in December, 1940, to Elaine Hirsch of Terre Haute, Indiana.

Father of two sons and one daughter, Richard, Robert and Jeanne.

Started with Lee Enterprises in the advertising department of the Kewanee *Star Courier* in 1936 and worked his way up the ladder as printer, pressman, stereotyper, reporter, and advertising representative before entering the ranks of management. Transferred to the advertising department of the *Davenport Times* in 1942.

Served in the U.S. Navy during World War II while on leave of absence from Lee. Participated in the invasion of Sicily and the capture of a German U-Boat.

Promoted to business manager of the *Times* in 1949 and to general manager of Lee Newspapers in 1959. In 1967, he became general manager and executive vice president of Lee.

Initiated a joint venture between Lee and Japan's Nippon Paint Co., Ltd. in July 1972 to form NAPP Systems Inc. to manufacture and distribute an advanced photopolymer plate for the printing industry.

Elected president and chief executive officer of Lee Enterprises in January 1970, upon the retirement of Philip Adler.

Active in numerous professional societies, particularly the American Newspaper Publishers Association.

Served as vice president of the ANPA Foundation and president of the ANPA Research Institute. Director of the Newspaper Advertising Bureau.

Received numerous honors as one of the nation's foremost experts in the field of production research and automation and was active in many educational and civic organizations including the Community Chest, the Boy Scouts, St. Ambrose College, the Red Cross, and the Crippled Children Society.

Died unexpectedly July 4, 1973, of a heart attack.

"I was working late the other night, actually past midnight, when I heard our elevator click," wrote columnist Bill Wundram of the Davenport *Quad-City Times* in a letter to David Gottlieb's son, Dick, now president of Lee.

"I jumped, for I was nearly alone in the newsroom, and for an instant I thought of but one person. Regularly, for many years when I was on the city desk, I would be startled at one or two or three o'clock in the morning by the click of an elevator. And there would stand Dave Gottlieb. He couldn't sleep, so he would come down to the office to talk.

"Usually, he would be wearing his overcoat over his pajamas and I knew it would be a long night because he loved to talk, and I loved to talk to him. We gabbed of many things, fools and kings, sometimes until daylight when the janitors would run us out. He'd tell me how all he ever wanted to do in life was to run a gasoline station, in a little town somewhere in Ohio, and talk to people and tinker with cars. What a guy!

"I owe so much to him, not alone in warm memories of friendship but in tangible things. I recall, as a newly married, moving into a crackerbox of a house that had no air conditioning. 'What you need is a nice screened porch,' Dave said to me during a visit one sultry afternoon. My wife agreed.

"Dave returned the next night to take measurements. He ordered the lumber, the cement blocks, and the following weekend he and I began building a screened porch. He was extremely handy. I was his flunky. But we built that porch together. You truly get to know someone after you have both bashed your thumbs a few times while nailing sheeting for the roof.

"In later years, he convinced me that I should get into the Laura Lee Stock Plan. It was an impossibly expensive purchase, but he worked out a time payment plan. That stock that I purchased is now gone, but it served its purpose in a magnificent way. I know Dave would be proud. The sale of that stock put two kids through college.

"Well, I don't know how this tribute began, but I suppose it was the other night when I heard the elevator click at midnight and thought of David K. Gottlieb. For a moment, I almost thought that I saw him standing there."

This heartfelt reminiscence came in the form of a spontaneous letter from Wundram a few years after Dave Gottlieb's sudden death. It says much about the thoughtful man who was head of Lee Enterprises for three years at the beginning of the 1970's.

"Printer's Devil"

The origins of this term have been lost in history and today it applies — as it did when Dave Gottlieb was getting his feet wet in the business — to "a young worker below the level of apprentice in a printing shop."

According to *The Reader's Encyclopedia*, by William Rose Benet, young boys were employed in the 17th century to remove printed sheets from the press. During the course of the day's work, they became so smudged all over from the ink that the others in the printing shop jokingly called them "devils."

But the term goes back farther than that, for a Venetian printer, one Aldo Manuzio, printed a whimsical "proclamation" which read in part, "I, Aldo Manuzio, printer to the Doge, have this day made public exposure of the printer's devil (a youth employed in his shop who was rumored to be an imp). All who think he is not flesh and blood may come and pinch him."

E. P. Adler, Gottlieb's mother's uncle, encouraged her to have young Dave spend his summer vacations living with him in Davenport and doing odd jobs at the paper. So, from age 15 on, Dave travelled from his home in Tiffin, Ohio, to Davenport every summer. His work with Lee began in the composing room as a "printer's devil," an industry term for a young worker below the level of apprentice. But no matter what task he was given, Dave tackled it with enthusiasm. He was a serious student of the business and paid intensive attention to every detail. He wanted to do everything right.

This pattern of summer jobs in Davenport continued through his years at Ohio State University, where he majored in journalism and had two years' experience as business manager of the college newspaper. An excellent student, Dave graduated near the top of his class and, to no one's surprise, immediately headed off to the Kewanee *Star Courier* where Phil Adler was publisher. His first job was in advertising sales.

As Dave rose through the ranks, first in Kewanee and later in Davenport, where he became business manager of the *Times* in 1949, Phil Adler recognized his unusual combination of vision, leadership, and drive. He also knew that Dave had a solid understanding of recent technological advances which had the potential to revolutionize the production of newspapers.

Adler looked to Dave as a man who could create new systems and procedures for Lee. Dave, for example, could visualize reporters pushing keys to retrieve stored information instantly from news libraries. He was among the first to use computers, phototypesetters, and video display tubes to produce newspapers. Although much of this technology was not commercially available at the time, Dave saw to it that when new plants were built for the *Billings* (Montana) *Gazette* and the *Corvallis* (Oregon) *Gazette-Times*, allowances were made for larger news rooms (where more of the future action would take place) and for engraving rooms that could be converted to another use when technology eclipsed the old plate-making techniques.

Asked about the origins of Dave's interest in technology, his devoted wife, Elaine, explained, "Dave had been a tinkerer since childhood. He could fix absolutely anything. If he didn't know how to do something, it only took him a few minutes to figure it out. He was interested in anything mechanical or electronic, especially things that saved time or made a job easier."

One area of newspaper production that quickly caught Dave's attention was the composing room. Reporters' stories (which may have already undergone several re-typings to incorporate editorial changes) required one final re-typing at the highly complicated keyboard of the Linotype machine which only the printers knew how to operate. This Rube Goldberg-type machine created individual lines of type cast from molten metal. But because each line had to be precisely the right width to fit the newspaper column, the printer operating the machine had the tedious job of justifying and/or hyphenating each line to make it fit. An experienced operator could set 10 to 12 lines a minute for short periods of time. Spacing frequently had to be adjusted and mistakes had to be corrected.

Dave knew computers could flawlessly perform this function for the Davenport paper even though it had not been done anywhere else in the country. He bought and installed an IBM 1130, the industry's first computer adapted for the composing room. Once the computer was installed, a reporter's story would be re-typed onto punched tape and fed into the 1130. The computer justified and hyphenated each line and punched a new tape which ran the Linotype machine with no further human involvement. While the process produced no more than the 14 lines per minute the Linotype machine could handle, the type was always clean and accurate, and the complicated Linotype keyboard that required special operators was eliminated. Significantly, the computer could run uninterrupted for days on end. (By comparison, today's computers and photo-typesetters can set more than 2.8 lines per second.)

A row of Linotype operators was a common sight in all newspaper composing rooms. Operators had the responsibility of hyphenating and justifying each line of type to make it fit into the column. It was demanding work.

After the Davenport machine proved successful, an 1130 was installed in Billings, Montana, and Lloyd Schermer and Wally Walsmith, Lee's production manager, took the technology a step further. Punched tape machines were added in the Missoula composing room and the tapes were transmitted to Billings via dataphones to be run through the 1130 and then transmitted back to Missoula. It was a harbinger of things to come when keystrokes could be transferred to distant computers for processing.

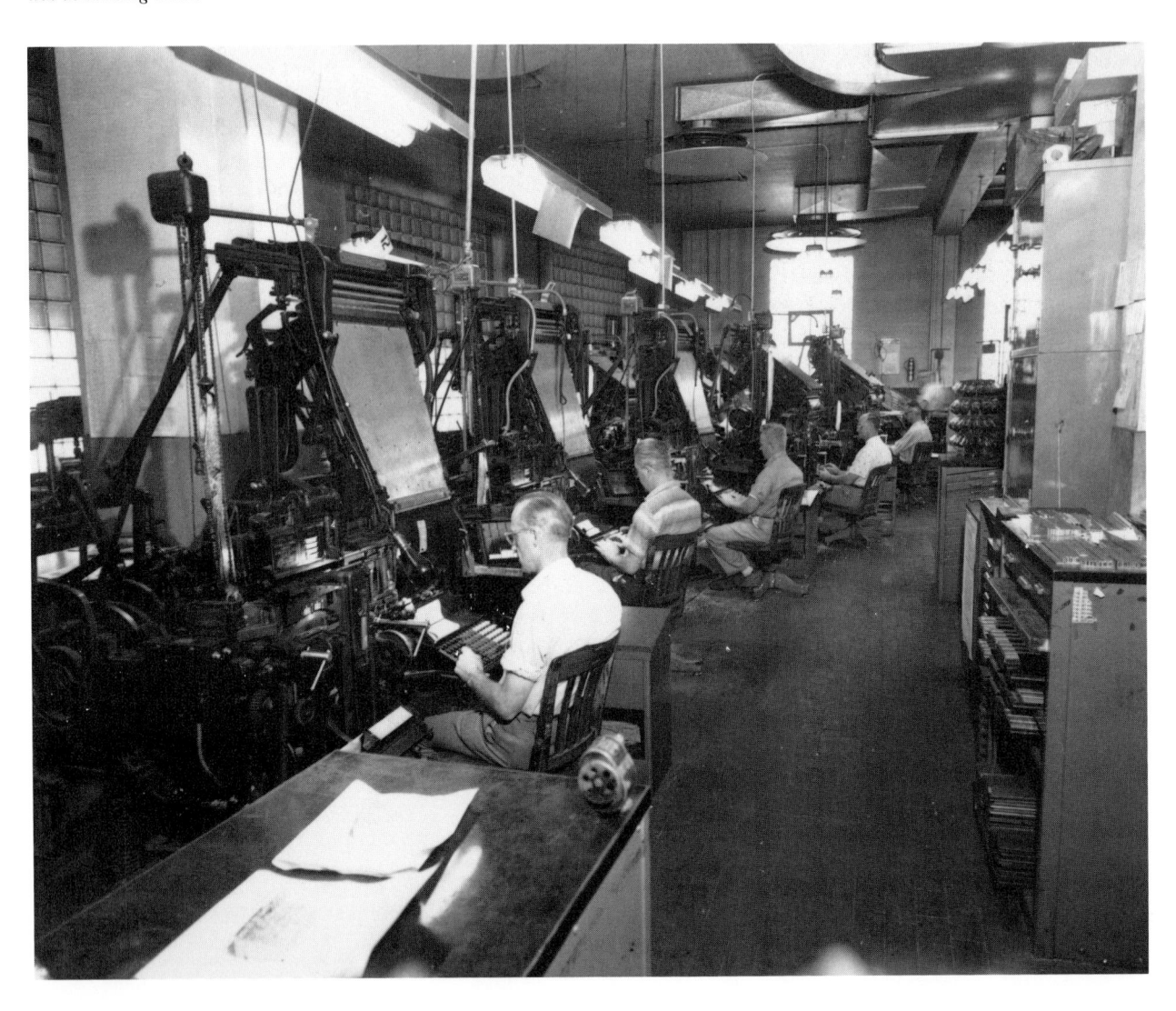

Gottlieb and the capture of U-234

Taking a leave of absence from the advertising department in Davenport, Dave joined the U.S. Navy during World War II. In one of the most unusual exploits of the war, Gottlieb was involved in the capture of an enemy submarine, the German U-Boat 234, shortly after VE Day.

The sequence of events began when Dave's ship, the destroyer escort USS *Sutton*, was assigned to duty in the North Atlantic. On May 14, 500 miles east of Cape Race, Newfoundland, the *Sutton* encountered a German submarine and ordered it to heave to and surrender.

Once it surfaced, the officer assigned the ticklish and dangerous task of boarding the submarine was Lt. David K. Gottlieb. As gunnery officer, Gottlieb was selected to be in command of a small boarding party.

As he headed for the surfaced submarine in one of the *Sutton's* gigs, Gottlieb and his men had no idea whether the Germans would surrender peacefully or suddenly start firing and try to escape.

It was with some relief that Gottlieb pulled alongside and found the German officers on deck waiting resignedly. "We had no trouble whatsoever with the Germans," reported Gottlieb later. "They seemed very happy that the war was over. The crew of this sub was quite young and didn't seem quite so Nazified as some of the older men might have been."

Upon boarding her, Gottlieb and his men got an astonishing surprise. The 2,086-ton craft, Germany's largest submarine — larger, in fact, than the USS *Sutton* — was carrying an incalculably valuable cargo destined for Tokyo: uranium supplies for use in atomic bomb tests by the Japanese. Also found were many important diplomatic documents and blueprints for both submarines and jet-propelled aircraft.

It was also carrying some "special" passengers: a top Nazi official, Luftwaffe Lieutenant General Ulric Kessler and members of his staff; a jet propulsion expert with plans for V-2 rocket bombs; and two Japanese naval officers who had already committed hara kiri.

Lt. Gottlieb had the distinction of being assigned as the temporary commander of the captured submarine to bring her to U. S. port. His first responsibility was to make certain the Germans couldn't scuttle the boat.

"After getting all the information and checking the torpedoes especially," said Gottlieb, "we transferred 37 men to our destroyer escort, keeping 29 aboard, as well as 14 [of our] men. We then got underway, with the Germans running the machinery, but with me as officer-in-charge. It took us until May 19 to get into Portsmouth, where Commander Kincaid Kimmel, the admiral's son, relieved me and took over."

With a twinkle in his eye, Gottlieb added that the most satisfying episode of all came when the German general saluted him upon going ashore. He also saluted the *Sutton's* coxswain, an enlisted man, who said without batting an eye, "That's all right, General, carry on!"

The success of the Montana operation prompted Dave and Wally to initiate a plan whereby the Davenport computer would justify and hyphenate type for all the Lee papers in the Midwest. While the system improved accuracy and speed, the unions, as might be expected, objected to this technological advance vehemently. They were suspicious and belligerent.

The most serious problem arose in Mason City, where the printers refused to use the punched tape when it returned from Davenport. So Dave got in his car and drove to Mason City.

"Once he arrived in the composing room, we transmitted the tape," recalls Tom Williams, then general manager of the *Times-Democrat*. "Dave rolled it up and handed it to one of the union men and asked him to put it in the Linotype machine. The printer refused. Dave said, 'You're fired,' and turned to the next man. This one also refused to handle the tape. Dave fired him, too. Without waiting to be asked, a third printer stepped up and took the tape, put it on the machine and it's run that way ever since. That's the way Dave was — when he knew something was right for the company, one way or the other, he got it. I don't know if the men really lost their jobs, but that shows how Dave handled problems. When he gave instructions, he expected them to be followed without hesitation."

The next step in the modernization of newspapers took place during the late 1960's and into the 1970's. The company was an industry leader in "conversions," or replacing the old method of typesetting, which involved a costly and time-consuming "hot" metal type process with a new photo "cold" type technology. Cold type involved electronic devices that read the punched tape and set type photographically, eliminating the Linotype machines and the individual lines of type they formed from molten lead. Gottlieb investigated numerous methods for cold-type printing, especially to determine which gave the most improvement to newspaper quality and profitability.

The move from hot to cold type

Lee Enterprises was one of the early leaders in the move to convert from hot type to cold type, that is, employing photocomposition methods instead of hot-metal casting and foundry type in the printing of its newspapers.

There are numerous advantages in using cold type: radical cost reductions; high-quality reproduction in color and black and white; greater flexibility in preparation and making last-minute editorial changes; the need for fewer compositors and pressmen; and lower energy costs.

As a result of its decisive campaign to convert from hot to cold type, despite opposition from labor unions, Lee newspapers, one by one, began to use photocomposition systems coupled either with offset presses or letterpress processes using photopolymer printing plates.

Dave also recognized that many newspapers would want to take advantage of this new typography technology while still printing on their old letterpress presses. He became intrigued by a Japanese plate-making process being developed by Nippon Paint Company, a century-old firm in Osaka, Japan. It utilized a photopolymer letterpress printing plate that could be engraved using ordinary tap water. He saw the magic of this technology — that any paper could use it to lower their costs by eliminating acid-etched zinc plates — and that it would give scores of newspapers the opportunity to marry their letterpress presses to the new cold-type composing rooms.

To make sure the technology worked successfully in an actual newspaper environment, Dave set up a development program at the Davenport *Times-Democrat*. At one point, disheartened by mounting technical problems, Tom Williams had the young project manager, Gary Benshoof, write a memo listing the overwhelming problems they were encountering.

An aerial view of the NAPP facility in San Marcos, California. The company is the largest shipper by rail, sea or truck in the entire San Diego County.

Tom took the memo to Dave and told him the process just wasn't working. Dave looked up at Tom and said simply, "Make it work." A week later, a breakthrough solved the toughest problem; everything else fell into place very quickly. Dave was determined to make it work, and work it did.

With the implementation of the technology documented, Gottlieb formed a joint venture with Nippon Paint to produce plates under the trade name, NAPP Systems Inc. Dick Galligan, Lee's Director of Financial Services, explained, "It speeded up the plate-making process so efficiently that it now requires only half as many people to do the same job." More than 400 newspapers worldwide are using the plate today.

Richard Sonnenfeldt, current chief executive officer of NAPP and a director of Lee, reflects on the wisdom of Dave's decision to pursue NAPP.

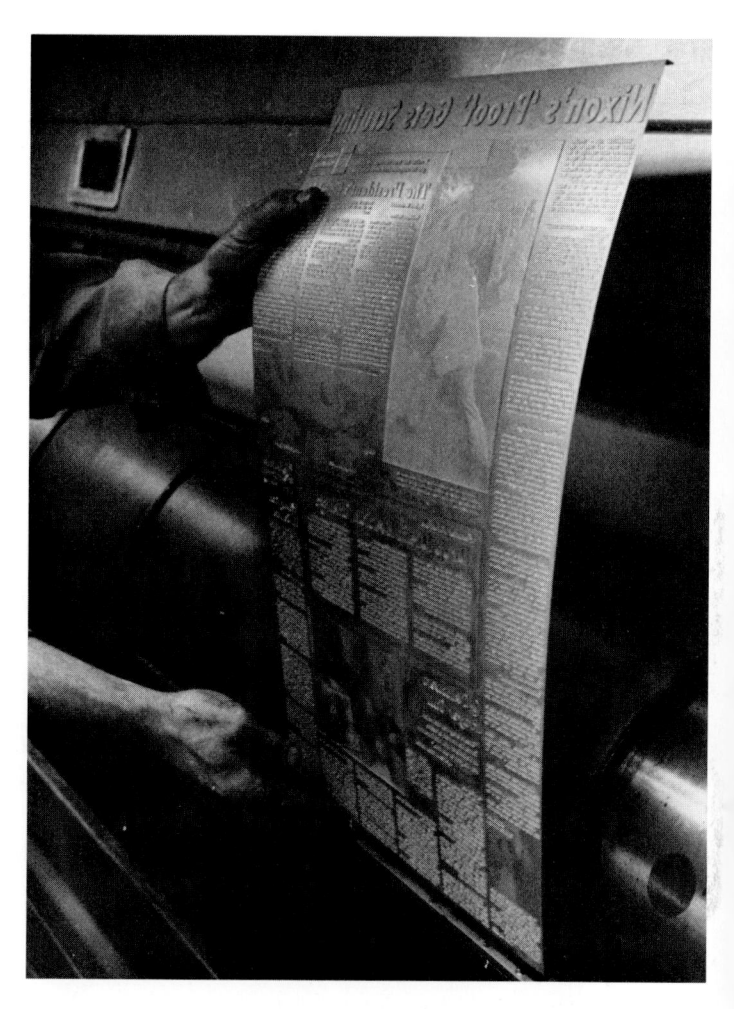

NAPP Systems, producer of this new type of photopolymer printing plate, was formed as a joint venture of Lee Enterprises and a century-old Japanese chemical company, Nippon Paint, which had spent five years developing a prototype before offering it to the newspaper industry.

An interesting sideline to this venture was the fact that during World War II the Japanese company had furnished supplies for the manufacture of the same thermite fire bombs Philip Adler was investigating during his tenure in Washington, D.C.

"We hosted a press party for our NAPP partners in San Diego," recalls Lloyd Schermer, "and didn't realize this wartime relationship until Mr. Obata, the chairman of Nippon Paint, rose to make a toast and began talking about the company's role in manufacturing those balloons.

"Well, several Lee attendees had been combat Marines in the Pacific. I could see them getting pasty-faced. Then Mr. Obata remarked, 'For what the Japanese did to America, your bombers leveled everything that our company owned — literally. We had to rebuild from the rubble.'"

As Lloyd Schermer remembers it, "The simple truth is, the unions were becoming an anachronism. If you deal with people in situations where everyone is to be treated the same, then the unions fit. But in companies where everyone is treated as an individual and jobs can be tailored to capitalize on a person's strengths, then unions don't make sense. We simply established a climate where the people knew they could grow in new directions.

There were no shortcuts to page make-up in the old days. It was an obvious place for computers to speed the process and improve the quality of the work. Because so many men could be replaced by so few machines, the union battles Lee faced were inevitable.

"I made it very clear," says Lloyd, "that we were not going to give any employees lifetime job guarantees. Why? Because you destroy people's self-esteem when you make them technologically obsolete, then tell them to come into 'work' every day, but sit in a corner and play cards."

Persuasiveness, logic, and resolve finally wore the unions down, and they realized that computers were as sure to come to the newspapers as they were to banks and other businesses. Retraining began and typographers became electronic technicians, reporters, photographers, or were assisted in finding new jobs in other businesses. "We retrained them for new jobs,"

remembers Lloyd Schermer, "either inside or outside the company, but we did not offer them a lifetime handout. That would have been like putting them on welfare."

The conversion was completed without a strike, and years later the union membership voted to leave the union, ending the ITU's control at the paper. Some of the former labor members and leaders joined the company and today are numbered among its best managers and employees. Over the next 15-year period, more than 60 bargaining units were decertified. Lee no longer has unions in its newspapers.

In describing how Lee dealt with strong union resistance, Walter Johnson explains, "We were successful largely because Dave had a precise understanding of what should be done to run the paper efficiently, because Lee had a realistic plan of action for publishers under strike conditions, and because Dave let us, his labor consultants, proceed effectively without being questioned or interrupted. We, for our part, provided continuing reports about what was going on so that Lee management was always fully aware of the situation and the progress of the proceedings."

The concept of "capturing the original keystroke" means that the reporter's initial typing of a story into a computer produces the words that finally appear in the paper. Naturally, the editorial process changes some of what's written. But in the days before computers, each editing would require retyping; even the finally approved version required one more retyping by the Linotype operator. Opportunities for typos and other errors abounded, not to mention the duplication of effort.

The world's first computerized system was conceptualized in Davenport, built by the Harris Corporation and de-bugged back in the Davenport news room before being sold to other newspapers.

102 Lee's Legacy of Leadership

One of Lee's strong points was that the company was then earning a strong reputation as a leader in production technology, a factor that made it difficult for the ITU to support its contentions that labor could stop the introduction of new technologies. "Much of this recognition came about," says Johnson, "because Dave Gottlieb had started with a vision of what could be done and because Lee's management made it happen.

"But our success in dealing favorably with the unions, either during a strike or in separate negotiations, was the result of a constructive attitude that, to me at least, was unique. The Lee people whom I dealt with directly were all able to see the goals and objectives quickly and clearly."

Dave Gottlieb was successful because he was a hands-on manager. When it came to printing and production, he never balked at rolling up his shirt sleeves and doing a job himself. During the strike in Davenport, he was able to lead by example when workers walked out, and officers of the company produced the newspaper with their own hands.

"Dave was a real genius in production," says Lloyd Schermer. "He could perceive the way it should be done and was determined to effect the necessary changes. From Dave I learned how to get my hands dirty and get the paper out even under strike conditions. There is no substitute for leading by example when major changes appear to threaten your people's means of livelihood."

Another reason for Dave's success with union situations was his unusual sensitivity to all employees, whatever their status in the company.

The Davenport news room as it may have looked during one of Gottlieb's trips through the office. Most employees considered Dave a friend; some viewed him as a father figure. He was quick with friendly conversation and was always willing to hear personal concerns, even reaching into his own pocket to help with financial problems whenever he could.

"Those people really loved Dave," says Bill Reinhardt of the American Newspaper Publisher's Association. "He went out of his way to greet employees and he knew all their names. It took a tremendous effort, but it seemed as though Dave knew not only the employees' names, but those of their family members, as well. Anytime someone was hospitalized or had a serious family problem, Dave was there by their side. He was a super human being. He knew everyone, loved everyone, and everyone loved him in return.

"I remember him picking me up at my hotel one morning and driving me to the office. Getting out of the car, I headed towards the front door. 'Not that way,' Dave explained, 'I go in over here.' We proceeded to the loading dock, through the pressroom and finally into the front office. Dave had a friendly word for everyone, stopped frequently to exchange some pleasantry or to kid a worker in a personal manner. They were his friends."

Tom Williams remembers, "Dave was a father figure to many of the younger people at Lee. Some people absolutely adored him. He had an unusual attentiveness to people's personal problems. He'd write someone a check at the drop of a hat: one person with medical bills; the next needing help with a down payment on a

During the strike in Davenport, everyone pitched in to get the paper out.

In this composing room picture are, left to right, Charles Fish, Dave Dale, Richard Petkunas, John Kable, Dave Gottlieb and Phil Adler.

Dave, Phil, and other managers and employees of the paper not only performed their own jobs, but worked throughout the printing plant to get each edition out on time. They never missed an edition. The paper then went on to become a world leader in newspaper production innovation.

house. They always paid him back, but without interest and on whatever time schedule suited the recipient. He was a kind person and fostered a real personal loyalty."

Another highly regarded trait was his belief in the dignity of fellow employees. "When I was in Butte," remembers Williams, "Dave came through on one of his visits. He was in the composing room and stopped to see how well a Linotype operator was doing. The printer happened to be a staunch union member and bristled at being scrutinized. Dave recognized the man's irritation, but rather than putting him down or having words with him, he simply asked him to move over so he could sit at the machine. Dave typed for a minute or two, then got up and left without saying a word. Whatever message he had for the Linotype operator soon came out in hot lead. The printer looked at it, put his head back and had a hearty laugh."

Dave was able to see beyond the realities of the present to the possibilities of the future. "Most of us are able to see the horizon," said long-time friend Judge Nathan Grant. "Dave could see way over it. He was one of the brightest people I knew." He saw, for example, how different broadcast bands could be used for transmitting facsimile copy over the air waves.

Dave was earning a reputation around the country as a newspaper man who came up on the mechanical side of the business and knew all its operations; from the receiving platform to the shipping dock, from advertising sales to the most complicated financial matters. What's more, he knew what technology could do to improve production and profits.

Gottlieb also understood the importance of broadcasting to the future of Lee and worked to bring the separate Lee Broadcasting, Inc., into the fold as part of Lee Enterprises. He recognized what the addition of the broadcasting properties meant to the value of the company and its attractiveness to investors.

The Davenport Municipal Stadium was renamed in honor of Times-Democrat *sports editor John O'Donnell on May 26, 1971. O'Donnell gained national fame for his "Dear Joe" columns written during World War II.*

It was Dave who began the move from the small stations that fit well with the medium-sized, mainly rural markets Lee newspapers served so well, into purchases of major broadcasting properties. A major purchase in 1970 took the company east rather than west when one of Dave's many friends in the industry told him the dominant station in Huntington-Charleston, West Virginia, WSAZ-TV, was being sold. The NBC-affiliated station covered a market exceeding 550,000 households.

Dave and Phil Adler, who was president at the time, went back to the Northern Trust Company for the $18 million needed for the WSAZ purchase. Even though this was the bank they used for funding the Montana purchase, negotiations dragged on. A determined Gottlieb went to First Chicago, got the approval, and the purchase was completed.

At the time, this was the largest market served by the Lee broadcasting division, which today includes other major market stations such as KGMB-TV in Honolulu, KOIN-TV in Portland, Oregon, KMTV in Omaha, Nebraska, KGUN-TV in Tucson, Arizona, and a partial ownership of KGGM-TV in Albuquerque, New Mexico.

In January, 1970, Gottlieb became president of Lee. The *Quad-City Times* was already being visited by journalists and publishers from all over the world who were interested in seeing how efficiently a newspaper could be published when using advanced technology. The computer and cold-type technology he pursued was well ahead of its time, and it had won him important recognition from his peers in the industry.

These two views show how WSAZ looks today, 20 years after the purchase of the station in 1970. In the master control room, Charlie Miller, foreground, and Mark Watts mind the equipment while the news room is a bustle of activity. Seen in this picture (from left) are: Kathy Brown, Nita Wiggins, Roger Lyons, Annette Walker, Bill Cummings and Randy Yohe.

WSAZ continues to be the number one affiliate of NBC in terms of delivering the largest share of audience of any station of any network in the country.

In the early '60s, Dave was asked to become a member of the ANPA Technical Committee. This was the branch of the ANPA that pinpointed industry requirements for technology. Later, Dave was asked to join the ANPA Research Institute, Inc., and became its chairman in 1972 and 1973. These important positions gave added stature to the Lee organization, especially in light of its relatively small size.

In 1973, Dave conceived the idea to dissolve the ANPA Research Institute and merge it into the ANPA. He felt both groups would be stronger under this arrangement. Dave won support from the board and the merger was effected. "He knew what was best and people believed him," says ANPA's Bill Reinhardt.

David K. Gottlieb, seated, as the newly elected president and treasurer of the board of directors of Lee Enterprises, Incorporated. Also shown are board members, standing left to right, Walter J. Rothschild, vice president and assistant to the president; Charles W. White, publisher of the Lincoln Star; Harry A. Fischer, partner of Paine, Webber, Jackson and Curtis; Dr. Earl F. English, dean of the School of Journalism, University of Missouri; J.S. Hilleboe, publisher of the Billings Gazette *and Western Divisions Operation manager; Alfred Magnusson, general counsel, partner Lane and Waterman, lawyers; Lloyd G. Schermer, vice president and assistant to the president and publisher of the* Missoulian; *and William T. Burgess, secretary and publisher of the* La Crosse Tribune.

108 Lee's Legacy of Leadership

Because of the technology Dave Gottlieb envisioned and brought to reality in the Lee papers, many U.S. and foreign newspaper dignitaries came to Davenport to learn how they could benefit from the new techniques.

In an article titled, "World Spotlight Shines On Times," that was published two years after Dave's passing, reporter John Willard wrote, "The guest book at the Quad-City Times *reads like a world atlas of editors and publishers who have crossed the oceans to Davenport in search of the latest newspaper production technology."*

He reported that in the past two years, people from 20 nations and 300 newspapers had spent time in Davenport.

Some of them are seen in this picture that accompanied the article on May 25, 1975.

Dave Gottlieb was president of Lee Enterprises for little more than three years, until his untimely death in July, 1973. Lee was the only employer he ever had, and his love for the company was second only to his love for his wife and family. Sadly, he passed away before seeing the commercial success of NAPP — the plant in north San Diego County was still under construction and wouldn't be operational for another year.

His period of administration as Lee's general manager and president saw numerous advances in technology which helped the company pioneer in new directions. It was significant, though, that while computers, electronic phototypesetters, and new devices were making it possible to process the news more quickly and accurately than ever before, the employee — not the process — was more important. Dave Gottlieb was a key figure in spearheading the entire newspaper industry's technological revolution. He brought to Lee the best of the new technology which was already beginning to shape the company's future. Dave was successful in incorporating these changes without disturbing the people-oriented, community-focused traditions established by A. W. Lee, Lee Loomis, and the Adlers.

Milestones during the Gottlieb administration

- October, 1969 — The *Corvallis Gazette-Times* installs an ultra-modern facility with the latest offset press.
- April, 1970 — Lee acquires station WSAZ-TV in Huntington-Charleston, West Virginia, an NBC affiliate then rated as 33rd in the nation.
- November, 1970 — Radio station WMDR-FM in Moline, Illinois, begins broadcasting.
- 1965, Forward — A new program is undertaken to upgrade production facilities and procedures at all Lee locations.
- July, 1972 — NAPP is formed as a joint venture to produce a new type of photopolymer printing plate.

The growth of Lee Enterprises 1970-1973
(boxed properties are new)

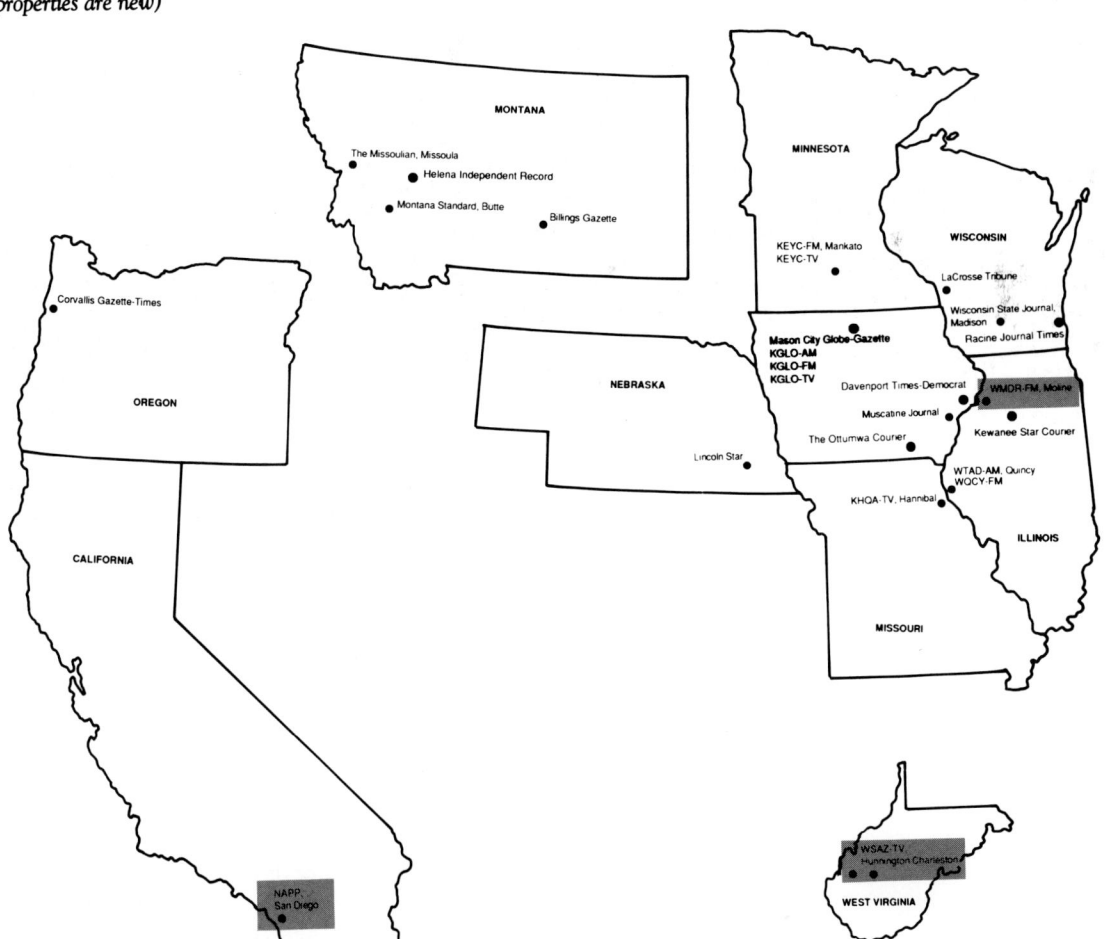

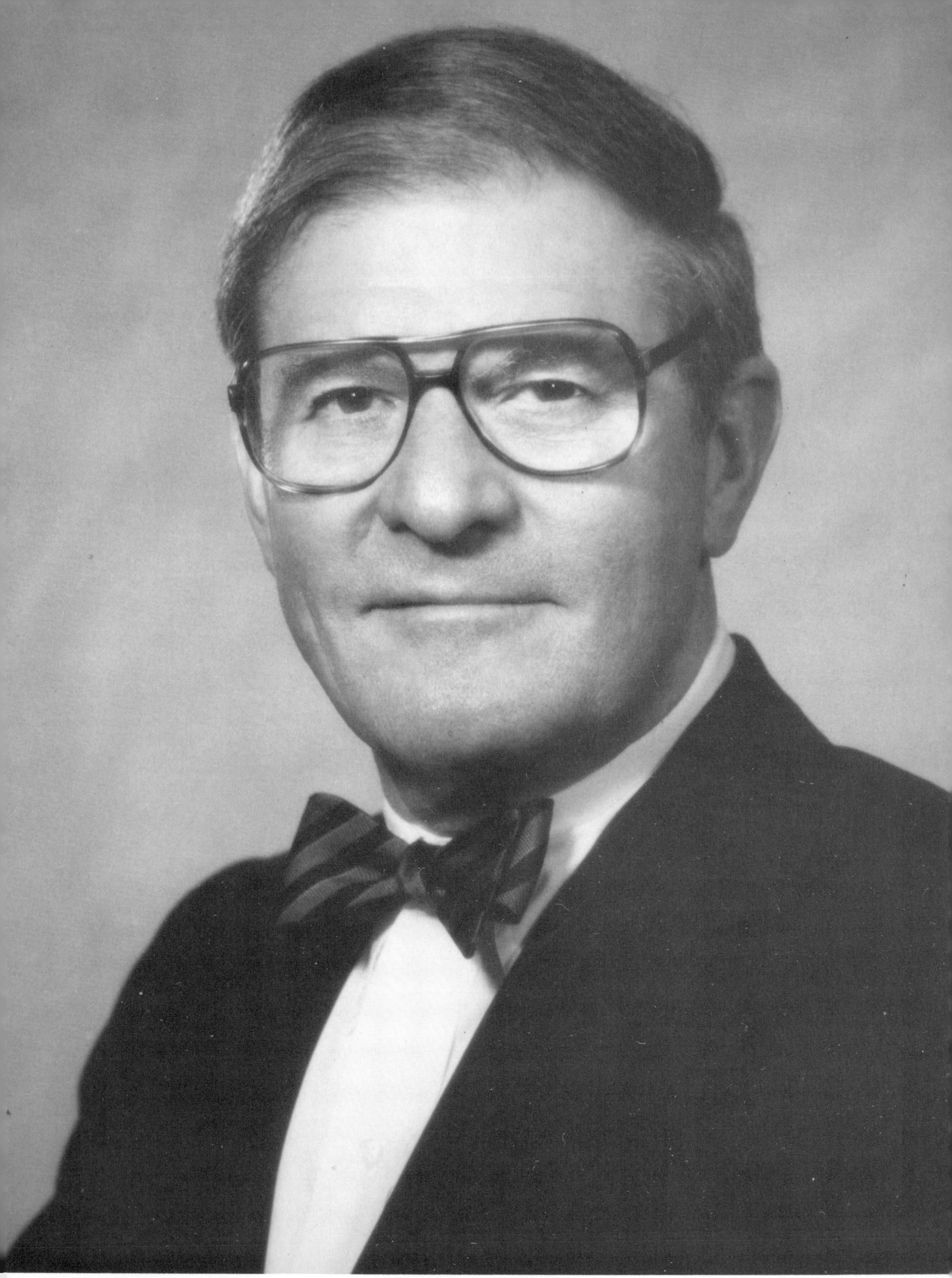

Chapter Six

A Winner who Doesn't Know there is a Second Place

1973-   *Lloyd G. Schermer*

Born January 27, 1927, in St. Louis, Missouri.

Graduated cum laude from Amherst College in 1950 and received an MBA from Harvard Business School in 1952.

Married in 1951 to Betty Adler II, daughter of Henrietta and Philip Adler.

Father of two sons, Gregory, June 1, 1954, and Grant, September 3, 1957.

Served in the U.S. Navy during World War II.

Started with Lee Enterprises in 1954 in advertising with the *Daily Times*, where he worked as a reporter, engraver, printer, photographer, and pressman before entering general management in 1958 as business manager of the Kewanee *Star Courier*.

Became business manager of the Missoula *Missoulian* in 1959 and was named publisher in 1961. Elected a director of Lee in 1963 and vice president of Lee Newspapers of Montana in 1965.

Returned to corporate headquarters in Davenport, Iowa, as Vice President - Newspaper Operations and Assistant to the President in 1970.

Elected president and chief executive officer of Lee Enterprises and Chairman and CEO of NAPP Systems Inc., in 1973. NAPP is a joint venture with Nippon Paint Co. Ltd., Osaka, Japan.

Assumed the newly created position of chairman and chief executive officer in 1986.

"A newspaper," Lloyd Schermer has said, "is one of the few institutions in America that can still cause things to change in a community, and it has an obligation not only to report accurately what is going on, but to take an active role as a catalyst for change."

Lloyd has made good on that commitment during his years at Lee. It's been part of a challenging agenda that also included formulating strategies, following through on the implementation of new technologies, developing new strategies used with unions and employees during the implementation of new technology, defining and adapting to a changing business environment, and introducing new concepts in management.

Though his vision of the activist newspaper is squarely in the Lee tradition, in some respects Lloyd's personal history represents a departure from Lee's past.

Unlike most of his predecessors, Lee was not Lloyd's original career destination nor did he spend any part of his youth in a Lee environment. Lloyd grew up in a family of entrepreneurs. His father, who had immigrated from Austria-Hungary as a youngster, started a grocery store and eventually built it into a small group of supermarkets. His mother, along with his Russian-born grandmother, opened a millinery shop in St. Louis in the depths of the Depression and expanded it into 60 stores in nine states.

So it is not surprising that early in his life Lloyd began to take leadership roles in scouting, summer camp, during his service in the navy, and then as an undergraduate at Amherst College.

Lloyd is the first of Lee's leaders to hold an MBA. His degree was awarded by Harvard University in 1952, but work on "my Ph.D.", he says, began when he returned home to St. Louis to run a heating and air conditioning contracting business in which his father had invested. His objective was to get his father's investment out,

Lloyd's father, Mannie, immigrated from Austria–Hungary when he was a young boy. He settled across the river from St. Louis in Granite City, Illinois with his six brothers. There he built a chain of grocery stores and was one of the first innovators of the "self-service" concept that ultimately turned them into small supermarkets. He also built one of the first shopping centers in that area.

"Dad was one of the kindest persons I knew," says Lloyd. He let all of us, including my mother, 'do our thing.' We all loved and respected him."

Lloyd's mother, Burdie Hurwitz Schermer, as she looked in 1954. She still lives in St. Louis where Lloyd was raised. "Lloyd is as devoted a son as any mother ever had," says one close family friend. Lloyd has two sisters, Eileen and Jean, who also live in St. Louis.

Lloyd's mother, who was working as a legal secretary, quit and opened a millinery store with her mother in St. Louis in 1930. They built the business into a successful chain of 60 stores spread over nine states and ran them for almost 20 years.

"She's a remarkable woman," says Lloyd. "She's enormously talented and not only raised a family with tender loving care but ran a successful business back in the days when women weren't supposed to do that sort of thing. But then Mother always did do things women weren't supposed to do and did them well. I guess I learned how to break new ground from both my mother and father," he says.

Lloyd joined the Navy when he was 17 and went to boot camp at the Great Lakes Naval Training Center north of Chicago. He was made a platoon leader and had his first experiences as a leader of men who were several years older than he. World War II ended while he was in boot camp. He considers the months he served as a platoon leader to be one of the most important early experiences he had in leadership.

In 1938, when Lloyd was 11, he went to Muggs Lorber's Camp Nebagamon in Wisconsin, where this picture was taken.

Muggs, an All-American quarterback and a former assistant coach for Knute Rockne and an exceptional role model, was one of those rare individuals who understood the intricacies of building campers' self-confidence and self-esteem. He was a master at using the camping environment as a character-building experience for young men.

Lloyd worked for Muggs for a number of year, both at the Wisconsin camp and on trips to remote areas of Ontario. He learned about nature and backwoods survival, and had his first real experiences in leadership. At one point, he seriously considered a career as a camp director.

not to make a career as a contractor. In a few years, the nearly bankrupt business was transformed into a significant packaged air-conditioning company. In the process, however, Lloyd faced a tough and potentially dangerous union situation that was resolved when his company got one of the first permanent injunctions under the secondary boycott provision of the newly enacted Taft-Hartley Act (against members of the council of building trades unions in St. Louis). During the dispute, the company also helped the FBI put several business agents in jail for racketeering.

The struggle with the unions in St. Louis left a lasting impression on Lloyd. "That's where I learned what I had to do to be effective in a job that involved skilled crafts. I realized I didn't necessarily have to be a craftsman, but I had to understand the people and their jobs. Only then can you understand where the people doing the work are coming from and get down to the real issues when you're talking with them about change, their problems, and their jobs.

"We won the battle but lost the war," remembers Lloyd. "There was no way we could win against the combination of corrupt contractors, unions and politicians in St. Louis. So I closed up the business and drove north to Davenport with my family."

Lloyd's friend, Don Anderson, then publisher of the Lee-owned *Wisconsin State Journal*, had persuaded him to join Lee. Although Lloyd had a job offer to become assistant to the president of Inland Steel in Chicago, "Anderson convinced me being an 'assistant to' wasn't for me," says Schermer, "whereas the Davenport paper needed someone with my background and provided very real growth opportunities. Don was a great editor, a gifted writer, and a wonderful human being. He had taken a newspaper in Madison that had little to offer its readers or advertisers, and

The Taft-Hartley Act

The Taft-Hartley Labor Act, also known as the Labor-Management Relations Act, was named after its sponsors, Senator Robert A. Taft and Congressman Fred A. Hartley. The law was enacted to help control labor disputes and provided, among other things, that unions or employers must serve notice on the other party before terminating a collective-bargaining agreement.

It also specified that the government was empowered to initiate an 80-day cooling-off period instead of permitting any strike that it deemed a peril to safety or health. Furthermore, it prohibited "secondary boycotts," that is, tie-ups against an already organized company doing business with another company with which the union was having a dispute.

turned it around. I was convinced that he knew what he was talking about and decided to take his advice and give it a try."

Lloyd's wife, Betty, was naturally delighted with the decision, as well. Her father was Philip Adler, then vice president of Lee, and she would be returning home. "People sometimes ask if my marriage to Betty was responsible for my joining Lee," says Lloyd. "It helped, but the truth is Phil offered me a job while I was at Harvard Business School but I turned him down. Don Anderson was the one who persuaded me to join Lee."

Lloyd's career with Lee thus began. The year was 1954. His first assignment was in advertising sales and his starting salary was $70 a week. But because the printers were on strike, he was presented with an unusual opportunity to spend his evenings and weekends working in the composing room. Although he was eager to learn all there was to know about the newspaper business, some of his experience came earlier — and faster — than even he expected.

Betty and Lloyd as they looked in 1951 shortly after they became engaged.

Davenport Eagle Refuge

Known as a naturally inquisitive person, Lloyd's interest in his surroundings will permanently benefit an important part of the Davenport area's wildlife, the bald eagles that migrate south during the winter to feed on fish in the open water below navigation dams on the Mississippi.

Lloyd's house overlooks Lock & Dam 14. Noticing 17 eagles perched in a single tree near the dam, he called the U.S. Army Corps of Engineers (who are responsible for the dam) and asked them to protect the dead tree. Within six months, the Corps had cut it down.

"That really got me going," says Lloyd. He donated a parcel of land he owned along the river to The Nature Conservancy and got two other prominent Quad Citians, Bob VanVooren and Sandy Nelson, to do the same, creating an eight–acre site.

While it took seven years to formalize the refuge, close to 100 eagles at a time now use the area. The site is the only one on the Iowa side of the Mississippi and was noted in an issue of *National Geographic* in 1989.

"Several months after I started," he recalls, "the engraver's union went on strike. Dave Gottlieb came by my desk one day and said, 'Come with me. You're going to be an engraver.' I hardly knew what an engraving was. But I went upstairs and the production manager, a great guy named Buck Weaver, taught me the ropes. I was already working in the composing room and the press room, and in a few days, I was an engraver. I'd sell advertising space by day, set type and spend the night engraving."

Buck Weaver has taught the nuances of production to any number of young Lee executives. "Lloyd ended up making some pretty good cuts," says Weaver. "He had the drive to learn it and do it right."

"My stint as an engraver would prove to be invaluable to me throughout my career, especially as CEO of NAPP. I worked my way all through the plant, learning everything from reporting the news to setting type and printing the papers," Lloyd says. "I was motivated by my experiences in St. Louis, where I saw firsthand how managers could be manipulated if they weren't fully aware of job requirements and skills. I said to myself, 'Lloyd, never again are you going to put yourself in a position where people working for you know more than you do about their jobs or operations.'

"I was determined to learn everything possible so I could communicate intelligently with the people I supervised and lead by example. That's what 'getting your hands dirty' is all about. I didn't have to be the best engraver in the world or the greatest reporter or printer. But I certainly had to know the techniques, the language, the skills, and the problems."

Buck Weaver came to Davenport from New Orleans in 1952 to help keep the paper going during the tough International Typographer's Union strike. Promoted many times, he was Production Superintendent of Davenport Newspapers when he retired.

Buck is seen here in front of the newest Lee press, a Goss Colorline, which was recently installed at the Quad-City Times. The 96-foot long, 43-foot high press prints up to 75,000 papers an hour and can run up to 128 pages at a time, producing two completely separate papers.

Three years later, Lloyd was on his way from Davenport to Kewanee to become business manager of the Kewanee *Star Courier*. Here he applied his production, management and leadership skills not only to the newspaper, but also to community improvement efforts.

It's consistent with Lloyd's interests and background that many of the battles he has waged have involved environmental issues. He often says, "We don't own the land any more than we own the planet Earth. We're just stewards of it for future generations." Lloyd has been an outdoorsman, conservationist, and wildlife supporter since he worked as a guide and counselor in the canoe country of Wisconsin, Minnesota, and Ontario. He is as much at home in a trout stream, on horseback, or exploring wilderness areas of the West or Alaska, as he is in a newspaper office or in the boardroom. As an editor and publisher and an active member of the board of the World Wildlife Fund, The Conservation Foundation and the National Board of Smithsonian Associates, he has had the opportunity to combine his vocation and avocation in efforts to protect the environment.

One such opportunity was waiting for him in Kewanee. Editor Jerry Moriarity alerted him that a major coal company was acquiring strip-mining rights to more than 6,000 acres of land in Henry County, Illinois, a development that would not only destroy the county's tax base but have serious environmental effects.

"I'd seen what these mines are like and what the strip-mining machines do," says Lloyd. "They dig down 150 feet to reach a two-foot layer of coal. When they're done, the once-fertile land looks like the barren surface of the moon.

"That land in Henry County is literally the richest soil in the world. You can measure the black topsoil in feet, not inches. Strip-mining would have ruined the land forever, and I thought the whole thing was immoral. There had to be some way of preserving the soil and the farm-based economy of the area.

Lloyd Schermer's interests

The groups and associations to which Lloyd contributes time are indicative of his varied interests. He is currently a director and Chairman of the American Newspaper Publishers Association and also holds directorships in the following: NAPP Systems Inc., American Newspaper Publishers Association Foundation, World Wildlife Fund, the Conservation Foundation, the Trout and Salmon Foundation, and the National Board of Smithsonian Associates. He is past chairman and remains a director of the Newspaper Advertising Bureau, he is a trustee of the Maureen and Mike Mansfield Foundation, a trustee of St. Ambrose University, a member of the advisory board of the Institute of Bill of Rights Law at the College of William and Mary, Williamsburg, Va.

His hobbies and interests include fishing, hunting, camping, skiing, rare books, American Indian lore, photography, tennis, and golf.

Lloyd is active in many professional, educational, civil, and social organizations and is the recipient of numerous honors including the Missoula George Award, Iowa Arts Council Outstanding Achievement Award, and an honorary doctorate in business administration from St. Ambrose University.

"This acquisition seemed to hinge on a corridor of land between two larger tracts which had to be breached in order to move those huge shovels back and forth. Knowing the sale of this corridor would make or break the company's plans, we began an editorial fight to block it by running stories and photographs on strip-mining devastation in the next county.

"We persuaded our local state legislator to introduce a bill in Springfield to control strip mining in Illinois. Then, we flooded the state legislators with reprints of all the articles and pictures we'd run in the *Star Courier*. Some included photographs showing a hold-out farmer's house bordered on three sides by a 100-foot drop into a strip mine."

It seemed like a David and Goliath encounter when the Kewanee Star Courier, with a circulation of barely 13,000, challenged a major coal company that was backed by unions and a small army of employees and supporters of strip mining. Once a minute, behemoths like this electric stripping shovel can gulp 270 tons of earth and rock in a single bite, swing it 450 feet away and dump it on a pile as high as a 15-story building. The shovel can move over 4.5 million cubic yards of topsoil a month to get at the coal seams below.

The state legislature passed the bill, but the governor vetoed it, so Schermer and Harry Harper, a past publisher of the *Star Courier* and the man who started Mail-O-Graph, went to work to block the miners in Henry County with zoning. They set up a booth at the county fair in Cambridge, Illinois. "As farmers came in," recalls Schermer, "we'd show them exhibits and photographs and ask if they were in favor of strip mining. They invariably said no, and we'd ask them to sign a zoning petition to the county board of supervisors. Then we loaded up three or four Greyhound buses with people from Kewanee and went to the decisive county supervisors' meeting in Cambridge. The board was stacked against us. Some of the coal miners came armed, looking pretty mean. But we stuck with it and got restrictive strip-mine zoning passed. Later, the state passed a reclamation act that the governor had vetoed, which was the right approach, permitting coal to be taken out but requiring the good topsoil to be replaced." There still is no strip mining in Henry County.

Another instance when Lloyd was able to use the newspaper as an agent for community betterment occurred when the *Star Courier* became involved in a strike at Kewanee's largest employer, the Kewanee Boiler Company. The stakes for the town were high. The Walworth Company, previously Kewanee's largest employer, had closed its doors the same day Lloyd started work at the *Star Courier*, throwing 1,800 people out of work. "We knew," says Lloyd, "that the American Standard Company, Kewanee Boiler's new owner, was going to close the plant if the strike couldn't be resolved satisfactorily. Loss of another major employer and an additional 900 jobs would have been too devastating a blow for Kewanee."

"The acrimonious strike at the Kewanee Boiler plant provided one of our greatest challenges because of the personal criticism we received and overcame," recalls Jerry Moriarity. "All we were trying to do was get the two sides talking so the strike could end and the men could get their paychecks again. For days on end, Lloyd and I met alternately with key union officials and company management to try to obtain a balanced

This 1950's photo shows a technician running a final pre-delivery test on one of Kewanee Boiler company's many boilers.

picture of what was going on. This continued even while the two groups were deadlocked and wouldn't speak to each other. When Lloyd had painstakingly worked out new contract jurisdiction language with the union strike committee, he went to management with a solution he felt would most likely be accepted by the union. It proved to be a major breakthrough and the *Star Courier* gained the confidence of both sides.

"At the meeting preceding the vote, the belligerent leader of the local foundrymen's union double-crossed us, took the floor and condemned the *Star Courier* for meddling, claiming the strike would have been over long before if it had not been for our interference. I heard this all firsthand because union members had sneaked me into the hall.

"When his scathing attack on the paper was over, I rushed to the speaker's platform — perhaps foolhardily — jabbed my finger into his chest, and demanded to know 'Who the 'ell writes your stuff?' Before he could answer, a wave of union members came to my defense, agreeing that the paper was helping to resolve the strike. I still savor that scene," Moriarity said.

The first vote was against settlement. The company then started action to close the plant. Lloyd recalls the international representative and the strike committee, alarmed by recent events, came into his office and asked his advice. He responded that he thought they should drive to Peoria, Rock Island, Moline and Sterling to look for new jobs.

Then their international representative said they did not want to change the jurisdiction clause. They only wanted certain other clauses "reinterpreted." Lloyd asked them to write their reinterpretations down and initial the sheet.

He then took the paper out to the plant and caught the plant manager as he was leaving for his home office in Youngstown, Ohio. Lloyd asked him as a personal favor to go back into his office for one more discussion. Upon seeing the terms, the plant manager agreed to one more meeting with a federal arbitrator.

Lloyd took the request down the street to strike headquarters and got their agreement for the final and successful meeting. Moriarity was asked to supervise and count the secret ballots, and the result of the vote was the union's acceptance of the contract. "The union contract was a personal triumph for Lloyd, who directed the *Star Courier*'s role and assembled the final package," Moriarity concludes. "We saved 900 jobs for Kewanee."

Lloyd recalls the international representative of the boilermakers union coming into his office after the settlement and saying, "I understand you're being transferred out west. Would you be willing to let us use you as an arbitrator for our boilermaker locals on the West Coast?"

He answered, "John, you've paid me the highest of compliments — your trust. I did what I had to do to save this town. But don't misread where I'll be coming from out in Montana. Here I was at the middle of the table; out there, I'll be on management's side.

"Few things have meant more to me in my career than that union man's offer," Lloyd recalls.

Whether fighting strip-miners or working to keep paychecks coming to employees of an important local business, Lloyd often finds himself in the middle of the fray, especially when a community's best interests are at stake. He remembers writing one editorial during the boiler strike that "lost the paper 800 or 900 subscribers out of a total circulation of 13,000 in one day.

Shown here are Don Anderson, Betty and Lloyd. Don and his wife, Florence, were fast friends of the Schermers.

Don talked Lloyd into working for Lee and arranged for Lloyd's pivotal move to Montana. They were frequent companions on pack trips in many of the mountain areas of Montana.

The Anderson's daughter, Sue, married John Talbot who worked on Lee newspapers in Muscatine, Iowa, and Madison, Wisconsin. He later became publisher of the Missoulian. He has retired with his family in Missoula, where he is a faculty member at the University of Montana.

But the newsstand sales went up by 1,300. People who hadn't been reading the paper started reading it and those who joined the boycott bought it anyhow at the newsstand. They couldn't afford to miss it."

Despite the rewards in Kewanee, Lloyd became aware of his need for new challenges and opportunities. He was not sure that Lee would be able to provide them. "I didn't think the company was exciting for young people," Lloyd said. "I didn't see my career taking me much further than Kewanee, and that wasn't enough."

At the time, the Lee Syndicate was a loose confederation of newspapers, with almost no central management. "During those days, the only time all the members got together was at weddings or newspaper conventions," remembers Murph Wolman, retired general manager and publisher of the *Wisconsin State Journal*. "No one felt they worked for people in Davenport. No one there told us what to do."

Once again, Don Anderson stepped in at a pivotal moment for Lloyd. Don was to represent the University of Wisconsin, where he served as President of the Alumni Association, at the installation of a new chancellor at the University of Illinois at Champaign/Urbana. He stopped en route to visit the Schermers. When Lloyd expressed his dissatisfaction, Don said he had heard Anaconda was selling their six Montana papers and he would look into it. Don was especially interested in following up on the possibility because he and his wife, Florence, grew up in Montana, where their parents had been homesteaders. Several months later, Don phoned Lloyd at home one evening. He had a proposition. Lee's offer for the Anaconda newspapers had been accepted. If Lloyd would move to Missoula, he would be appointed business manager of western Montana's leading newspaper, the *Missoulian*. There were no "publisher" positions in Montana in those days, which meant the business manager actually ran the newspaper.

Lloyd consulted with Betty and accepted without even knowing where Missoula was located. "It didn't matter," recalls Lloyd. "This was a challenge and we wanted to go west. I remember Betty asking me, 'Where is Missoula?' We looked at each other and laughed because neither of us had any idea where Missoula was. We got out an atlas, spread it out on the floor, and located our new home."

Phil Adler opposed the move. He and Betty were very close and he enjoyed having her and Lloyd around. He also didn't want them to move, with his grandchildren, to what — realistically, at that time — was such a remote place in the West. Anderson told him, "If you want me to be president of the Montana papers, then Schermer goes to Missoula. Otherwise, get someone else." Phil agreed and the Schermers headed west.

Lloyd, Betty, and son Greg arrived in August, 1959 — their younger son, Grant, was to come later with the Adlers by train — and started unpacking. That night, as John H. Toole tells the story in his book, *Red Ribbons: A Story of Missoula and Its Newspaper*, he and Betty felt their bed shaking violently. They grabbed Greg and dashed out into the yard. As soon as the shaking ceased, Lloyd ran back inside and phoned the night line at the *Missoulian*.

"Has there been an earthquake?" he asked.

"Could be," came the laconic response. "Who are you?"

"My name is Schermer and you'll find out pretty quick," answered Lloyd, in no mood to talk further. He threw on his clothes and drove down to the office.

Going directly to the newsroom, he asked the night staff where the quake was located. No one, including the wire services, knew or seemed much concerned. So Lloyd suggested they try making phone calls in each compass direction, thinking whichever area they could not reach by phone would probably be where the quake was centered. The plan worked and they soon knew the epicenter was near Yellowstone Park's western entrance.

Shortly after dawn, Lloyd heard the senior *Missoulian* editor arguing on the phone. Reporter-photographer John Forssen was calling from the Missoula airport asking if he could charter a plane to fly over the earthquake site.

Taken in 1960, a year after the Schermer's arrival in Missoula, this picture shows Betty with Grant (left) and Greg.

"No way," he was told. "It's against company policy. And besides, it's too damned expensive." With his hackles already up, Lloyd interrupted his cost-conscious editor. "Who made that policy?"

"*They* did," came the reply to this unexpected intruder, who then asked who "they" were and how long such a policy had been in effect. The editor confessed that he had no idea who these mysterious makers of policy might be, though he had been working at the *Missoulian* for almost 30 years.

"The policy just changed!" Lloyd said curtly. "Tell Forssen to rent the plane and fly right down to West Yellowstone."

Forssen found what he was looking for at the head of the Madison Valley where the Madison River emerges from the mountains. He was astonished at the enormity of the damage. A gigantic mountain north of the narrows had collapsed and slid across the canyon, burying 35

The Daily Missoulian

Vol. LXXXVII. No. 111. Missoula, Montana, Wednesday Morning, August 19, 1959 Price: Five Cents

Death Toll Revised Downward From Devastating Earthquakes

8 Bodies Recovered With Possibility Of Finding More

HELENA (AP) — Earthquakes rocked mountain country of southwest Montana just west of Yellowstone National Park Monday night and Tuesday leaving at least eight dead. The death toll was revised downward from 19 late Tuesday night by Hugh Potter, Montana's civil defense director. He said confusion at the scene of the quake and a lack of communications led to the belief more lives had been lost. At least 60 persons were injured seriously enough to require hospital care. A driving rain and overcast skies added to difficulties.

Rescue of 30 injured, a dozen of them reported in serious condition, was accomplished by helicopter from the Hebgen Dam area. Pilots estimated that 125 persons remained trapped and prospects were they could not be removed before daylight. The dam was cracked and battered by the earth shocks but still held. A mountainside toppled into the Madison River, famous among Western fishermen, throwing up a 200-foot barrier.

Large sections of a highway rimming the lake formed by the dam were ripped loose and flung into the water. Engineers said there is a possibility a number of persons might be buried beneath hundreds of tons of debris at the Rock Creek campground below the dam. The worst shock came shortly before midnight. It was followed by numerous aftershocks. These continued during the day, leaving the ground "shaking like jelly," as a telephone repair crew described it. Shocks were felt in Yellowstone Park, where 22,000 to 25,000 persons were vacationing. Slides closed a number of roads in the park, including the main highway to the west, but no one was reported killed or injured in the vast summer playground.

Old Faithful Inn was closed after a water main burst but officials expected to have one wing reopened during the night. Old Faithful geyser continued spouting on its hourly schedule.

Five bodies were in a mortuary at Virginia City, historic town in western lore, and two more were reported being taken there. Three bodies were in a mortuary at Ennis.

The University of California estimated the shock at 7.8, compared to the 8.2 magnitude of the 1906 quake in San Francisco, the most powerful in modern times.

Dr. Charles Richter, an authority on earthquakes at the California Institute of Technology, said he thinks it was somewhat less severe, possibly 7.1.

Death reports were fragmentary and possibly duplicating.

A helicopter pilot told Sheriff Lloyd Brook at historic Virginia City he had seen six bodies during a trip over the area.

Idaho State Police, in a broadcast heard by Montana Civil Defense headquarters, said they were told there were eight deaths near Reynolds Pass, on the Idaho-Montana border.

J. D. Coleman, who flew over the area, said he was told at least five persons were buried in the bigges' slide which blocked the Madison River. Coleman said the devastation was unbelievable.

Early reports said 100 to 150 persons were marooned between the slide, which created a barrier 200 feet high, and a leaking dam on the river.

The hospital at Ennis, north of the slide area, was crowded with injured persons and others were taken to Bozeman.

IDENTIFIED DEAD

HELENA (AP) — Identified dead in Montana's earthquake:
Purley Bennett, 45, Coeur d'Alene, Idaho.
Carole Bennett, 17, his daughter.
Tom Bennett, 11, his son.
George Stryker, Berkeley, Calif.
Mrs. Stryker.
Unaccounted for:
Susan Bennett, 5, Coeur d'Alene.

Parents Receive Message Daughter Safe

A telegram stating simply "I am okay but roughing it," climaxed nearly 16 hours of waiting by Mr. and Mrs. Dwight Massey, 201 E. Central Ave. Their daughter, Diane, 18, who will be a sophomore this year at Montana State University, is working on a dude ranch located near West Yellowstone, where the main brunt of the earthquake struck Monday night.

A second girl, Donna Goodrich, 18, of Plains, also a sophomore at the University, was working on the ranch with the Massey girl. She is also believed to be safe.

The Masseys received the message about 3:30 p.m. Wednesday and took it to mean that the residents of the ranch in the Hebgen Lake area, had been cut off from outside roads. The ranch is located near a turnoff 10 miles south of West Yellowstone. The message was sent from Gallatin Gateway.

The 'amily said they were waiting additional word so they can drive to the area to pick up the girls.

Quake Refugees Taken to State College

By JOHN A. FORSSEN

White faced, shaken, and bearing the marks of fatigue and pain, more than 150 refugees from devastating earthquakes arrived at a luxurious Montana State College dormitory late Tuesday night and early Wednesday morning. Except for those remaining buried under the huge and minor slides, none of the trapped tourists and campers remained in the area below Hebgen Dam. "I was never so scared in my life," said a Salt Lake woman who survived with her husband and two small children. "My husband went through the war with bombs falling around him and he said he had never experienced anything like this." The survivors told terrible tales of violent upsets in the earth's surface throughout several miles where the quake hit hardest.

Leland L. Sanders of Roy, Utah, a Salt Lake City suburb, told of his narrow escape from death during the catastrophy. "We passed several trailer camping spots but didn't like the looks of them and finally pulled farther up the river. The places we passed are all buried by the big slide." When asked if he thought there were persons buried under the slide, he said, "I know very well there are. You just don't realize how much that mountain slipped. I was in the trailer when it started shaking. I tried to go out the door but it was shaking so hard I couldn't get across to the door. Finally I got outside and the rocks were pouring down."

"It's a miracle we weren't killed," said a Salt Lake City tourist, "we had stopped there for the night. There were cracks three inches wide in the ground, with water spurting up through them." Mrs. Charles Rogers of Roundup said, "We didn't get it as bad as some."

President Pushes Hard For Strike Settlement

WASHINGTON (AP)—President Eisenhower decided Tuesday to push for a steel strike settlement by giving the public basic facts about the dispute.

Secretary of Labor James P. Mitchell announced the decision after a 45-minute discussion with the President.

"We hope as a result of these background statistics that the parties will bargain a little harder and reach a settlement," Mitchell told newsmen.

Mitchell has been working for weeks, with a huge staff, gathering statistics from both government and industry sources. Data he will release Wednesday, cover prices and some related subjects. His report will be purely factual Mitchell said, with no recommen-

every week it continues it costs 300 million dollars in production and 70 million in wages. Half a million workers are on strike with 150,000 in related industries idle.

The union is demanding pay raises and fringe benefits which the companies contend would be inflationary.

Eisenhower has favored a hands-off attitude for the government, and it is known the administration has planned to hold off invoking the Taft-Hartley Act at least until Sept. 15. Officials are convinced there will be no damaging steel shortage until then.

The Taft-Hartley law requires a cooling off period for 80 days, but no major strike has been ended by using this provision. The strike usually just resumes at the end of the 80 days.

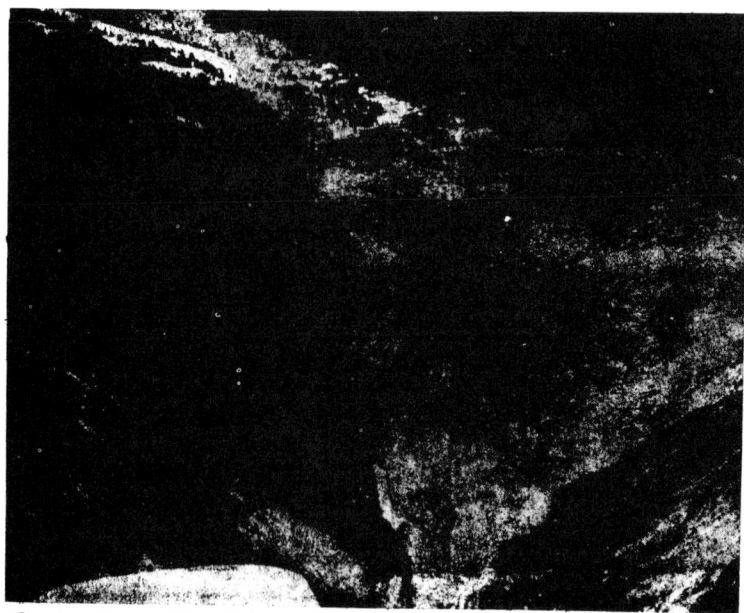

Quake Pours Five Million Yards of Rock Into Natural Dam

An estimated five million yards of rock, earth and trees roared down the mountainside early Tuesday shortly after the earthquake jarred the Hebgen Lake area. The unbelievable rock and debris stretches over an estimated 4,000 feet of canyon floor and is probably at least 300 feet deep. Many campers were in the area Sunday and Monday and it is not known how many are still alive. In the picture, water can be seen rising in the trees which line the banks of the Madison River. The highway is shown at bottom center. Hebgen Dam is five miles upstream and the reservoir which backs up the dam was nearly full at 325,000 acre feet of water. Rescue workers were helping stranded persons to safety Tuesday. (Photo by Dick Engstrom, Montana Power Co.)

Ministers Conclude Peace Discussions

SANTIAGO, Chile (AP)—American foreign ministers wound up their Caribbean peace conference Tuesday by signing a 10,000-word final act aimed at starting tension-easing machinery in motion.

Meanwhile Chile, the host nation, threw out a party of Cuban soldiers and newsmen who landed in a Cuban air force transport, uninvited and without authorization, as the advance guard for a professed good will visit by Cuban Prime Minister Fidel Castro's brother Raul.

Cuba joined, however, with 19 other Latin American nations and the United States in signing the act at the closing session of the seven-day conference.

Among the others was the Dominican Republic, whose Generalissimo Rafael L. Trujillo has been accused by Castro of attempting to overthrow Cuba's revolutionary regime.

U.N. Secretary of State Christian A. Herter told newsmen he believed the conference "will have a long-range effect that will have great significance.

Although the ministers agreed to give special temporary powers to the Inter-American Peace Committee in an effort to curb further moves by revolutionaries and their sympathizers, they called no names and slapped no wrists.

It was plain they were banking on public opinion to bring moral pressure to bear on those responsible.

Weather

Missoula and vicinity — Partly cloudy Wednesday, Wednesday night and Thursday. Scattered light thunderstorms possible in the area Wednesday evening. Continued cool temperatures Maximum both days near 75, the minimum Wednesday night 40 to 45.

West of divide — Considerable cloudiness through Thursday with a few isolated thunderstorms south; little temperature change; highs Wednesday and Thursday 70-80; lows Wednesday night 45-55.

YESTERDAY IN MISSOULA
Maximum 77 Minimum 46
At 6 a.m. 47 At 6 p.m. 53
At midnight 62 Precip Trace

YESTERDAY ELSEWHERE
City High Low Pcp
Billings ...... 82 63 T

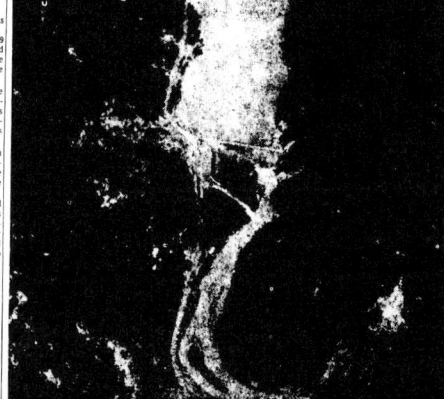

Says Slide Dam Will Protect Madison Canyon

HELENA (AP) — Only a tre-

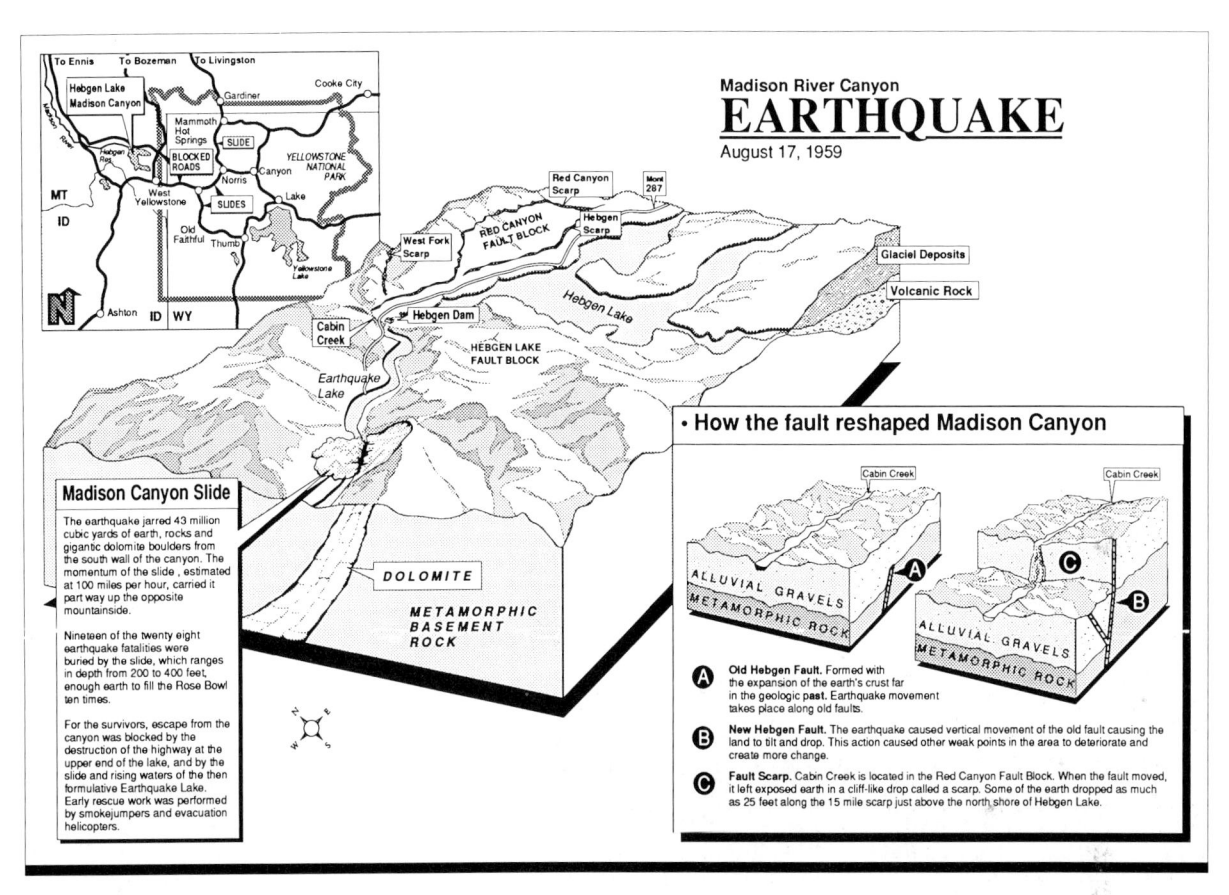

Madison River Canyon EARTHQUAKE
August 17, 1959

Madison Canyon Slide

The earthquake jarred 43 million cubic yards of earth, rocks and gigantic dolomite boulders from the south wall of the canyon. The momentum of the slide, estimated at 100 miles per hour, carried it part way up the opposite mountainside.

Nineteen of the twenty eight earthquake fatalities were buried by the slide, which ranges in depth from 200 to 400 feet, enough earth to fill the Rose Bowl ten times.

For the survivors, escape from the canyon was blocked by the destruction of the highway at the upper end of the lake, and by the slide and rising waters of the then formulative Earthquake Lake. Early rescue work was performed by smokejumpers and evacuation helicopters.

How the fault reshaped Madison Canyon

A Old Hebgen Fault. Formed with the expansion of the earth's crust far in the geologic past. Earthquake movement takes place along old faults.

B New Hebgen Fault. The earthquake caused vertical movement of the old fault causing the land to tilt and drop. This action caused other weak points in the area to deteriorate and create more change.

C Fault Scarp. Cabin Creek is located in the Red Canyon Fault Block. When the fault moved, it left exposed earth in a cliff-like drop called a scarp. Some of the earth dropped as much as 25 feet along the 15 mile scarp just above the north shore of Hebgen Lake.

---

campers under 500 feet of rock and damming the river. Behind the blockage, a new lake was already forming (later to be known as Earthquake Lake). He had the pilot fly up the river bed, where he spotted and photographed massive fractures in the highway and huge faults lining the mountainsides. Forssen returned to the *Missoulian* with many outstanding photographs. The paper's office became the Associated Press's national center for news coverage of what turned out to be one of America's greatest earthquakes, measuring 7.9 on the Richter scale — only slightly less severe than the famous 1906 San Francisco earthquake.

This "throw out the old rules" response to one of Montana's most significant natural disasters was a harbinger of things to come at the paper in Missoula and at the other Montana Lee newspapers, as well.

The earthquake that shook southern Montana, near Yellowstone Park, on August 17, 1959, was a major tremor. Registering 7.9 on the Richter scale, it packed more force than the devastating earthquake that struck the San Francisco/Oakland area in October, 1989.

In the Madison canyon, the earthquake dislodged 5 million cubic yards of earth, rocks and giant dolomite boulders. At speeds estimated at 100 miles per hour, the debris slid down the mountain and part way up the opposite side, damming the Madison River and creating Earthquake Lake.

This is how Lloyd looked in 1961 when he became publisher of the Missoulian. He didn't spend a great deal of time in his office. He spent as much time as possible in the plant and in the community. He always believed an effective leader had to be close to the people who were doing the work.

"Almost everyone says they believe in an 'open door' policy," comments Lloyd. "I think it's more important to walk through your open door going the other way and be out there in the trenches rather than waiting for someone to walk in."

By accepting the offer to come to Montana, Lloyd found himself squarely in the middle of the action. Lee's Montana newspapers were the setting for some technological changes that were revolutionary at the time. "For example," says Lloyd, "we had a single computer sitting in Billings, 300 miles away. We got the telephone company to put in a dataphone. News stories would be punched on tape in Missoula and sent over the wire to the *Billings Gazette* computer. We'd run it through the computer for hyphenation and justification, then send the tape back to Missoula over the wire where it would run our typesetting machines. We couldn't get our paper out without the telephone and our computer 300 miles away." Thus began Lloyd's involvement with telephones and their use by newspapers.

Lee was in the process of converting its newspaper operations to cold type and grappling with the unions' response to the change. "My job in Montana," Lloyd says, "was to make the first conversion to cold type and offset. It was to be a total conversion, and our objective was to do it with or without the help of the unions, even though they were very strong in the state."

Not surprisingly, the printers' union dug their heels in and prepared to resist these changes. A major confrontation threatened, but Lloyd made it obvious that he was ready to publish without the unions, if necessary. His firmness on production issues, however, was coupled with the promise to help those displaced by change to find new jobs or careers.

"I strongly believe you have to deal with people truthfully," says Lloyd, "and that means telling people, as far ahead of time as you possibly can, what the impact of a new process will be on them and their job in terms of retraining or facing the probability of no job at all. Then you try to help them keep their means of livelihood either by retraining them within the company or getting them new jobs on the outside — even to the extent of paying for their training for work at another company.

"One of our union people became a game warden, for example. Another one started a TV repair company. A number, like Butte pressman Don Berryman, who recently retired as publisher of the *Montana Standard* and was a group manager, stayed inside Lee. Some became photographers, reporters, ad salesmen, technicians, you name it. But under no circumstances would we leave somebody in a job that was obsolete and irrelevant. There's more to work than just getting a paycheck. A person has to maintain dignity and self-esteem."

The negotiations in Missoula resulted in an unprecedented agreement. The original contract with the International Pressmen's Union included a standard clause referred to as a "manning clause," which specified how many men it took to run each press unit. It was featherbedding which, at that time, was the "holiest of holies" in the pressmen's contract. "We made a deal with the international leaders of the IPU in New York," says Lloyd, "that we would give the pressmen the page-making camera — which the printers claimed in those days — and platemaking in exchange for the total elimination of the manning clause. The IPU agreed. So back in 1965, we had the first contract in the U.S. underwritten by the IPU that agreed to the total elimination of the manning clause and a no-strike clause as well. We were successful because we convinced the pressmen's union leaders in New York that their future did not lie in featherbedding new printing technologies but in productivity and the best work flow."

For the first few years after Lloyd became vice president of the Montana newspapers, he negotiated contracts in Butte, Billings, Helena and Livingston until the local publishers took over the negotiating role.

Don Berryman remembers representing the Butte pressmens' union in the first negotiating session with Lloyd. "I was surprised, and frankly impressed, with the input he wanted from me and the others. During Anaconda's ownership, they didn't want anybody from production suggesting anything. I'd been told to keep my mouth shut more than once.

128 *Lee's Legacy of Leadership*

"After hearing what Lloyd wanted to discuss, I told him about the previous policy. 'That's a lot of crap,' Lloyd said. 'You people are the source of our best information. We want you to make suggestions and help us run this newspaper,' he told me.

"I was astounded," Don remembers. "Actually, I thought he was nuts, that this was some kind of negotiating ploy. I certainly didn't think the guy was serious. But over time, I learned he was dead serious. As a matter of fact, I even learned that the opportunity I had with Lee was a hell of a lot better than I could expect if I'd stayed on the other side. I knew if I wanted to build a career in newspaper management, I'd have to leave the union." And leave he did.

Similar problems existed in other Lee Montana papers. Tom Williams, hired by Lloyd to be Butte's production manager (and who later became business manager, publisher of the *Quad-City Times*, president of NAPP, and a Lee board member), remembers what the old days were like in Butte when the *Standard* had a circulation of 25,000. "Blatant stealing, gross feather-bedding, absolute insubordination, and determined sabotage were rampant, especially in the composing room. We were using antiquated cast-off hot-metal equipment which at best, ran only sporadically and at worst, not at all. The paper was often late, as much as 10 to 12 hours. Matrixes were scattered on the floor or in the parking lot. There was a lot of drinking and the general pervasive attitude was, 'Screw it.' Not surprisingly, the *Standard* was running at a loss.

"The news room couldn't cope and the advertising department had thrown up their hands in despair. Neither the business manager nor the publisher could handle the situation, and the paper was drifting slowly, but inexorably, to the end of its long and illustrious life.

"That's exactly the way it was when I arrived," Williams recalls. His job, as production manager, was to help Lloyd get it straightened out. Otherwise, the paper would be sold or shut down.

During one union session, which came after months of negotiations, the international representative of the printers union from San Francisco launched a tirade of complaints against Tom, using abusive and foul language. Lloyd listened, then gathered his papers to leave and said, "You guys better get one thing straight. Williams is going to be here for a long time. I'm backing him 100 percent, and as of this minute I'm promoting him to business manager, so get used to working with him."

Lloyd then asked for an apology, otherwise the negotiations were over and they could "hit the bricks." The negotiating committee left the room for about an hour, came back with an apology, and Lee was on its way to getting the *Montana Standard* on the road to recovery. Eventually, the workers saw that Lloyd and Tom meant business, that they genuinely weren't trying to hurt anyone but just wanted to get rid of the bad actors.

The year after Lloyd arrived, western Montana had several big forest fires. Missoula was a fire-fighting center for the smoke jumpers and fire-retardant bombing planes. Early one morning, Lloyd hopped into one of the old torpedo bombers refitted for retardant bombing and went out to cover the story with his camera. Lloyd's picture shows a smoke jumper who has just exited a plane.

When Phil Adler received a copy of the Missoulian *and saw that Lloyd had bylines on the story and pictures, he called and said, "Schermer, what the hell are you doing flying around in airplanes out there, taking pictures of fire fighters? We're paying you to run the* Missoulian."

"My career as an action reporter/photographer was over before it began," Lloyd remembers.

"The truth is," says Lloyd, "the vast majority of people who work for you want to give you an honest day's work. They want to succeed every day they come to work and want to be recognized for what they're doing successfully. It's the same for most people whether they're in or out of the union."

Strikes were avoided throughout Montana. Years later the employees voted to decertify, and the papers became nonunion operations. "It took a lot of heart-to-heart talks," says Berryman, "to show them how much better off they'd be with the company providing benefits than what they could negotiate through union contracts. But we did it."

Years later, on one of his visits, Lloyd found himself in a conference room with a number of former union leaders who had become the managers who were running the *Standard*. The irony of the situation moved him to exclaim, "Here we are sitting around drinking coffee in this very room where we used to fight and negotiate. For all these years, I thought I had won. But I realize you guys won, because now you're the ones who are running the joint!"

Tom Williams remembers what it was like to work for Lloyd. "He gives you responsibility, tells you what he expects and turns you loose. And he always backs you up all the way. He's an excellent trainer. He introduced all of us to budgeting, and believe it or not, neither Lee nor Anaconda had any budgeting process before Lloyd arrived. Montana was the testing ground for the entire company. We made Lloyd's new methods work."

The conversions in Montana and elsewhere and the resulting struggles with the unions did not arise from any desire to simply "beat the unions," Lloyd explains. This new approach reflected both a new reality in the business culture and a different concept of how a company should deal with all of its employees.

Lee's adoption of new technologies became mandatory as the company faced an increasingly competitive environment. "My years at Lee," Lloyd says, "have been during the period when we had to make the transition from newspapers and TV stations with strong, profitable franchises and little or no competition, to very competitive situations. Technological innovation, changing lifestyles, government deregulation and competition have given our customers many more choices. We have moved from a time when the information receivers had to take what we gave them to today's environment, where they can pick what they want, when they want it. Lee took a hard-nosed position on production and management development because it was a matter of survival."

Ultimately, unions have disappeared in the company's newspaper operations because of a management focus that tends to make them unnecessary. "There are some companies in which unions are absolutely necessary in order to prevent people from being exploited," says Lloyd. "People must always have the right to organize. But at Lee, we recognize every human being is different and unique and needs an opportunity to grow and reach his or her potential. In companies that are able to manage people and meet their psychic and financial needs on the job, autocratic managers and unions become irrelevant."

That approach to management has been articulated and expanded by Lloyd over the years, and so has another principle of leadership that was impressed on him by an early experience in Montana.

Soon after he arrived in Missoula, Lloyd recognized that the newspaper's composing room was in such bad shape that it was dangerous, unpleasant, and inefficient. "There was a parquet floor in the composing room," he says. "The cracks were filled with coal soot belched from steam engines that had passed near the building for many years. There was dirt all over. It was dimly lit by tiny pull-chain bulbs and bare three-phase electric wires came up through pipes in the floor. If anyone had touched them, they could have been electrocuted."

The citizens of Missoula gave this plaque to Lloyd when his promotion to Vice President-Newspapers required him to return to Davenport.
"I'll never forget them," reminisces Lloyd when asked about the plaque. "I cherish my Montana years and still have many wonderful friends out there."

Lloyd set to work to change the production environment, preparing layouts showing how the equipment could be repositioned for better efficiency; improved lighting and ventilation was also planned. "I called the printers into my office one at a time to show them this new layout and get their input," Lloyd says. "I didn't realize it at the time, but that was an unfair labor practice; by law, you had to go through the union to make changes in the work environment. The printers were stunned because I valued their opinions enough to ask them. Once we started talking, they made suggestions, and together we finalized the new layout.

TRIBUTE

TO

Lloyd G. Schermer

HE BROUGHT TO US THE FRESH AIR OF A FREE & INDEPENDENT NEWSPAPER. HE COMMITTED HIMSELF AND HIS ORGANIZATION TO A VIGOROUS AND EFFECTIVE ATTACK ON THE PROBLEMS BESETTING OUR COMMUNITY. ALL OF US HAVE BENEFITTED BECAUSE HE WAS HERE. WE SHALL NOT SOON FORGET HIM.

FROM

The Citizens of Missoula

"I got Walt Hoefler, a good friend and our machinist printer, to help me recruit some men from the Bar of Justice, a saloon across the street. We worked several nights between shifts from midnight to 5 a.m. to get the place moved around and fixed up. Production skyrocketed.

"Some of the effectiveness had to do with the physical changes and improved environment, but what really happened was that these men and women were asked for their input, and a lot of them saw their suggestions incorporated into the new setup. They knew I respected them and their opinions. That was my first experience with what is now called consultative management. I didn't ask them *if* I could move the equipment around, I

The irrigation ditch, seen in the foreground of this 1985 picture of the new Missoulian building, was what caused all the problems in the creation of Caras Park. The park, which the newspaper played a major role in creating, is on the other side of the river.

asked them for their thoughts about my proposal to move the units, and it turned out to be not my plan but *our* plan. They acquired ownership in the new plan and ownership of its success. Together, we made it work."

Before moving to Davenport as Lee's Vice President - Newspapers in 1970, Lloyd served as publisher of the *Missoulian* and Vice President - Lee Newspapers of Montana. In those Montana years, he also found numerous opportunities to act on his vision of newspapers as catalysts for change. "When Lloyd was here," says Phil Blake, present publisher of the *Missoulian*, "much of his attention was on a number of community projects that significantly changed the town. For instance, shortly after Lloyd arrived, the Clark Fork of the Columbia River, which runs through the middle of the town, turned rusty orange periodically because of mining pollutants such as copper, arsenic, and sulphur released by the Butte mines 125 miles to the east. There were junked autos lining the banks. It's really quite incredible to look back on it because today it's absolutely gorgeous, a pristine mountain river full of trout.

"First Lloyd worked on the Anaconda Company to use proper water treatment techniques and then on the town of Missoula, which was dumping raw sewage into the river, to build its first sewage treatment plant. The newspaper led a public awareness campaign that was ultimately successful in the rebirth of the river.

"Then it occurred to Lloyd and some other civic leaders that a seven-acre island in the middle of the river, adjacent to the downtown business area, would make an ideal public park. Citizens trying to develop the island were stopped by an irrigation company's water rights claim. Lloyd personally wrote a full-page feature story about the stalemate that included pictures and a map.

A retired county engineer saw the article and produced a 20-year-old agreement signed by the irrigation company president who was blocking the project. The agreement gave the city the right to develop the island anytime it chose. The island is now joined to one bank and is a beautiful park with picnic and seating areas, along with a lovely summer theater."

The *Missoulian* led a four-year effort to bring Frontier Airlines (now Delta) into western Montana, connecting it with Denver and Salt Lake City. Lloyd started the United Fund of Missoula and increased awareness of the importance of contributing to its work. He initiated highway construction to the new interstate and the rebuilding of part of Missoula's main thoroughfare.

The *Missoulian* became the driving force behind Montana's air and water pollution legislation, some of the earliest and best in the country. In 1962, they brought more awareness of the issues of local and statewide political campaigns by providing a "political forum" for comparing candidates' unedited answers to questions on important issues. Each candidate was asked the same questions and their answers were run in a column of space under their pictures.

Caras Park was created from an island in the Clark Fork of the Columbia River. It is located in the center of Missoula's downtown area.

The Missoulian worked with John H. Toole to connect the island with the north bank, making the park possible. The park contains a lovely summer theater, picnic and recreation areas and is a popular oasis for Missoulians.

Toole later became mayor of Missoula and wrote an interesting book called, Red Ribbons: A Story of Missoula and Its Newspaper. He was one of Lloyd's closest friends.

In one race, the 1962 gubernatorial election, one of the candidates refused to join the forum. After several futile weeks of trying to get him to respond, the *Missoulian* ran the one candidate's answer and a column of blank space under the other's picture with "No Comment" in the column. This went on for several weeks. The candidate who refused to participate was defeated, despite having been the early favorite to win.

The *Missoulian* also campaigned to protect the natural beauty of the region. One effort began with a pack trip into the million-acre Bob Marshall Wilderness Area of western Montana, below Glacier National Park.

"I loved to go into the Bob on a horse," Lloyd explained, "especially to the Middle Fork of the Flathead River to see wildlife and fish for cutthroat trout. We were near a place called Spotted Bear Station and noticed bulldozers pushing out roads along the northern side of the wilderness area.

"I asked our packer, Smoke Elser — the best in the West — but he didn't know what was going on either. I knew once a road was built, the area around it could never be declared a 'wilderness.' What was happening didn't look right. This was high, fragile alpine country, noted for its wildlife and trout streams. So when we reached our destination at Essex, I found a pay phone and called Dale Burk, our environmental reporter on the *Missoulian*.

"Because Dale could throw a diamond hitch on a pack horse with the best of them, I asked him to pack into the area the following week as Smoke's wrangler with several officials from the U. S. Forest Service. He might just hear something around the campfire.

As comfortable on horseback as he is in the boardroom, Lloyd values his lifelong love of the wilderness. "Getting out into the country is always a rewarding experience for me," says Schermer. "Sometimes it's the people I'm with and the experiences we have; other times it's the new perspective the environment gives me on everyday problems and opportunities."

"Burk went up there with Smoke, confirmed that they were indeed planning to build logging roads, and returned to Missoula to write. The Forest Service vigorously denied our assertions about new road construction. Then we had a real break when an anonymous Forest Service informant slipped us an official Forest Service map with 'existing' and 'proposed' roads clearly marked. The *Missoulian* ran the map and a story in a two-page color spread. The roof blew off all the way to Washington, D.C. Our two senators, Mike Mansfield and Lee Metcalf, quickly took up the controversy. The outcome was not only an abrupt halt to the road building but also the creation of the new 300,000-acre Great Bear Wilderness Area that now joins the Bob Marshall with Glacier National Park.

The one-million-acre Bob Marshall Wilderness Area is characterized by mountains and valleys and contains the South Fork and Middle Fork of the Flathead River, known for its superb wildlife and fishing. The Missoulian was responsible for the creation of the 300,000–acre Great Bear Wilderness Area that joins the Bob with Glacier National Park.

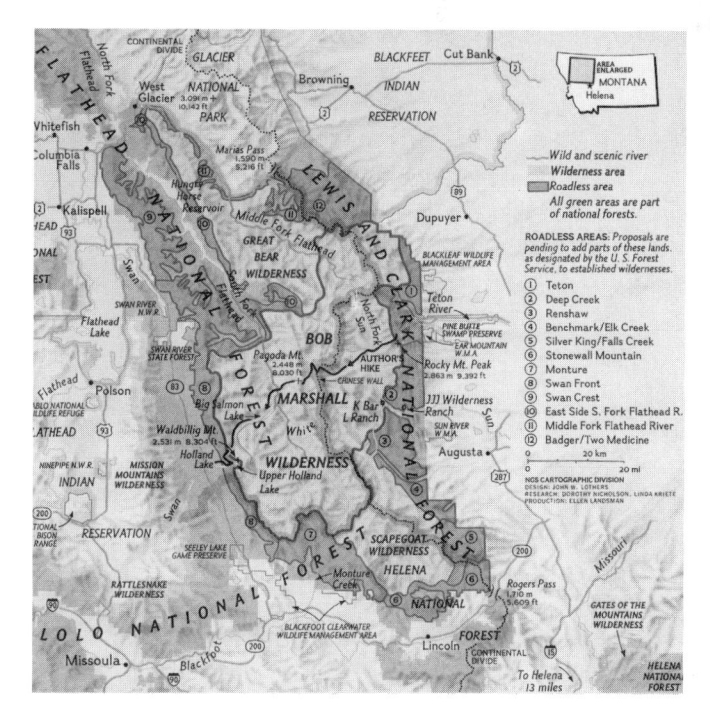

Because of Lloyd's involvement with the communities his papers serve, many townspeople remember him well. In 1960, for example, the *Missoulian* published a special 200-page centennial edition. "We had a 'Pony Express' arranged with 35 riders from our sheriff's posse to take the first copy 125 miles over the Continental Divide and deliver it to Governor Hugo Aronson at his mansion in Helena," Lloyd remembers. While it was being put together, Lloyd travelled all over western Montana talking to people about the paper, picking up historical news stories and pictures, and selling advertising for the centennial edition. "I really learned what people thought of our newspaper, our city, and our state," he said.

"Readers either loved or hated what we wrote," says Lloyd. "There was no middle ground. We sure weren't ignored. We reported on issues and had many editorial page controversies. It was good for us and good for the community. I remember one fellow who wanted a story reported in the paper. 'Get it on the editorial page if you can,' he asked. 'That's the one page everyone reads.' What a change from the days prior to Lee's ownership when letters to the editor were not accepted at all and editorials discussed the price of eggs in Afghanistan."

Lloyd's next challenge was when Dave Gottlieb asked him to come back to Davenport as Vice President - Newspapers. Dave's objective was to duplicate Lloyd's western successes in other Lee properties. Lloyd's work took on a new immediacy when Dave suffered a sudden heart attack and died on July 4, 1973.

There was boardroom intrigue, remembers Harry Fischer, a Lee board member for more than 20 years, who was impressed that Lloyd, unlike some others, didn't actively campaign for the job. "He knew we knew he was ready," says Fischer. Others agreed, and Lloyd was elected president.

Fishing the Middle Fork of Idaho's Salmon River was one of the trips Lloyd often enjoyed with his young sons.

"Dad gave us the best introduction to the wilderness any kid could have," remembers Greg. "One of his great joys is sharing his love and knowledge of the wilderness with others. He taught us everything about fishing, from stream entomology, to selecting the right fly, and then making it produce fish.

"The campfires, the great ghost stories, the grown-up discussions we participated in were all an enriching part of our youth," Greg continues. "I also learned the only place Dad will stand absolutely still, with incredible concentration, is when he has a fly rod in his hand."

Dave Jaquith, then president and CEO of Vega Industries and a highly regarded American Management Association lecturer, was also a member of the board. Jaquith said, "Schermer, we have great confidence in you, but instead of meeting quarterly, we're going to meet once a month for a while."

It was well they did, because the first few months of Lloyd's tenure were fraught with complications. "The going was tough at first," says Jules Tewlow, Lee's director of special projects. "First, he had to build a loyal team to help him run the company. Almost immediately he faced the threat of a newsprint shortage which could have left the company without any paper to print on. The NAPP plant was just being built, and there were big problems out there. And a few months later, it looked like someone was making a run on the company's stock. Several other media companies wanted to buy Lee. Everywhere he looked, major problems loomed. Lloyd had the guts to face all the issues. He made all the tough decisions — no shirking or delaying them. I don't know how he managed it, but he looked like a leader every second of every day."

"I remember the challenges of those early days," says Harry Fischer. "When the crises were over, Lloyd instituted many of the management systems he learned at Harvard and from the AMA —things he had perfected in Montana. All those management programs you see at Lee today were started by Lloyd. There's no question in my mind that if Lloyd had not been elected president when he was, Lee would not be an independent company today."

Lloyd quickly saw the need to develop a strong second leg for the company, and Lee Loomis' and Dave Gottlieb's ventures into broadcasting provided the perfect framework. But instead of adding more small and medium-sized stations in the largely rural communities Lee's newspapers had traditionally served, Lloyd's plan called for purchasing more stations in larger, urban markets. Building on the earlier purchase of WSAZ-TV in Huntington, West Virginia, Lloyd soon added the market-dominating CBS affiliate in Honolulu, KGMB-TV, and then turned his attention to the CBS affiliate in Portland, Oregon, KOIN-TV.

Dick Belkin, a former Vice President - Broadcasting, remembers how determined Lloyd was to make the KOIN-TV purchase. "It was a tough situation," Belkin says. "Newhouse Broadcasting owned 50 percent of the station; a Portland family owned the rest. And ownership of just 50 percent doesn't give anyone real power. Many companies were interested in the property, but none would buy because they couldn't be sure of being able to acquire both pieces. Lloyd intuitively knew he could do it and was willing to take the risk," says Belkin.

The process began in a meeting room at O'Hare airport. Lloyd and Lee's CFO at the time, John Stemlar, met the senior Newhouse Broadcasting executive for preliminary discussions. Lloyd walked into the room, extended his hand, and said, "Nice to meet you." He shook Lloyd's hand and replied, "Nice to meet you, Lloyd. I want $13 million."

Lloyd was stunned. "We haven't even begun negotiating," he said.

The Newhouse officer replied, "It doesn't matter. $13 million is the price. That's what we want."

Excusing themselves and stepping into the hall to discuss the situation, Lloyd said to Stemlar, "This is crazy. We just came here to dance; they want to have sex!" But Lloyd knew the price was fair and the deal was made.

"Then he flew to Portland," remembers Belkin, "met with the family owners, and told them the vision he had for the station. He told them of Lee's management philosophy, the company's historic value system, and how other acquired properties have thrived under Lee ownership. Lloyd's a great closer. He pulled the deal off — and at a very attractive price. But it was Lloyd's willingness to take the risk of buying the first 50 percent, and his belief in his ability to close the deal, that made it happen. He was determined to build a successful, prestigious broadcasting operation for Lee." After KOIN-TV was purchased, Lloyd bought the CBS affiliate, KMTV, in Omaha, Nebraska; KGUN-TV, an ABC affiliate in Tucson, Arizona; and a 42-percent stake in Albuquerque's KGGM-TV.

This picture, taken in May, 1990, at a ceremony commemorating the opening of the new Davenport Quad-City Times *plant, shows Lloyd with his management team, from left: Robert D. Ross, Vice President, New Ventures: Michael J. Riley, Vice President - Finance and Chief Financial Officer; Richard D. Gottlieb, President and Chief Operating Officer; Lloyd G. Schermer, Chairman and Chief Executive Officer; Ronald L. Rickman, Vice President - Newspapers; Gary N. Schmedding, Vice President - Broadcasting; and Floyd Whellan, Vice President - Human Resources.*

appreciates you and makes you feel that you're part of the team. He's an exciting guy to be around."

Harry Fischer says, "Lloyd is a man of great, absolute integrity. If he says something is done, it's done. If he says it's going to get done, it will get done."

"Challenge" is a crucial element in the environment that Lloyd strives to create. Lloyd is often described as a "caring" person, but he is adamant about distinguishing his attitude from the type of paternalism that just makes people feel good. In conversations and speeches, he has shown a deep respect for the individual's need for self-realization. "One of the only institutions left," he has said, "where individuals can do the best they are capable of doing and be recognized and rewarded for it, is in the work organization where they spend most of their lives. Workers are aching to make a commitment if given the freedom to do so. Management's role should be to create a nourishing environment for growth — not to make people feel good all over, but to have a climate where they feel challenged and can satisfy their psychic and financial needs."

Ask Lloyd where his management philosophy comes from and he'll quickly tell you from his value system and his experiences in Montana and with the President's Association of the American Management Association. They had more impact than the Harvard Business School.

"At one point," says Lloyd, "I was asked by the Inland Press Association to talk about this new thing called budgeting we were doing in Montana. I got up, talked a little bit about budgeting and a whole lot about managing. I thought I'd done a pretty good job.

"Then a guy named Allen Mathis stood up and gave a talk about the management process that absolutely knocked me over.

"I thought, 'Good Grief! I've been out in Montana for years working on management development and somebody else is far ahead of me.'

"I went up to Alan afterwards and I said, 'You know, you just shook me up.'

"'Why?' he asked.

"'Where does this all come from?' I wanted to know.

"'Well, I head up the President's Association of the American Management Association and this is what we teach.'"

"'Where do I sign up?'"

"'Are you a president?'"

"I said that I wasn't — not yet anyway — and he told me no one could participate without their company president attending first. But they made an exception and stuck me into one of the sessions in Florida anyway. It was a week-long program and a profound experience for me. The best lecturer there — the best the AMA ever had — was Dave Jaquith, a successful businessman who later became a Lee board member. Dave's thinking was light-years ahead of anyone else. I knew these were programs we needed to implement for our people.

"Gradually, we developed our own program at Lee, using much of what I learned from the AMA. Most important, I had the help of Dave Jaquith and Bert Hayward. Bert was a unique and outstanding behavioral psychologist."

"It certainly wasn't easy," says Dick Gottlieb. "I remember some of the first sessions where some of the officers and managers didn't even show up. Today, all of us teach these classes to our people. We've put over 900 people through the managers' training program. Training is the life-blood of the organization." Lloyd became a lecturer at President's Association meetings.

Murph Wolman remembers the early days of management seminars. "Lloyd was the only advocate of this new professional management system — none of the rest of us understood it. We had a meeting in New York where they brought in Dave Jaquith and other President's Association guys. We were all captive in this hotel and had nowhere to go, so we had to listen. Most of us were smart enough to know we'd have to learn it sooner or later."

Lloyd has described human resources as a "competitive edge" for the future, and stresses the need to foster innovative and risk-taking behavior that will enable the company to adapt to change and ambiguity. "I think a lot about the future," he says. "I represent a transition away from the old elitist media school and toward new forms of marketing communications — driven by our customers and enhancing our ability to innovate and meet their needs. As a part of that effort, I've tried to build an environment for motivating Lee people to be creative and to contribute new and productive ideas to the company."

Looking at communications from a national viewpoint, Schermer treasures his 12-year participation on the board of the American Newspaper Publishers Association, which elected him chairman in April of 1990. Previously, Lloyd was chairman of the Newspaper Advertising Bureau, the marketing arm of the industry.

"It became very apparent to me early in the 1980's," he explains, "that major problems impacting our industry could not be solved by individual companies alone, no matter how big or forceful and dedicated they might be. We've all wrestled with such industry-sensitive issues as postal rates or telecommunications policies or other regulations that challenge the First Amendment. Because these matters stem from pressure groups and government policies, they are difficult to resolve at anything other than a national association level, and that points to Washington, D.C. The word 'lobby' wasn't even in our vocabulary, and we needed to put it there."

As a case in point, he recounted the part he and the American Newspaper Publishers Association played in successfully opposing federal legislation that would have rewritten the Communications Act of 1934 in such a way that telephone companies would have gained an unfair advantage with their monopoly networks over newspapers and other information providers. It required a coordinated effort and meetings with a multitude of legislators to voice the Association's viewpoint and convince Capitol Hill that the proposed bill simply was not equitable and would be injurious to all information providers.

Arthur Ochs "Punch" Sulzberger, chairman and CEO of the *New York Times*, explains that people are elected to ANPA's board of directors on the basis of what they have done for the industry, compatibility, and the ability to get things moving. "I give Lloyd high marks on what he has done for ANPA. He's a real leader and he has a great sense of humor — the kind of person people like to work for and one of the reasons why Lee has a reputation in our industry as a fine place to work.

"He has done yeoman's work for our association on the telecommunications project; he worked extremely hard and long hours. It was very demanding and required a tremendous amount of homework and travel back and forth to Washington, as well as meetings with multitudes of telephone company executives and politicians.

"Lloyd has a certain bulldog streak, and when he has something that seems to be moving along, he'll grab hold of it and keep after it. A while back, he saved all the junk mail he and Betty received during a year's time so he could display it to make the point that junk-mail producers are getting a free ride at the expense of newspaper publishers and other first-class mailers who must pay higher postal rates. His strategy was effective and has resulted in important postage revisions."

"Media people consider Lloyd to be one of the great futurists in the industry," says Edward W. Estlow, former Chief Executive Officer and now Chairman of the Executive Committee, Scripps Howard, and another ANPA board member. "He looks down the road a long way to determine where this industry is going, where Lee Enterprises should be going in relation to the industry, and then he plans. He's done more planning for his company than anyone else I know. He really is a world-class planner and a world-class analyst. He's just a little bit ahead of almost everybody else.

"He is highly informed on telecommunications and the moves that the phone companies are making in contrast to what the newspapers are doing in this same area. His analysis and forecasting have been very helpful to the industry. On the other hand, if it's something that is of advantage competitively for the Lee newspapers, then he is going to keep his cards close to his chest. That's just the way he is. He is generous in sharing his industry analysis, all of which is extremely helpful in planning for the future. He has already done things that we found out about later (voice mail, for example), that others of us are just beginning to learn about. He's one of the world-class executives."

Bob Erburu, Chairman and CEO of The Times Mirror Co. and another long-time friend and ANPA associate, puts it this way. "Status quo is not one of Lloyd's long suits. He has that rare ability to find a way to make anything better. Lloyd has brought bright new leadership to ANPA — professional leadership, just like he's done at his own company. Things always happen when Lloyd is involved."

When new postal policy lowered third-class mail rates and raised first- and second-class rates, the effect was to "subsidize" third-class mailers. An entirely new industry was created that delivered printed advertising material through the mail — at the expense of newspapers.

To dramatize the unfairness of these new regulations, Lloyd and Betty saved every piece of third-class mail that arrived at their home in 1985. The result: almost seven feet of material consisting of 1,403 pieces and weighing 175.8 pounds.

Because of the low third-class rate, this postage cost about half as much as regular first-class rates ordinary people would have to spend to mail the same material.

Lloyd's involvement in telecommunications

The evolution of telephone technology and its future impact on newspapers has been an area of interest to Lloyd since he first used a dataphone tied into a computer 300 miles away at the *Billings Gazette* in 1967 to produce the *Missoulian*.

He participated in a seminar at Harvard that focused on this subject in 1978. It was there he decided to take a very active role in what appeared to be a great opportunity for newspapers as high-tech technology was beginning to gather momentum for telephony.

Lloyd was one of the moving forces that captured the interest of the American Newspaper Publishers Association when he addressed that organization's convention in 1981. Lloyd has continued his efforts into 1990, serving as chairman of the ANPA Telecommunications Strategic Steering Group whose objective has been to block the seven regional Bell operating companies from using their monopoly telephone lines to sell information owned by them in competition with others, such as newspapers. Lloyd wanted to guard against setting policy today that might give the phone companies an unfair advantage in the future. ANPA maintains its watchdog posture and is a formidable opponent to the phone companies in Washington.

In 1983, Lee created a new company, Call-It Co., doing business today under the name "Voice Response, Inc." to do research and development because he viewed the telephone network as a medium distinctly different from radio and television or print on paper.

During those R&D years, Lee has developed a voice information process that allows callers to interact with computer databases without agent or operator intervention, and the extent of the interaction is controlled by the database owner. The process transfers the information retrieval and data entry functions from operators and agents to callers and customers. Independent research services forecast the total voice information market will grow to $4.2 billion by 1992.

Call-It Co. was granted a patent in 1989 on its voice information process. The company is currently exploring opportunities for the use of this patent.

Schermer says, "The voice response field is high-tech, high-risk, high-reward territory. We are going forward knowing there is risk. We are approaching the end of a ten-year odyssey in which we have developed a body of proprietary property that we hope will play an important role in the development of this new information medium."

"This is exciting new technology," says VRI President Bob Ross, "and we are committed to staying out in front of it. Interactive telephony is already gaining an important foothold in American life and Lee hopes to be a player in this growing field."

Lloyd's "bulldog streak" has been recognized by others who describe Lloyd's tenacity and competitiveness in situations that range from the boardroom to fly fishing to bird shooting.

Ed Estlow is one who has experienced Lloyd's competitiveness. "We were up in British Columbia, 250 miles north of Vancouver, on the Dean River. It's a trophy river for steelhead trout. While Lloyd is a great fly fisherman, he hadn't done well this particular trip. On the last day, dusk came and Lloyd was still casting for his fish, determined to catch at least one steelhead in the 'trophy' category.

"While the rest of us were drinking and relaxing, Lloyd stayed in the river, right in front of the lodge, and finally hooked into a 20-pounder that gave him a merry time. He landed the thing and, of course, he was tickled to death. He simply had to satisfy his drive to achieve what he set out to accomplish. He wasn't competing with anyone but himself. Lloyd demands the best of himself, and he always delivers. I'll always remember that of Lloyd. He is really competitive. It doesn't make any difference what the activity is, he wants to be the winner. He's tough."

Don Berryman agrees. "Lloyd is a hard-nosed, tough son of a bitch who gives everything 100 percent. He really cares about the people in this company. He's incredibly sensitive. Lloyd doesn't know how to lose; he doesn't know there is a second place. That's just his nature."

Ron Rickman knows that about Lloyd's characteristic tenacity, too. "Lloyd heard that Guy Palmer, our former ad manager in Butte, and I knew of a good goose-hunting spot near Ennis,

Lloyd cherishes his ability to spend time in the wilderness, whether hunting, fishing or just enjoying the spectacular beauty of the American West. Tom Williams, whom Lloyd hired as Butte's production manager, has been a frequent companion and tells stories of the wonderful camaraderie the outdoors generates among friends.

"Where else," Tom asks, "could I wake up the chairman of the board by chopping wood next to his tent at 4:00 a.m.?"

Montana, and urged us to set up a shoot. On the appointed morning, Lloyd arrived on time but was almost crippled with a bad back from a herniated disc — it had kept him in a hospital for the past two weeks. Lloyd wanted to hunt and wasn't going to let the pain stop him.

"While we carried most of his gear, Lloyd trudged through the field to the blind, obviously in excruciating pain. We set him up in the blind, actually laying him down on some old timbers, and left him there while we went to another blind and tried to move some geese around.

"As luck would have it, a flight of geese came along and started to pitch into the decoys. While flat on his back, Lloyd managed to raise his gun and bag a pair.

"But the most sheer determination I've ever seen in him or in any other person," continues Rickman, "was Lloyd's decision to create a super-voting class of stock."

"In the mid-eighties," explains NAPP chairman and Lee board member Dick Sonnenfeldt, "there were rumors that Lee, like other media companies, was a possible take-over candidate. The stock price was less than one-half of the company's market value. Someone might have tried to offer a high price for the shares to take control and then dismember the company to retire the debt and make a quick profit.

"Lloyd was bothered by the distraction this caused. 'Because we have the votes, I'm going to get rid of these threats,' he told us. The only choices were to take the company private or to establish a new class of 'super-voting' stock.

"The approach provided that on the day the new class was approved, a new share of stock (a one-for-one split) would be issued for each existing share. Each new share carried ten votes, but would revert to one vote each if it was ever sold. New shares issued carry only one vote, too. It puts the real voting power of the company into the hands of existing, long-time shareholders, making it virtually impossible for a raider to buy enough stock to assume control.

The first Official Guidebook of China was one of the number of projects Lee produced after Lloyd was invited to China in 1980 shortly after the Cultural Revolution began. The picture shows him entering a room at People's Daily in Beijing with An Wenyi, secretary general of the paper. Lloyd spoke about American management.

Lee Enterprises held exclusive rights to create books and TV documentaries, and to place advertising in Chinese newspapers and magazines. Unfortunately, the relationship came too early in China's push towards democracy. While the exclusive arrangements are no longer in effect, a solid relationship exists to this day.

"The reason it was a bit of a gamble," continues Sonnenfeldt. "is because you really need well over 50 percent to agree to that provision. If the vote was close to 50 percent it would be an open invitation for a raider because there might be a chance management would not have the full support of the shareholders."

"At the time," remembers Rickman, "only three or maybe four other companies had done this. We knew we had over 50 percent of the votes, but weren't sure how far over the 50 percent mark we could get. The New York Stock Exchange even threatened to throw us out. But Lloyd never quit. He knew he wanted it, knew it was right for the shareholders and for the employees, and he made it happen."

Harry Fischer remembers, "It was Lloyd all the way. He put on his traveling hat and went to see everyone who controlled big blocks of stock all across the country. He had all the shares charted and knew where everyone stood. Nothing was left to chance."

"There are not many CEO's who would dare do this, or who feel they know their shareholders well enough," concludes Sonnenfeldt.

The vigorous effort Lloyd put into that vote, which was endorsed by 76 percent of all Lee shareholders, is characteristic of his approach to life. "Lloyd never completely relaxes," says Dick Gottlieb, president of Lee. "He always wants to learn more. He's an incredibly inquisitive person.

The Institute of Bill of Rights Law

Laura Anna Lee, the daughter of A. W. Lee, retained a lifelong interest in the company her father had founded. When she was in her seventies, she decided that she would like to pay tribute to her parents, Alfred Wilson Lee and Mary Walker Lee, in a way that would be meaningful and of service to mankind. Thus, she conceived an idea which saw fruition in the founding of the Institute of Bill of Rights Law in 1982.

Miss Lee had long been interested in the Bill of Rights, the formal statement of the fundamental rights of the people of the United States, incorporated in the Constitution as Amendments one through ten, and in all state constitutions. She knew that it had been inspired by the Declaration of Rights, created in England in the 17th century during the reign of William and Mary.

With this in mind, she decided that it would be appropriate to base the Institute at the Marshall-Wythe School of Law in Williamsburg, Virginia, recognized as one of the finest law schools in America. She was aided by Tim Hanson, who served as the Lee company's attorney in Washington and who had graduated from this law school, a part of the College of William and Mary.

Miss Lee's goal was to create an institution that would help to preserve the freedom of speech to which her father devoted his life, but would also serve a broader function for scholars interested in constitutional law. Thus, the Institute of Bill of Rights Law has become a center for information and activities relating to this field, especially to the First Amendment.

The Institute serves, too, as an educational resource for journalists and sponsors a number of programs on topics related to news-gathering and reporting to the general public on constitutional issues.

Through an ironic twist of fate, Miss Lee did not get to William and Mary to see what she was creating. The week before a planned visit to Williamsburg from her home in Washington, she slipped and broke her hip. Within a few more days, she had died of an embolism.

It was fitting that the administrators of the new Institute decided to dedicate it to Laura Anna Lee as well as to her beloved mother and father. It was appropriate, too, that after Hanson died in 1989, Greg and Lloyd took the remaining funds from the Laura Lee Trust and made them available for a fund to endow a chair in Hanson's name at the Marshall-Wythe School of Law. Greg and Lloyd continue as trustees.

If someone close to him develops a new kind of disease, Lloyd will read up on it and know more about it than the person himself. He loves to learn new things."

There's no question Lloyd moves fast. "Intense and fast-paced though he may be," says Gottlieb, "you can count on his attention and support when you need it. One part of Lloyd is a very anxious, intense, rush, rush guy — but he never forgets his people. If I need him, everything, and I mean *everything*, comes to a halt."

A strong supporting team at home backs up his efforts. Betty Schermer's presence is understated, but extremely important. Her knowledge of the company comes from a lifelong intimacy which she cherishes. She enjoyed a storybook relationship with her grandfather, E. P. Adler, and traveled with him whenever school vacations allowed. Betty made friends wherever E. P. and her parents took her, such as Sue Anderson, whose father was the publisher of the *Wisconsin State Journal* and played such a pivotal role in Lloyd's career. E. P. took her to New York for ANPA meetings and to Chicago for Inland Press Association meetings. "They really adored each other," remembers Murph Wolman.

Betty was fortunate to have the same loving relationship with her father. When she was in college, Phil wrote to her every day, and the love was reciprocated in many ways. Phil, and E. P. before him, talked about the newspaper business with Betty and involved her in its many phases. She has a degree in journalism and worked as a reporter at the *Daily Times* in Davenport, so her awareness of current Lee events is instinctive.

Betty is always willing to head off anywhere, to Montana, Japan, China, Russia, or wherever, and do what she can to have fun and make Lloyd's life easier. She is extremely proud of Lloyd's accomplishments. "I know both E. P. and Phil would be very proud of him, too — especially the stature he's given the Lee papers through his activities with the ANPA," reflects Betty.

St. Ambrose University awarded Lloyd a honorary doctorate in business administration. Lloyd and Betty are seen here walking on the campus after the awards ceremony.

Over–the–counter trading of Lee Enterprises, Incorporated, began in March, 1966. By March, 1970, trading had begun on the American Exchange.

On April 11, 1978, Lee began trading on the New York Stock Exchange under the ticker symbol "LEE." The opening price was 28-3/8.

In this photo, William Batten, left, Chairman of the New York Stock Exchange, and Lloyd Schermer listen to NYSE specialist Robert Shaw of Shaw & Adrian explain the specialist book during listing ceremonies on the Exchange trading floor.

THE NEW KID ON THE BLOCK

The national monument to Presidents Washington, Jefferson, Lincoln and Theodore Roosevelt atop Mount Rushmore looked much more familiar once Lee Enterprises purchased the nearby Rapid City Journal.

The Schermer's have two sons, and both spent much time in the company while they were growing up. Grant was the classified advertising department manager at the *Missoulian*, and Greg is currently corporate counsel in Davenport. Predictably, the family shares the same closeness that both Betty and Lloyd have had with their respective families all their lives.

"Betty is not a flamboyant person who likes to see her name on every list of contributors," says Harriet Gottlieb, Dick's wife. "The things she does, she does quietly. But if something needs to be done, her help is always there. Sometimes the help is financial; other times it's as personal as spending Thanksgiving serving food to the needy, which Betty and Lloyd have done together for years."

Others, like Tom Williams, call Betty "an elegant first lady. When she talks to you, she looks you in the eye because she's genuinely interested in what you have to say. Her incredible breadth of life experience makes her fascinating to talk to. Betty is a perfect complement to Lloyd, and Lloyd's a perfect complement to her," he says.

Lloyd is also backed up at Lee by a strong second-in-command in the person of Dick Gottlieb, who has a growing reputation as an excellent leader with a strong value system. "Dick is a good balance," says Ron Rickman. "He's meticulous, rarely gets excited, and is thorough. He also has the uncanny ability to keep a lot of balls in the air. He handles a tremendous volume of work."

The Schermer family in 1987. Left to right: Grant; Greg's wife, Jenifer; Greg; Betty; and Lloyd.

Others in the industry, such as John W. Madigan, publisher of the *Chicago Tribune*, have interesting perspectives on Lee's management team. "I've been fortunate enough to watch both Lloyd and Dick in operation. Those are two great people. I see Dick as one of the future stars of our industry," says Madigan. "He's one of the most highly regarded young leaders and a role model for others in his company and in the industry."

"Dick is decisive, extremely intelligent and has a superb value system," says Lloyd. "He respects other people and earns their respect in return. He has the unusual ability to be both hard and soft. He understands tough love. With Dick, people know where they stand. Most important, he's constantly growing. He is self-confident and never afraid to take a stand on an issue, express an opinion that might not be popular or anticipated, or fight for what he thinks is right. He even spits in my eye from time to time.

"Dick attracts the kinds of people we want and inspires them as a role model. As a result, Lee has acquired highly capable and experienced managers from outside the company as well as growing them from within," says Lloyd. Buck Weaver, Davenport's retired production manager, says simply, "Dick knows when to talk nice and he knows when to holler."

Still some Lee people were surprised when Dick was named president. "I was one of them," confides Ron Rickman. "I told Dick, 'I'm not sure you can do this, but I'm going to support you in every way I can.' We haven't had a bad day since. I was wrong and Lloyd was right."

Others echo this sentiment and give Dick high marks for his human relations as well as managerial skills. Like many staff members who followed relatives into the company, Dick, as Dave Gottlieb's son, had to earn his stripes the hard way. Fortunately for him, and for Lee, the process appears to be working successfully once again.

Dick Gottlieb was born in Davenport on June 12, 1942. He spent many summers working for Lee during high school and college. After graduation from the University of Arizona in 1964, he joined the advertising department of the Quad-City Times.

A year later, he went to Madison, Wisconsin, where he worked as a management trainee in the advertising, circulation, production and editorial departments. He was elected treasurer and director of Madison Newspapers, Inc. in 1972, and named general manager in 1973.

He was named publisher of the Journal Times, *Racine, Wisconsin, in 1980 and was promoted to Vice President - Newspapers, of Lee Enterprises in 1985.*

In November, 1986, Dick was elected President and Chief Operating Officer of Lee Enterprises and elected to the board of directors. He also serves on the boards of Madison Newspapers, Inc., NAPP Systems Inc., and the Newspaper Advertising Bureau.

The Gottlieb family on a 1989 trip to Colorado. Left to right: Michael; Meghan; Dick; his wife, Harriet; Jason; and Allison.

Lee's latest acquisition, the 19th paper to be published by the company, is the *Rapid City (South Dakota) Journal*. It is an example of Dick Gottlieb's growing influence in the company.

"That was Dick's deal all the way," boasts Lloyd. "I was involved to the extent I needed to be, but Dick and Ron Rickman get all the credit for identifying the situation, analyzing it properly and then making it happen."

Assuring a strong presidency is one of many achievements Lloyd can look back on at Lee. When he joined the company, television was in its toddler stage and the possibilities of the computer were a distant dream. Lloyd has been the driving force behind the immense technological changes Lee has undergone, and he has, as its leader, directed the growth that's reflected in financial statistics and geographic expansion.

"Broadcasting holds special promise for us, too," continues Lloyd. "We have a lot of very accomplished people, many of whom have grown up in broadcasting. Coupled with our financial strength, we have the human resources to go even further than we are today."

With the future in mind, Lloyd has focused much of his energy on the creation of a senior management team that can carry on after him. "The professionalism that Lloyd has nurtured in that team," says Bob Fusie, "is his major accomplishment and holds tremendous promise for the future.

"Lloyd Schermer," Fusie continues, "clearly took us from a kind, friendly, positive paternalism to professionalism — a management that's highly sophisticated in the way we deal with each other and the way that we grow as individuals. We're a strong, independent company because we act independently as managers. That's why I think Lloyd Schermer has prepared not simply his senior management team, but the whole company, for the year 1990, the year 2000, and beyond. Thanks to his management, Lee is ready for the future."

Milestones during the Schermer administration, from 1973:

- July, 1973 — Lloyd becomes CEO of NAPP Systems, Inc.
- August, 1974 — NAPP begins production at its new facility in San Marcos, Calif.
- April, 1976 — Station KGMB-TV, the CBS affiliate in Honolulu, Hawaii, is acquired.
- October, 1977 — KOIN-TV, Portland, Oregon, is acquired. Later, ground is broken for a new center with a 50,000-square-foot television facility.
- August, 1978 — The *Bismarck* (North Dakota) *Tribune* is acquired.
- September, 1978 — NAPP begins operations from new NAPP/Europe headquarters in London and starts a letterpress expansion project in California.
- October, 1979 — The purchase of Lindsay-Schaub Newspapers, Inc., gives Lee the *Southern Illinoisan* in Carbondale, Illinois, and the *Herald & Review* in Decatur, Illinois.
- August, 1980 — The Winona (Minnesota) *Daily News* is purchased.
- March 26, 1985 — Lee acquires an interest in the New Mexico Broadcasting Company, owner of KGGM-TV in Albuquerque.
- December, 1986 — KGUN-TV, Tucson, Arizona, and KMTV, Omaha, Nebraska, are acquired.
- 1988 — A concerted effort is undertaken to acquire additional Pennysavers and other shoppers for Lee.
- March, 1990 — The *Rapid City Journal* is acquired from Cowles Media Co., bringing the number of Lee-published newspapers to 19.
- July, 1990 — Lee purchases the remaining 50 percent of NAPP Systems Inc. for approximately $100,000,000.

In April, 1990, Lloyd was elected chairman of the 1,400-member American Newspaper Publishers Association. He is the 50th newspaper executive to head the ANPA in its 103-year history.

The new ANPA officers pictured here are: standing (from left), Secretary Frank A. Bennack, Jr., (president and chief operating officer of The Hearst Corporation), Treasurer Donald E. Newhouse (president of the Newark, New Jersey, Star-Ledger), and Jerry Friedheim, president of ANPA; seated (from left), former chairman William H. Cowles 3rd, (president and publisher of the Spokesman-Review *and* Spokane Chronicle*), Lloyd, and Vice Chairman Robert F. Erburu (chairman and chief executive officer of the Times Mirror Co.).*

The growth of Lee Enterprises 1973 - present
(boxed properties are new)

OBJECTIVES
Present Overview + Consistency
Position Descriptions
Performance Standards
Performance Apprai
Coaching and Counseling
STAR PARTICIPANT'S MANUAL

Chapter Seven
Growing the Leaders of the Future

Six strong individuals have steered Lee Enterprises through its first century. Each one has left his unique imprint on the company's development, reflecting his philosophy, temperament, talents and interests, as well as his reaction to the challenges presented to him by his place in history. Underlying their differences, however, has been an important body of shared beliefs that have been strong and sure enough to serve as a foundation for the increasingly complex structure that has grown on it since 1890.

One person in a position to evaluate the company, both currently and historically, is Dick Gottlieb, president of Lee. When asked what he feels is the real backbone of Lee, he quickly replies, "The value system. Each of the six men who headed Lee over the last 100 years shared similar values, even though they were completely different from each other as personalities and in

As part of Lee's comprehensive training program, Kewanee Star Courier staff members (from left) Nancy Belcher, Rocky Stuffelbeam, Ken Miller, Jill Dekeyser and Wilbur Rogers attend a STAR (Supervisor Training and Review) session designed to establish a common ground for supervisors to share skills, language and basic management philosphy.

their respective management styles. These men were as different as night and day, but each possessed four similar attributes: they saw Lee as a medium for growth; they cared about people; they had magnificent value systems; and they were unbelievably honest."

Looking back at the past century, some unmistakable themes emerge to form a profile of Lee's value system. Different times have seen different emphases, but Lee's leaders have always expressed and acted upon a strong sense of responsibility to the company's customers, employees, communities, and investors. Their management styles recognized the importance of risk-taking and innovation, of employee motivation, and of open communication. Furthermore, colleagues who have described the personal characteristics of these six men have echoed the same phrases: personal honesty, respect for the opinions of co-workers, the gift of listening patiently and communicating accurately, and the ability to create a climate where

"Management and development are very important, and we have programs to proceed in these matters," reports Floyd Whellan, Vice President-Human Resources. "Every manager completes a Development Profile and a Career Profile, the latter to determine what managers want to be and where they want to be.

"You can talk forever about career and development opportunities, but until you have something in place to make things happen, they are unlikely to do so. Our management training sessions help to clarify objectives, and they are attended not only by those in training but by the very top managers in the company, including Lloyd Schermer and Dick Gottlieb. All those in attendance at these sessions, which usually last three days, come away with a better understanding of themselves as well as the company."

employees can satisfy their needs and feel challenged. It adds up to picture a company that has never lost sight of the needs and talents of the individuals with whom it's involved.

The major elements of Lee's historic value system are very much alive today and are reflected in virtually every facet of the company. Far from being relegated to a dead and distant past, they have become wedded to new perceptions to form an invigorating vision of the company's future.

Lee Lodge, located on beautiful Flathead Lake in western Montana, was purchased in 1962. It has grown to where it now contains five homes and a conference center, tennis courts, a swimming pool and other recreational facilities. It is used 100 percent by Lee employees and their families. Everything is provided with the exception of food. Each year, over 600 use this facility.

"What's interesting about Lee," says Bob Erburu, Chairman of The Times Mirror Company, "is what they do to strengthen the bond between the company and their employees. If you don't have good people, you don't have a good business."

"We have a great team," says Lloyd Schermer, who spends significant personal time and corporate resources fine-tuning his staff. "Every year the officers of the corporation spend three days at Adler Haus, Lee's conference center in Galena, Illinois, with 35 to 40 new managers at Lee who have either been promoted or hired from the outside," says Schermer. "The objective of these sessions is two-fold. First, we want to help them acquire, modify, or reaffirm a clear and precise image of the management process and the management behavior that will attract, retain, and motivate talented people. The second purpose is to encourage and assist them in professionalizing and upgrading the management process with their own group of people."

Nancy Chapman, Director of Finance, who recently joined Lee from CBS headquarters in New York, saw this process work at her first management seminar. "I thought Lloyd and Dick were there to introduce the speakers. I was astonished when they served as 'faculty' themselves, along with several V.P.'s. They were learning as well as teaching. They asked as many questions as they provided answers, probing the experiences of others to stimulate dialogue. 'This is a value system that really works,' I said to myself, 'because it is passed along directly in a one-on-one manner; there are no go-betweens to dilute the meaning.'"

Nancy is one of many women in important positions at Lee, including the board of directors. Lee was one of the first media companies to have a woman on their board. Phyllis Sewell, a Lee director since 1977, was formerly a senior vice president at Federated Department Stores.

Talented women have found the company a congenial place to apply their skills and receive recognition for their accomplishments. Vicki Wessling, account executive at KMTV in Omaha is one of them. Asked about opportunities she sees for her advancement, she replies, "They're virtually unlimited. Just look at Molly," referring to Molly Carroll, publisher of the *Muscatine Journal*, one of the up-and-coming young publishers.

Floyd Whellan, Vice President - Human Resources, who came to Lee from another media company, describes Lee's efforts to support this kind of growth. "We have a formal program in which we encourage, coach and counsel people on their personal development plans. If someone says, 'I want to be a publisher some day,' we map out a program showing them exactly what steps in their development, what skills and job experience, etc., will be required. We tell them what's needed and help them get there. When we talk about a positive climate for growth, that's the kind of program we're talking about."

The importance of training is underscored by Lloyd, who predicts there will be a serious shortage of qualified managerial people in the future. "The difference between a company's success and failure will be directly related to the quality of its human resource management," he says. "All these programs are designed to insure that we will always have the best people. Right

Seventy miles northeast of the Quad Cities is located the Adler Haus, named after Phil Adler. This is used as a conference center by the corporate office and Lee's Midwest divisions. It is located on a 13-acre tract and is perched on a 200-foot cliff overlooking the Galena Territory, a wooded recreational/residential area with several golf courses. Wild turkeys and deer are often seen on the property.

now, we don't have much trouble getting the people we want. They want to buy into our system," Lloyd says. "While few people ever choose to leave Lee, I've been told that having the 'Lee' name on a resume looks pretty good to future employers."

Some of the new employees seem surprised to find the kind of "family" environment usually identified with much smaller companies. "I came from Roy Disney's Shamrock Broadcasting," says Dick Grimm, general manager of Honolulu's KGMB-TV, "which really was a small company. I was amazed to find the wonderful 'extended family' atmosphere that is so much a part of Lee.

"I remember telling Lloyd that his company was, 'ohana' — Hawaiian for the 'family feeling' that pervades the company. I felt at home from the first day." Grimm, who has worked for competitors for 22 years, has seen a lot of broadcasting properties in a lot of markets, "but never a company with the culture and caring attitude of the Lee people," he says. "There's something here that the employees seem determined to pass on to newcomers."

Shirley Fatchett, Corporate Director, Training and Development, exemplifies the many Lee managers who earned repeated promotions, growing into positions of considerable stature and responsibility. She attributes much of the company's success to Lee's ability to train and "grow" managers who are both professionally skilled and actively involved. "We all have a shot at really succeeding," she says.

Advancement is the norm at Lee, and most managers are home-grown. Many people have mentors who are always available for guidance and advice. This informal, yet powerful support system has been influential to many Lee managers, who point with pride to the mentor who assisted them as well as to the younger employees they're helping in the same way.

Lee's focus on employee growth has led observers to describe it as a company that has an unusually strong "caring" attitude about its people. There's an edge of challenge to its caring, however. It's as if the company were saying, "We care enough to expect you to reach for the highest achievements you're capable of, and we'll help you do it."

What these systems, practices, and philosophies try to produce is a self-confident manager who can keep in step with how the world is changing. "This is not a 'cover-your-ass company,'" says Dick Gottlieb. "You never see people wasting their time protecting themselves with memos.

Occasionally, major events trigger opportunities for Lee's various newspapers and broadcasting properties to publish books. The eruption of Mt. St. Helens provided one such occasion for KOIN-TV in Portland, Oregon. Yellowstone On Fire! was created from the outstanding coverage of the Billings Gazette of that conflagration. The newspaper was runner-up for the Pulitzer Prize for its impressive coverage of the fire.

Where we do spend time is in the process of getting everyone's thoughts out on the table. The fights in management meetings can be fierce. We want people to speak their piece, and believe me, they do. We have a group of strong-willed people who, when they believe in an idea, will fight for it until the end. But after all this heated debate is over and a decision is reached — and it isn't always a consensus — we walk out of the room without a grudge, without a negative thought in our minds. We leave with a plan that each of us will work equally hard to accomplish."

Watching the management process work has been a 30-year study for Ron Rickman, who speaks enthusiastically about a practice that might send shivers up the spines of managers at many companies. Rickman was selling commercial printing for the *Montana Standard* in Butte when Lee arrived.

"Dick and Lloyd have a more in-depth understanding of what's going on in our company than others in the newspaper business," says Rickman. "This means they're always in the field, visiting divisions and studying the marketplace. Part of these visits always involves questioning people carefully about the problems and opportunities they see for themselves and for the company.

"Knowing your boss is in the field, digging into things that are clearly your area of responsibility, can be an unsettling experience. In fact, it's been real tough for some of the new managers. Seems as though every time you have trouble with a particular person, the next thing you know, either Lloyd or Dick happen to be there hearing their side of the story. But these things have a way of

Growing the Leaders of the Future **165**

In May, 1990, Dan Killoy was named publisher of the Butte Montana Standard, succeeding Don Berryman who retired after 33 years with the paper. Ron Rickman, vice president – newpapers, was on hand to announce Dan's promotion.

Dan started his career in 1963, stuffing funnies into the paper in the Butte mailroom. Before his printing apprenticeship began in 1965, he worked as a fly-boy for Berryman, who was then pressroom forman. Dan remained a printer and was president of Butte Local 126 of the International Typographer's Union from 1972 until its decertification in 1977, often negotiating against Berryman, Schermer, and Rickman.

In 1978, Dan took a job selling advertising for the paper, "I didn't even own a necktie," remembers Killoy. "They handed me an account list and an order form and said, 'Go sell ads.' That's the extent of the training we got in those days. Opportunity is the key word for Lee employees. For those who are willing to work hard and learn, the sky is the limit."

Standing (from left) are Rickman, Wendy Dinsmore, George Toy, Bob Henderson, Norm Hovis, Fred Mandl, Larry Spiecer, Killoy, Jim Ruark and Chuck Roberts; seated, Jim Edgar.

working themselves out. Management wants to do it the most expeditious way, not the way the business schools might say it should be handled. Our system really works.

"I imagine this openness would be intimidating to managers at many companies," he says, "but it's part of the drill here. There's a genuine feeling of trust. If my boss can get a handle on a problem faster than I can, that's good for everyone. These things never result in a 'gotcha' – we never get bit by anything they find out. It's always for the good of the company. We're all in this together."

What helps make this rather unorthodox communication work is that while Schermer and Gottlieb are in the field, they never offer opinions or make decisions. "They listen, they question, and then they come back here and discuss it with us," says Rickman. "They might tell me they want something done, but they never let the field know what they're thinking. The decisions come from here, following the chain of command, if you will, and that's what makes it work."

Ask Floyd Whellan how he finds people who are comfortable with this environment and he says, "Managers know what's going to happen because they're told. It's explained as part of the open climate we describe to prospective employees. And it's not just Lloyd and Dick; anyone can talk to an operator on the floor and get that kind of feedback. There's a tremendous amount of personal contact in this company at all levels."

Elaborating on the kind of leaders Lee hires, Dick Gottlieb adds, "We're most interested in their overall value system. We assume the talent, technical, and administrative skills are already there. What we want to see are their human behavior skills. If the person has the right integrity, trust, and values, then we want to know about their ability to manage people. Our leaders must be able to develop their people."

"We also look for people who can handle ambiguity," says Lloyd Schermer. "It's easy to listen to what the boss wants, and then go out and do it. But when you get out into the field, nothing is ever the way you thought it would be. The ability to adapt to changing situations is a fundamental skill of a good manager.

"Although it may seem like a trivial thing," says Lloyd, "our policy manual makes an interesting statement about the way we operate. It's only 1/2" thick — which tells you how much emphasis we put on the judgment of our employees. That's another aspect of dealing with ambiguity.

"Here's the attitude we're looking for: we want leaders who are active rather than passive; who are consultative and decisive, but not authoritarian; leaders who are more interested in developing people than just performing tasks. Above all, we want people who are honest with each other, a quality that we have inherited in full measure from those who preceded us."

Many of those leaders happened to be related in one way or another, and nepotism is a subject that can be highly sensitive in any company that started as a family-owned business and still has evident family ties. "You'll see family relationships running all through the history of Lee Enterprises," explains Henry Hook, who retired after four decades and knew all of the leaders except A. W. Lee himself. "Lee Loomis was related to A. W. Lee; Phil Adler was E. P.'s son; Lloyd is Phil's son-in-law. Dave Gottlieb was a distant relative of the Adlers, and now Dave's son is president. Then there was John Talbot, whom we sent to Madison, Wisconsin, after he married publisher Don Anderson's daughter. And there were the Whites. And the Burgesses — including Frank, Bill, Bob, Jim, and Steve, who all ended up with important jobs. Ron Rickman has three sons in the company; Lloyd Schermer has one, as well.

"And then there's my son, Sandy, who has served as publisher of three different papers at one time or another. That's 'nepotism' in some people's books. But at Lee, these relationships

Native American Journalism Student Scholarship Program

"One of our top priorities as an industry is to increase the number of minority people who are working in newspapers," Lloyd Schermer has said.

In 1989, Lee took a step towards that goal by endowing the University of Montana with $60,000 for scholarships for Native American journalism students. The endowment, created at the suggestion of *Missoulian* City Editor Frances Schjonberg, will fund annual scholarships for Native American students enrolled in the university's School of Journalism.

When the endowment was announced, Schermer pointed out that several Lee newspapers and television stations are located near reservation areas where there are significant numbers of Native Americans. Encouraging Native American journalists, he said, "is important to the pluralism of our society."

have been much more positive than negative. And if anything, it has always been tougher for the sons and daughters of managers to make their mark because they have been *expected* to perform better than those with no in-house family ties."

"Anyone knows that business skills are not inherited," said the late Don Anderson. "The children of Lee managers had to be twice as good as anyone else and prove themselves in order to get ahead. They have a harder row to hoe because everyone knows to whom they are related and can quickly spot any evidence of favoritism."

"The toughest thing you have to do when you let family members into a business is make damned sure they qualify," says Lloyd Schermer in commenting on the issue. "If they don't cut the mustard, you have to cull them out. That's what we've done. Otherwise, nepotism can destroy an organization. Look at Lee's roster of managers and of course you'll see the names of those related to others — it reads like the extended family this company really is. But you'll also see new blood like the Rileys, Whellans, Carrolls, Fusies, Blakes, Grimms, Schafbuchs, Rickmans, Rosses, Schmeddings and others who have no ancestors in the company and are in key positions, adding new strength and vitality to management.

"Remember how Lee Loomis slept on the police station bench just to make sure he got the stories first and was accepted for his diligence, not his connection to A. W. Lee? That determined attitude has been here since the beginning. Family members know that on a scale of one to ten for achievement, they have to do a 12. It's always tougher because of who we are."

"There's no question people often wonder whether someone got their job through nepotism or through brains," says Dick Gottlieb. "It's up to the individual to prove that the brains and ability did it. Look at it this way: the company really has nothing to lose. People with Lee in their heritage often work harder and smarter to keep the tradition going. This emotion produces some pretty hard-charging people."

Who's related to whom may be of interest to some, but the world of business is generally more impressed with the bottom line. An evaluation from that perspective would have to conclude that Lee's managers and the Lee management style are working well. They have produced a company recognized for its leadership as well as its financial solidity.

"Lee is one of the best small-business operators in the country," says J. P. "Rick" Guerin, a private investor and member of Lee's board. "They have an extraordinary ability to get the maximum result from what they own in terms of market penetration, good economic results, and a terrific management structure. It has been a sensational investment."

Since Lee went public 21 years ago, its net income has increased 20 of those 21 years, excluding gains from property sales. Net income has increased 1,383 percent from $2.9 million to $43 million in 1989 — that's an average increase of 14.4 percent.

One hundred shares of stock purchased at the first public offering in 1969 have split into 1,350 shares today. One would have paid $2,050 for those 100 shares in 1969; today they're worth about $40,000; an increase of 1,851 percent.

"The analysts who know us," says Michael Riley, Vice President - Finance, "give us pretty high marks. Our financial results are probably in the top one or two percent and we are frequently on the Forbes list of best-managed companies. Lee creates a caring atmosphere for employees, not in a paternalistic way but in a manner that encourages productivity. The analysts evaluate Lloyd Schermer as being innovative, truthful, and tremendously good for the shareholders. Better than anybody I know, he has found a good mix for what's right for employees, what's good for communities, what's beneficial for customers, and what's best for stockholders."

Riley, who holds a Ph.D. in finance from Harvard and recently came to Lee from a Fortune 100 corporation, turned down other offers in order to have the freedom to innovate as well as to contribute ideas and skills. He estimates Lee is "financially stronger than 99 percent of the companies in this country — in any field."

Nancy Chapman offers one sound explanation for Lee's continuing economic health: "The top managers, present and past, have always controlled the budgets as though they were spending their own money, with care and consideration. You won't find Lee executives flying first class, staying in expensive suites, or entertaining lavishly. When I think of company entertainment, I picture picnics or barbecues — often with Lloyd and Dick turning steaks at the grill and handing out sodas."

"We don't intend to fall into the overspending trap that gets many companies in trouble," says Lloyd. "Lee will continue to be the best small company in our industry, with planned growth for both our shareholders and our employees. Our focus is on providing financial rewards for our stakeholders and *both* financial and psychic benefits for our employees."

Creating a climate for personal and corporate growth, maintaining a meeting ground in which people share mutual understanding, continuing a value system perfected through many generations, and in all things honoring a rich tradition of forthrightness and integrity — these are serious and sober endeavors. Yet it would be a substantial omission in the story of Lee to overlook a facet of the company that has constantly been cited by managers and employees, past and present: its reputation as an environment in which things happen, in which there is an immense joy of living, and where the frustrations and rigors of work are generously spiced with liveliness and good humor.

Lee people work hard and play hard. Many of the senior managers are rugged outdoors people who like to hunt, fish, and enjoy the natural resources of the areas in which the company operates. New arrivals in the corporate ranks are often invited on hunting and fishing trips to help them feel part of the Lee "family," even though they may have had little or no exposure to this kind of wilderness setting. Floyd Whellan, who grew up in New York City, had an unusual initiation into this aspect of the company ethos. Whellan had never owned a shotgun or hunted. Dick Gottlieb and Ron Rickman decided to fill this gap in his experiences. The introduction was more dramatic than planned. Dick picked off a pheasant overhead and the bird dropped, landing on Whellan's head. The incident was memorialized at the next management meeting when Whellan was presented with a hard hat as a trophy.

Lee often gathers its employees for company-sponsored outings, to which all family members are invited. Traditionally, these take the form of barbecues, picnics, and other recreation that can be enjoyed by all ages. The "chefs" often turn out to be Lee managers, as was the case when this photo was taken showing Lloyd Schermer barbecuing steaks, an activity to which he brings considerable talent.

Employees talk about meeting the chairman for the first time at an outdoor reception where they found him flipping steaks over an open fire. Those who have been with the company for awhile and have done an outstanding job in some field of endeavor are likely to end up being "mugged," presented with a coffee mug that says, "I was mugged by the chairman of Lee," in recognition of their special contribution. The mugs are prized by their recipients, and the involvement of senior management is recognized and appreciated.

This is a company where some top managers sometimes dress in cowboy boots and Stetson hats because they are more comfortable that way, and where conferences and seminars are frequently enlivened by comical T-shirts or cleverly designed hats. It is also the company where 46 officers, board directors, and other executives once arrived, poker-faced, at a corporate meeting in bow ties in a humorous salute to the chairman's well-known preference for this sartorial style. It's no wonder that employees' descriptions of the company so often include the words, "Lee is a fun place to work."

On trips to the field, Lloyd Schermer often singles out employees who have performed some deed or service "above and beyond the call of duty." These selectees then are awarded a coffee mug that reads, "I've been mugged by the chairman of Lee."

Lani Renneau, Racine Journal Times *ad department, received hers for achieving performance goals despite a two-person shortage. "She was a one-person band," Lloyd remembers. "The mug was well deserved."*

Improving the communities Lee papers serve is a serious pursuit for the company, and some exceptional programs have developed due, in part, to the enthusiastic leadership of Lee people.

Bob Ross was publisher of the Racine Journal Times in the late 1970's. He worked hard to convince the city of the need for creating Tax Increment Financing (TIF) districts in which the town fathers could encourage construction. He was successful in promoting the purchase of land along the shore of Lake Michigan.

When Dick Gottlieb went to Racine as publisher in 1980, he continued where Ross had left off, trying to convince the city that the land was more valuable than anyone realized. Sam Johnson, of Johnson's Wax, Gottlieb and a few other visionaries initiated a drive to finance a renovation of the harbor. That turned out to be a $14 million project, the major funding coming from public and private sources.

Dick was a key leader in the effort to get the public involved and, through the paper, to visualize a dream that could be a reality. As a result, they remodeled the Racine waterfront into the largest secure recreational harbor on Lake Michigan, with more than 980 boat slips, a festival hall, and facilities for concerts and plays.

In addition, space was allocated for an $18-million condominium project and a $65-million, three-year development called Gaslight Pointe. "It's wonderful! It's beautiful!" exclaims Lloyd Schermer whenever he talks about what Lee helped to accomplish in Racine. "Today, it's a picture postcard."

Benefits of this revitalization process will continue to be felt for years. In large part because of the attractiveness of the area and the city's demonstrated commitment to preserving its downtown, J. I. Case, the major farm and construction equipment manufacturer, has already broken ground for a $100-million office tower in the heart of the downtown area.

Case president, James K. Ashford, recently said, "We're committed to making Case a world-class company, housed in a world-class facility in a world-class town."

Local government and business officials hailed the historic announcement and described the five-phase project as the largest single investment ever in the Downtown area eclipsing even the $65 million Gaslight Pointe project.

The new jewel on Davenport's riverfront is the Quad-City Times. *Built at a cost of $23.8 million, the plant includes a five-story Goss press, a distribution center, warehouse and offices. It is the home of 450 Lee employees.*

Board member Mark Vittert summed it up by saying, "If Norman Rockwell had painted a company, this is the one he would have chosen — it's the real McCoy. The people are genuine; nobody's trying to impress anyone else.

"Companies don't develop this way by happenstance," he continues. "You don't wake up one day and find you have a wonderful company, full of wonderful people. It comes from being around people who have strong values, a dedication to their work, and the confidence of knowing that individual effort is rewarded. This spirit comes from years and years of watching management operate and knowing everything you hear about the company is really true."

Lloyd Schermer has a way of bringing it all together by weaving in the company's guiding values with its business goals. "I never want to confuse my self-worth with my net worth. The wrong kind of ego can be counter-productive in building the kind of organization I think is important in today's world. I've had a personal commitment to build a unique and special kind of company where employees are turned on every day by their jobs and come to work because they want to, not because they have to. The single most important responsibility I have as head of this company is to insure that long after all of us are dead, Lee Enterprises will still be a viable, thriving corporation generating profits and leaders for the future. But it must ultimately come down to profit on the bottom line. Profit pays salaries, compensates shareholders, funds new plants and equipment, buys new opportunities for employees through overall company growth, and permits us to contribute not only money, but the time and skills of our people to public service and community improvement."

Lloyd Schermer and his predecessors have brought Lee Enterprises to a position of leadership disproportionate to its size — leadership in technology, in management, in service, and in human resource development. Lee's second century will bring new generations of leaders who will inherit a company with a core of values that have proven solid and supportive over time.

Whatever challenges those leaders may face, they will find in the legacy of the past a source of energy and direction, a launching pad into a dynamic future.

Lee Operations and Markets*

Broadcasting

KGUN-9 (ABC)
Tucson, Arizona

KGMB-9 (CBS)
Honolulu, Hawaii

KMTV-3 (CBS)
Omaha, Nebraska

KGGM-13 (CBS)[1]
Albuquerque, New Mexico

KOIN-6 (CBS)
Portland, Oregon

WSAZ-3 (NBC)
Huntington-Charleston,
West Virginia

Newspapers

Southern Illinoisan
Carbondale, Illinois
Daily: 30,753
Sunday: 36,231

Herald & Review
Decatur, Illinois
Daily: 43,035
Sunday: 56,351

Star Courier
Kewanee, Illinois
Daily: 7,990

Quad-City Times
Davenport, Iowa
Daily: 56,573
Sunday: 82,513

Globe-Gazette
Mason City, Iowa
Daily: 20,472
Sunday: 22,129

Muscatine Journal
Muscatine, Iowa
Daily: 10,986

The Ottumwa Courier
Ottumwa, Iowa
Daily: 17,395

Winona Daily News
Winona, Minnesota
Daily: 14,071
Sunday: 14,396

Billings Gazette
Billings, Montana
Daily: 54,677
Sunday: 60,860

The Montana Standard
Butte, Montana
Daily: 16,126
Sunday: 16,546

Independent Record
Helena, Montana
Daily: 13,359
Sunday: 13,917

Missoulian
Missoula, Montana
Daily: 29,385
Sunday: 32,165

The Lincoln Star[2]
Lincoln, Nebraska
Daily: 81,769
Sunday: 82,590

The Bismarck Tribune
Bismarck, North Dakota
Daily: 30,825
Sunday: 31,185

Corvallis Gazette-Times
Corvallis, Oregon
Daily: 13,326
Sunday: 14,737

Rapid City Journal
Rapid City, South Dakota
Daily: 34,708
Sunday: 36,061

La Crosse Tribune
La Crosse, Wisconsin
Daily: 35,139
Sunday: 39,106

Wisconsin State Journal[3]
Madison, Wisconsin
Daily: 108,749
Sunday: 153,643

The Journal Times
Racine, Wisconsin
Daily: 35,833
Sunday: 37,703

Specialty Publications

NewsLife
Atkinson, Illinois

Prairie News Shopper
Decatur, Illinois

Henry County Advertizer
Geneseo, Illinois

Tri-County Advantage
Kewanee, Illinois

Thrifty Nickel
Moline Sterling and Rock Falls, Illinois

The Orion Times
Orion, Illinois

The Globe
Port Byron, Illinois

Bettendorf News
Bettendorf, Iowa

Town Talk
Clinton, Iowa

Illinois Accent
Davenport, Iowa

The Advertiser
Davenport, Iowa

Classic Images
Muscatine, Iowa

Muskie Trading Post
Muscatine, Iowa

Wapello County Shopper
Ottumwa, Iowa

Thrifty Nickel
Billings, Montana

Yellowstone Shopper
Billings, Montana

Nickel Saver
Butte, Montana

Western Shopper
Deer Lodge, Montana

Trader
Dillon, Montana

Consumers Press
Great Falls, Montana

The Adit
Helena, Montana

The Western Montana Messenger
Missoula, Montana

Dollar Saver
Lincoln, Nebraska

Farm & Ranch Guide
Bismarck, North Dakota

Pennysaver
Dickinson, North Dakota

Mandan News
Mandan, North Dakota

The Finder
Mandan, North Dakota

Buyers Guide
La Crosse, Wisconsin

Sunshine Advertising News
Madison, Wisconsin

Pennysaver
Racine, Wisconsin

Racine County Shopper
Racine, Wisconsin

The Foxxy Shopper
Sparta, Tomah and Viroqua, Wisconsin

Printing Facilities

Bicon Publications
Atkinson, Illinois

Trico Communications
Davenport, Iowa

Western Publishing
Deer Lodge, Montana

Dakota Printing & Publishing
Mandan, North Dakota

Graphic Arts

NAPP Systems Inc.
San Marcos, California

Information Services

Voice Response, Inc.
Davenport, Iowa

---

* As of April 1, 1990

(1) Lee owns 42% of New Mexico Broadcasting Company, Inc., which owns KGGM-TV and KBIM-TV in Rosewell, New Mexico.
(2) Journal-Star Printing Co. publishes *The Lincoln Star* and the *Lincoln Journal*. Lee supplies news and editorial content for the *Lincoln Star* and owns 49.75% of Journal-Star Printing Co.
(3) Madison Newspapers, Inc., publishes the *Wisconsin State Journal* and the *Capital Times*. Lee supplies news and editorial content for the *Wisconsin State Journal* and owns 50% of Madison Newspapers, Inc.

Bold listings indicate photographs

Index

A

Adler, Bertha Blade, 25, 39
Adler, Betty. *See* Waterman, Betty Adler
Adler, Betty II. *See* Schermer, Betty Adler
Adler, E.P. (Emanuel Philip), 16, 22, 23, **24**-43, **38**, 64, 69, 71, **82**; bank crisis, 31-33; becoming president, 29-30; board memberships, 25; childhood, 34-35; chronology, 25; community involvement, 25, 31, 40; death of, 40; early days with A.W. Lee, 16-18; habits of, 28, 29; in Davenport, 27-28; kidnap attempt, 41; known as Mannie, 27; labor relations, 28; philosophy of, 37, 40, 84
Adler Haus, 162-163
Adler, Henrietta Bondi, 40, 63, **66**, **71**, 75, 81, **82**, **84**
Adler, Lena Rothschild, 25, **35**, 63, 71
Adler, Philip David, 25, 60, **62**, 63-89, **68**, **72**, **82**, **85**, **86**, 87, **104**; as editor, 71; board memberships, 63; childhood, 64; community involvement, 84-85; Montana purchase, 77-80; personality of, 72; public stock offering, 81; relationship with E.P., 69, 82; values of, 81, 86-87
Adler, Philip Emanuel, 25, 27, 34
Adler Theater, 139-**141**
Advertising, Bureau of, 60
American Management Association (AMA), 136, 145
American Newspaper Publishers Association, 88, 146, 148
American Stock Exchange, 152
American Trust Bank, 31
Amherst College, 111, 112
Anaconda Mining Company, 60, 77, 122, 133
Anderson, Don, **72**, 77-80, **78**, **85**, **86**, 114, **121**, 166
Anderson, Florence, 121, 122
Anderson, Sue, 121, 151
ANPA Research Institute, Inc., 107
ANPA Technical Committee, 107
ANPA. *See* American Newspaper Publishers Association
Aronson, Governor Hugo, 136
Ashford, James K., 170

B

Bank failures, 31-33
Batten, William, **152**
Bechtel Foundation, 141
Beiderbecke, Bix, 64
Belcher, Nancy, **159**
Belkin, Dick, 137
Bennack, Frank A., Jr., **156**
Benshoof, Gary, 76, 96
Berryman, Don, 127-130, 149, **165**
Billings Gazette, 93, 126-127, 164
Bishop's Cafeteria, 83
Bismark Tribune, The, 156
Blade, Bertha. *See* Adler, Bertha Blade
Blade family, 39
Blade, Max, 39
Blake, Phil, 133
Blue Ribbon News, 87
Bob Marshall Wilderness Area, 134-135
Bolivar, Betsy. *See* Waterman, Betty Adler
Bondi family, 82
Bondi, Henrietta Carol. *See* Adler, Henrietta Bondi
Bootlegging, 14
Brayton, Aaron M., 17, 23, 40, 42
Broadcasting properties (present and former). Current stations listed on p. 172
    Radio stations:
        KEYC-FM (Mankato, Minnesota), 48
        KFAB (Omaha, Nebraska), 42
        KGLO-AM (Mason City, Iowa), 42, 45, 47, 49, 138
        KGLO-FM (Mason City, Iowa), 48
        WMDR-FM (Moline, Illinois), 109
        WTAD (Quincy, Illinois), 42, 48
        WTAD-FM (Quincy, Illinois), 42
    Television stations:
        KEYC-TV (Mankato, Minnesota), 48, 88
        KGGM-TV (Albuquerque, New Mexico), 106, 137, 156
        KGLO-TV (Mason City), 48-49, 58, 60, 138
        KGMB-TV (Honolulu, Hawaii), 106, 137, 156, 163
        KGUN-TV (Tucson, Arizona), 106, 137, 156
        KHQA-TV (Hannibal-Quincy), 58, 60
        KMTV (Omaha, Nebraska), 106, 137, 161
        KOIN-TV (Portland, Oregon), 106, 137, 138, 156
        WSAZ-TV (Huntington, West Virginia), 48, 106, 109, 127
Brown, John, 82
Brown, Kathy, **106**
Bunker, Lloyd, **72**
Bureau of Advertising. *See* Advertising, Bureau of
Burgess, Bob, 166
Burgess, Frank H., **22**, 23, 166
Burgess, Jim, 166
Burgess, Steve, 166
Burgess, William T., **72**, 80, **85**, **86**, **107**, 166
Burk, Dale, 134
Butte Montana Standard, 79, 105, 129-130

C

Call-It Co. *See* Voice Response, Inc.
Capitol Times. *See Madison Capitol Times*
Caras Park, 132, 134
Carbondale Southern Illinoisan, 156, 165
Carroll, Molly, 161
Censorship, Office of, 63, 70
Chalupa, Rolla, 40
Chapman, Nancy, 161, 167
Chicago, Illinois, 11, 34
Chicago Times, 11, 13
Chicago Tribune, 14-15
China, The Official Guidebook of, 150, 164
Clark Fork of the Columbia River, 133
Clemens, Samuel L., 13
Congressional Record, 59, 60
Conroy, David M., 20
Consultative management, 132, 142
Conversion to cold type:
    Missoulian, 99, 127
    Quad-City Times, 96, 116
Corner Bar, 83
Cooper, John, 66-67
Corvallis Gazette-Times, 88, 93, 109
Cowles, William H., 3rd, **156**
Cummings, Bill, **106**

D

Daily Iowan, 63, 64
Dale, Charles, 14
Dale, Dave, **104**
Davenport Bank and Trust Company, 25, **32**, 33
Davenport, Colonel George L., 26

Index

Davenport Daily Times, 20, 23, **28**, 63, 87
Davenport Democrat, **27**, 31, **39**, 87
Davenport Eagle Refuge, 116
Davenport, Iowa, 26, 140
Davenport Municipal Stadium, 105
Davenport Newspapers, Inc., 60
Davenport papers, name changes of, 87
Davenport Quad-City Times, 75, 87, 129, 154, 171
Davenport Times, 7, 26, 42, 76, 87
Davenport Times-Democrat, 63, 76, 87, 96
Decatur Herald & Review, 156
Dekeyser, Jill, **159**
Dinsmore, Wendy, **165**
Dougan, Vince, **37**
Douglas, Bob, 50

E

Earthquake Lake, 125
Edgar, Jim, **165**
Einstein, Albert, 82
Elser, Smoke, 134
Emanuel, Temple, 33, 84
Emerson, Ralph Waldo, 10, 11
English, Dr. Earl F., **107**
Erburu, Robert F., 147, **156**, 161
Estlow, Edward W., 146, 148

F

Fatchett, Shirley, 163
Federal Bureau of Investigation (FBI), 114
Federal Communications Commission (FCC), 47, 48
Figge, V.O., 31-32
First Chicago Corporation, 106
Fischer, Harry A., Jr., **107**, 136, 137, 144, 150
Fish, Charles, **104**
Flathead Lake, 135
Flathead River, 161
Forssen, John, 122-125
Friedheim, Jerry, **156**
Friendly House, 84
Frontier Airlines, 133
Fu-Go balloons, 70
Fusie, Bob, 142, 156

G

Galena Territory, 162
Galligan, Dick, 97
Gardner, John, **75**
Gaslight Pointe, 170
Glacier National Park, 134-135
Globe-Gazette. *See Mason City Globe-Gazette*

Gottlieb, Allison, **155**
Gottlieb, David K., **72**, 80, **86**, **90**, 91-109; **107**, **98**, **104**, **107**, 116; broadcasting contributions, 106; childhood, 93; chronology, 91; community involvement, 91; conversions to cold type, 103; printer's strike, 73-74, **85**; relationship with employees, 103-104, 105; vision of electronics 93
Gottlieb, David S., 91
Gottlieb, Elaine Hirsch, 91, 93
Gottlieb, Harriet, 153, **155**
Gottlieb, Jason, **155**
Gottlieb, Meghan, **155**
Gottlieb, Michael, **155**
Gottlieb, Richard D., 91, **98**, **144**, 145, 150-151, 153-**155**, **154**, 159-160, 163; chronology, 154
Grant, Judge Nathan, 39-40, 75, 84, 87, 105
Grimm, Dick, 163
Guerin, J.P. (Rick), 167

H

Haines, Scotty, 99
Hakes, Margaret Anna. *See Loomis, Margaret Hakes*
Hall, W. Earl, 53, 59
Hannibal Courier Post, 7, 20, 23
Hanson, Major General Arthur B. (Tim), 72, 76, 88, 151
Harper, Betty, **55**
Harper, W.H. (Harry), 67-68, **72**, 118
Harrer, Don, 51, **55**
Harrer, Elizabeth Hakes (Betty), 45, 47, 52, **55**, 57
Harris Corporation, 101
Harvard Business School, 111, 112, 115, 145
Hayward, Bert, 145
Hearst, William Randolph, 8
Henderson, Bob, **165**
Henry County, Illinois, 65, 117, 119
Herald & Review. *See Decatur Herald & Review*
Hickey Brothers Cigar Store, 83
Hill, W.J., **22**, 23
Hilleboe, J. Strand, **72**, **107**
Hoefler, Walt, 132
Hook, Henry B., 36-37, 48, **58**, **72**, 76, 166
Hook, Sandy, 166
Hoover, President Herbert, **33**
Hovis, Norm, **165**
Huston, John, 15-16

I

IMB 1130 computer, 93
Inland Daily Press Association, 41, 151
Institute of Bill of Rights Law, 151
International Pressman's Union, 127
International Typographer's Union, 99, 101-103, 116
Iowa, University of, 63-64, 84
Iowan, Daily. *See Daily Iowan*

J

Jacobs, Randy, 78
Jaquith, Dave, 136, 145
Johnson, Sam, 170
Johnson, Walter, 99, 101, 103
Journal Times Company, 88
Journal Times, The. *See Racine Journal Times*

K

Kable, John, 104
Katz, Isadore, 29, 32-37, 77, 84,
Kelley, Tom, 27-28
Ketridge, Chris, 64
Kewanee Boiler Company, 119-120
Kewanee Star Courier, 31, 42, 64-70, **67**, 93, 117, 119-121, 159
Kewanee, Illinois, 65
Killoy, Dan, **165**
KOIN Center, 138, **139**

L

La Crosse Tribune, 7, 20, 23
La Crosse, Wisconsin, 18
Lakeview, Oregon, 70
Lane, Walter L., 16, 23
Laura Lee Stock Purchase Plan, 85, 92
Lawrence, J.E., 42
Lee, A.W., **6**, 7-23, 51-52, 151; acquisitions by, 13; chronology, 7; death of, 20, 28-29; early childhood, 10; family of, 19, **22**; integrity of, 8; philosophy of, 11, 17-18, **22**
Lee, Anna, 7
Lee Broadcasting, Inc., 105
Lee Enterprises, Incorporated, 60
Lee Foundation, 141
Lee Group, 45, 46, 80
Lee Group: Mid-America to the Mountains, The, 48
Lee, John B., 7, 9, 16
Lee, Laura Anna, 7, 16, **19**, 40, 60, 85, 88, 151
Lee Lodge, 161

Lee, Mary Walker (Minnie), 7, **19**, 30, 151
Lee Papers, The, 19
Lee Syndicate, 30, 37, 42, 80, 122
Lincoln, Nebraska, 30
Lincoln Star, The, 30-31, 42
Lindbergh, Charles, 53
Loomis, Elizabeth Hakes. *See* Harrer, Elizabeth Hakes (Betty)
Loomis, Lee P., 23, 42, **44**, 45-61, **55**, **58**; board memberships, 45, 60; broadcasting, 46-50; chronology, 45; community involvement, 45; early childhood, 45-46, 50-51; philosophy of, 60; versifier, 51, 57, 59; voluntarism, 52-53, 77
Loomis, Lewis, J., 51
Loomis, Margaret Hakes, 45, **58**
Loomis, Mildred Anna Lee, 51
Lorber, Muggs, 114
Lowe, Leo H., 64
Lyons, Roger, **106**

M

Madigan, John W., 154
Madison Capitol Times, 42
Madison River, 125
Madison Wisconsin State Journal, 31, 42, 46, 78
Magnusson, Alfred, **86**, **107**
Mahin Advertising Agency, 16
Mahin family, 16
Mahin, Frank, 16, 28
Mahin, Harold J., 10, 16
Mahin, John B., 7, 13, 23, 28
Mahin, John Lee, 16
Mail-O-Graph Company, 68
Mandl, Fred, **165**
Manhattan Project, 71
Mansfield, Senator Mike, 135
Marshall-Wythe School of Law, 88, 151
Mason City Development Association (MCDA), 54, 55
Mason City Globe-Gazette, 31, 42, 52, 54
Mason City, Iowa, 46
Mathis, Allen, 145
McKinley, President William, 10, **65**
Metcalf, Senator Lee, 135
Miller, Charlie, **106**
Miller, Ken, **159**
Milligan, Lester, 58
Missoula Missoulian, 79, 122-127, 133
Montana Standard, The. See Butte Montana Standard
Montgomery Ward, 67, 68

Moriarity, Jerry, 117, 119-120
Morrison, Dick, **72**
Mt. Hood, 138
Mt. St. Helens, 138
Mt. St. Helens: The Volcano Explodes, 164
Mugging, **169**
Muscatine Journal, 7, 13, 14, 16, 20, 23, 53, 161
Muscatine, Illinois, **13**
Muse, William F. (Will), 42, 52
Music Man, The, 59

N

NAPP Systems Inc., 71, 76, 91, **97**, 99 108, 109, 129, 156
Native American Journalism Student Scholarship Program, 166
Nebagamon, Camp, 114
Nebraska State Journal. See Lincoln Nebraska State Journal
Nelson, Luke, **72**
Nelson, George, **37**
Nelson, Sandy, 116
Newhouse Broadcasting, 137
Newhouse, Donald E., **156**
Newhouse, John, 80, 81
Newspaper Advertising Bureau, 60
Newspapers currently owned by Lee. *See* individual listings.
  Billings Gazette
  Bismark Tribune, The
  Butte Montana Standard
  Carbondale Southern Illinoisan
  Corvallis Times-Gazette
  Davenport Quad-City Times
  Decatur Herald & Review
  Helena Independent Record
  Kewanee Star Courier
  La Crosse Tribune
  Lincoln Star, The
  Madison Wisconsin State Journal
  Mason City Globe-Gazette
  Missoula Missoulian
  Muscatine Journal
  Ottumwa Courier, The
  Racine Journal Times, The
  Rapid City Journal
  Winona Daily News
New York Stock Exchange, 150, 152
Nippon Paint Company, Ltd., 71, 91, 96, 97, 98
Northern Trust Company, 80, 106
North Iowa Fair Association, 54

O

O'Donnell, John, 105
Ottumwa Courier, The, 7, **12**, 13, 15, 20, **21**, 23, 25

P

Pacific Northwest Newspaper Association, 99
Palmer, Guy, 149
Petkunas, Richard, 104
Photocomposition, 96
Photopolymer printing plates, 97
Powell, John F. (Jim), 16, **22**, 29, 30
Printer's devil, 25, 63; defined, 92

Q

Quad-City Times. *See Davenport Quad-City Times*

R

Racine Journal Times, The, 170
Radedeaux, Clyde R., 23
Radio stations. *See* Broadcasting properties
Rapid City Journal, 152, 155, 156
Reagan, President Ronald, **75**
Red Ribbons: A Story of Missoula and Its Newspaper (Toole), 122, 134
Reimers, Charles D., 23, 26, 28, 87
Reinhardt, Bill, 104, 107
Renneau, Lani, **169**
Rexroad, Carl, **165**
Richardson, D.N., **36**
Richardson, Mrs. D.N., **36**
Rickman, Ronald L., 139, **144**, 149, 150, 153, 154, **164-165**
Riley, Michael D., **144**, 167
Roberts, Chuck, **165**
Rogers, Wilbur, **159**
Rorick, Ray, **72**
Rosenauer & Adler, 34
Ross, Robert D., **144**, 148, 170
Rothschild family, 35
Rothschild, Lena. *See* Adler, Lena Rothschild
Rothschild, Walter J., 50, **86**, **107**
Ruark, Jim, **165**
Rusty Hinge Quartet, 59

S

St. Ambrose University, 111, 152
Salmon River, 136
Schermer, Betty Adler, 63, **66**, 81, **82**, **115**, 122, 123, 151-**153**

Schermer, Burdie Hurwitz, **113**
Schermer, Grant, 111, **123**, **136**, **153**
Schermer, Gregory, 88, 111, **123**, **136**, 151, **153**
Schermer, Jenifer, **153**
Schermer, Lloyd G., 66, 67, 71, **72**, **86**, 100, **107**, **108**, 111-157, **114**, **115**, **126**, **153**, **168**, 171; ANPA, 146; board memberships, 117; broadcasting, 137; childhood, 114; China, 150; chronology, 111; climate in workplace, 145; community interests, 117; consultative management, 132; environmentalist, 117; ethics, 143; function of media, 140; function of unions, 100, 114, 127-130; Kewanee days, 117; leading by example, 116, 142; move to Missoula, 122; telecommunications, 148
Schermer, Mannie, **112**
Schjonberg, Frances, 166
Schmedding, Gary N., 48, 139, **144**
Sewell, Phyllis, 161
Shaw, Robert, **152**
Sheppard, H.M., 16
Sonnenfeldt, Richard, 97, 149-150
Southern Illinoisan. See Carbondale Southern Illinoisan
Sparks, E.L., Jr., **72**
Spiecer, Larry, **165**
STAR (Supervisor Training and Review), 159
Star Courier. See Kewanee Star Courier
Standard Hotel, 83
Stemlar, John, 137
Strip mining, 117-119
Stuffelbeam, Rocky, **159**
Sulzberger, Arthur Ochs (Punch), 146

T

Taft-Hartley Act, 114, 115
Talbot, John, 121, 166
Television stations. *See* Broadcasting properties
Tewlow, Jules, 136
Throop, Frank D., **22**, 23, 42, 52
Toole, John H., *Red Ribbons: A Story of Missoula and Its Newspaper*, 122, 134
Toy, George, **165**
Twain, Mark. *See* Clemens, Samuel
Type, cold, 96, 127
Type, hot metal, 96, 99

U

U-Boat 234, 95
Union Bank, 31
United Fund, 133
U.S. Forest Service, 135

V

VanVooren, Bob, 116
Vittert, Mark, 143, 171
Voice Response, Inc., 148

W

Walker, Annette, **106**
Walker, Mary Ingalls. *See* Lee, Mary Walker
Walsmith, Wally, 94-96
Waterfront Park, 138
Waterman, Betty Adler, 25, **33**, 35, 71; as Betsy Bolivar, 33
Waterman, Selma, 27, 39, 69, 71-72, 74
Watts, Mark, **106**
Weaver, Buck, **116**, 154
Wessling, Vicki, 161
Whellan, Floyd, **144**, 160, 162, 165, 168
White, Charles W., **72**, **86**, **107**, 166
White, Walter W., **72**, **86**, 166
White, William Allen, 10, 11
Wiggins, Nita, **106**
Willamette River, 138
Willard, John, 108
William and Mary, College of, 88, 151
Williams, Tom, 96, 104, 105, 129, 130, 149, 153
Willson, Meredith, 59
Winona Daily News, 156
Wisconsin State Journal. See Madison Wisconsin State Journal
Wisconsin, University of, 46, 122
Wolman, Martin (Murph), 66, 80, 83, 122, 145
Women's Christian Temperance Union, 14
Wundrum, Bill, 92

Y

Yellow journalism, 8, 15
Yellowstone National Park, 125
Yellowstone on Fire, 164
Yohe, Randy, **106**

(6) KOIN-TV

Missoulian

He

Quad-City Times

NA
SYST

WS

Star ✱ Courier

theRap

9 KGUN

GLOBE GAZETTE
MASON CITY

13 KGGM·TV

W

Wisc

Helena Independent Record

Jo

Billings Gazet

LA CROSSE Tribune

THE LINCO